Praise for

Until Tuesday

"This story of an incredible service dog is both touching and warm. Some of the struggles are painful to read, because they are so real, but that only makes the triumphs more uplifting. In the course of these pages, Tuesday truly bécomes a hero, as does Luis Montalván. This book feels like more than a joy; it feels necessary."

—Vicki Myron, #1 *New York Times* bestselling author of *Dewey*

"This is a profoundly honest book filled with vital lessons about loss, friendship, war, and the loving bonds that can save us in our lowest moments. We are all lucky that Capt. Montalván and his dog Tuesday found each other, for in their story we see the possibilities in our own lives."

—Jeffrey Zaslow, coauthor of the #1 *New York Times* bestselling *The Last Lecture*

"Wow, what a book! I think I was crying on page 3. The collision of man and dog, and the unbreakable bond they form, made my heart leap. Everyone should read this book to better understand not only the ravages of war, but the amazing capacity of the human spirit to rebound. I dare anyone to read this book and not believe in the power of love to heal."

—Lee Woodruff, author of *In an Instant* (with Bob Woodruff) and *Perfectly Imperfect*

"[A] richly detailed narrative of true grit and psychological turbulence."

—*Seattle Kennel Club Review*

"Luis and Tuesday are two true American heroes. This powerful story is a testament to the courage of veterans both on and off the battle-field. Luis is a critical voice for our community, reminding every single veteran that they are not alone."

—Paul Rieckhoff, executive director and founder,
Iraq and Afghanistan Veterans of America (IAVA)
and author of *Chasing Ghosts*

"*Until Tuesday* explores the unique bond that can occur between dogs and people that ennobles both. This book is a moving tribute to the courage and perseverance of a man as well as the love and the devotion of a remarkable and unforgettable dog."

—Larry Levin, *New York Times* bestselling author of
Oogy: The Dog Only a Family Could Love

"A clarion call to all who profess to care about our veterans and an intense reminder of just how high a price they have already paid, Montalván's mixture of memoir, military history, and pet story results in an urgently important tale."   —*Booklist*

"A deeply moving story of service, sacrifice, and restoration. Years from now when critics assemble the canon of Iraq War literature, look for *Until Tuesday* to make everyone's short list."

—Andrew J. Bacevich, author of *Washington Rules: America's Path to Permanent War*

Tuesday's Promise

Tuesday's Promise

One Veteran, One Dog, *and*
Their Bold Quest to Change Lives

Former U.S. Army Captain

LUIS CARLOS MONTALVÁN

AND ELLIS HENICAN

NEW YORK   BOSTON

Hachette Books
Hachette Book Group
1290 Avenue of the Americas
New York, NY 10104
hachettebookgroup.com
twitter.com/hachettebooks

First Edition: May 2017

Hachette Books is a division of Hachette Book Group, Inc.
The Hachette Books name and logo are trademarks of Hachette Book Group, Inc.

The publisher is not responsible for websites (or their content)
that are not owned by the publisher.

The Hachette Speakers Bureau provides a wide range of authors for speaking events. To find out more, go to www.hachettespeakersbureau.com or call (866) 376-6591.

Lu Picard photo courtesy www.ecad1.org.
Al Franken photo by Dan Dion.
Service Dog Summit photo by Jo Arlow.

Library of Congress Cataloging-in-Publication Data has been applied for.

ISBNs: 978-0-316-31441-1 (hardcover), 978-0-316-31440-4 (ebook)

Printed in the United States of America

LSC-C

10 9 8 7 6 5 4 3 2 1

To Mamá
& Tuesday...

CONTENTS

PART II

Will and Desire

PART III

Paws Forward

High Flier

I NOTICED HIS CAP EVEN BEFORE I SAW THE MAN SITTING BENEATH IT.

"332nd Fighter Group," the hat read, and I knew immediately what that meant. The man had to be one of the legendary Tuskegee Airmen who'd fought so valiantly in World War II for a military and a nation still divided by race.

He was old enough. He was African American. And now he was parked in a wheelchair, unattended, in a busy hallway at the decrepit VA hospital in lower Manhattan, while his couldn't-be-bothered attendant was jabbering away on her cell phone.

Tuesday noticed him first. Tuesday often notices things before I do. He's more intuitive—and, yes, far better trained. As soon as we made it past the elaborate security checkpoint at the hospital's main entrance—always an ordeal with a service dog—Tuesday was tugging on his leash and signaling to me: *Luis! Wait a second! That man needs something!*

I'd read plenty about these flying aces, how they had trained in a tiny speck of dirt called Tuskegee, Alabama, and went on to complete 1,578 missions through heavy combat in North Africa and Italy. The Airmen flew hand-me-down Republic P-47 Thunderbolts and North American P-51 Mustangs with the tails and rudders painted bright red. That's why the Airmen were often called "Red Tails" by other fliers in the Army Air Corps, the predecessor to our modern U.S. Air Force. The Airmen's wartime accomplishments included destroying or damaging 409 enemy aircraft, 40 boats and barges, and 745 boxcars, rolling stock, and locomotives. Using only machine-gun fire, a Tuskegee Airman was credited with sinking the *Giuseppe Missori,* one of the fiercest destroyers in Mussolini's Italian Navy. Long before the modern civil rights era, the Tuskegee Airmen taught a lesson to a nation not quite ready to learn it: Talent, bravery, and patriotism have nothing to do with skin color. But until that day in the hospital, I had never personally met one of these humble heroes.

The man in the wheelchair looked old, old in a way that old veterans sometimes do—gnarled and twisted, blank and glum, like he'd seen a lot and done a lot but couldn't hide what the years had done to him. His spine was bent with scoliosis. His eyes were impossible to see behind Coke-bottle cataract glasses. He certainly didn't appear eager for chitchat.

Tuesday and I had come to the hospital for one of our biweekly counseling sessions, the standard-issue treatment for an Iraq or Afghanistan War combat veteran who battled raging, full-blown PTSD. The truth was that Tuesday, my golden retriever service dog, had done far more to ease my symptoms than any human Department of Veterans Affairs employee ever had, helping me secure the control and the confidence I needed to leave my apartment, quit drinking so much, finish graduate school, write a bestselling book, rebuild my relationship with my family, and begin traveling around the country advocating for America's battered and ignored military veterans, among others. But as good as Tuesday was at his job, talk therapy was important, too. I'd finally found a caring therapist at the VA. So here we were for another forty-five minute fuel stop on the long road to recovery.

All around us were sad-looking patients and overwhelmed or distracted staff. Veterans on crutches, veterans on walkers, veterans on canes, veterans in wheelchairs—the few who were walking without assistance shuffled along. Everyone else seemed to be waiting in lines that made the lines at the Department of Motor Vehicles look efficient and quick. There were lines to get prescriptions filled. Lines to see a doctor, a therapist, or a nurse. Lines to get a number to stand in another line. Old soldiers don't die, it seemed. They just shuffle down the hallway or wait in endless lines at the VA.

No one seemed to be complaining. Most of the patients looked heavily drugged to me, like zombies more than warriors, though clearly they had all once been vigorous and young. Almost everyone seemed to have a cap, a patch, a T-shirt, or some other insignia connecting them to a branch of the service and a recent or ancient American war. "Marines." "Airborne." "Korea." Many of them from an era when a patch or hat saying they'd served was enough to command instant respect. God bless 'em. They are my brother and sister veterans. They deserve so much better than this. But the disrespect they've gotten and the treatment they haven't received leaves far too many of them in hallways like this one.

Could Tuesday tell the man was in physical pain? Did his canine Spidey Sense detect that the man was having a combat flashback? Was it just a vibe that here was someone who could really use a hug? It could have been any of that. Or all of it. Over the past five years, he had woken me from enough nightmares, also known as night terrors, for me to recognize the signs: Tuesday picks up on all kinds of things.

We had time before our appointment. Given the lines, we always arrive early at the VA. And I trust Tuesday enough that when he says, "Stop," I say, "You bet! Right here!" It's almost always because someone needs something, and Tuesday thinks he can help. Most of the time, that someone is me. But sometimes, it's a total stranger.

I shot the inattentive attendant my stink eye, that powerful stare of negative energy, my sharpest nonverbal judgment of that's-not-cool-ignoring-your-patient-like-that. On this occasion, the stink-eye effort produced exactly zero results. The woman was still prattling away on her phone, totally useless in her blue scrubs. As Tuesday prepared to step forward, I turned my attention from the careless caregiver. I got a closer look at the man in the wheelchair.

The man seemed almost catatonic. His only expression was blank. The attendant still hadn't so much as glanced at him. I hated the idea that someone so uncaring might be taking care of my mom or my dad someday or one of America's veteran heroes. Her inattentiveness was the opposite of everything I had learned as an army leader, where initiative-taking and selflessness and working to the bone were what kept my soldiers and me alive and allowed us to accomplish the mission, no matter how tough the mission was. We do our best to look out for each other in far-away battle zones. We don't come home expecting to be treated like nearly invisible zombies shuffling down the hallways, pieces of meat rolled around in chairs. This man was someone who needed real attention, not the fake attention of a blue-scrubbed clock-puncher at the Manhattan VA.

"Go say 'hi,' Tuesday," I told him. "Go say 'hi.'"

Tuesday approached slowly.

He put his head gently on the man's left thigh just above the knee. The man didn't seem to notice.

He burrowed his nose into the crease beneath the man's leg, playfully smooshing around down there.

I figured I'd better say something. Without a word of invitation, my loyal service dog had just entered this stranger's personal space. Now Tuesday had his snout resting on the old man's lap.

"This is my service dog, Tuesday," I said, trying to sound upbeat. "He needed to say 'hello' to you."

Was the man going to respond? Did he understand what was happening? Was he even awake?

Ten seconds passed. It seemed like ten minutes.

It was like Tuesday was pulling the choke starter on an ancient lawn mower, struggling with all he had to get the old clunker to start. *This could take a few pulls,* I thought to myself.

Finally, the old guy lifted his chin.

"Tuesday?" he sputtered. "What kind of name is that?"

No hi. No smile. No nice-to-meet-you. I guess I was just glad he reacted at all.

Tuesday's eyebrows started dancing. His eyes darted back and forth. His tail began to wag. His snout brightened into a warm, welcoming smile.

"You're right," I said. "That's an unusual name for a dog. I didn't name him. Tuesday is the name he came with. No one really knows what it means."

The old man kept staring. At least now I could tell he was awake.

"He's my dog," I said. "And my best friend."

"I know he's a dog," the man answered.

This was hard. But a little grumpiness wasn't going to deter Tuesday. He was determined to turn this man's day around. So we stuck with it. Tuesday just needed a little verbal help from his wingman.

"Well, my dog saw you," I continued. "And he wanted to say hello."

That was all it took.

Tuesday pressed his furry golden coat against the man's spindly legs and let out a few affectionate doggie murmurs. The man's mood suddenly lifted. The tone in his voice softened, too. In those few seconds, he'd gone from catatonic to curmudgeon to grandpa. Believe me, that doesn't happen by accident.

To the casual observer, Tuesday was just saying hi. But I knew better. I knew he was also taking the old veteran's pulse, one of many things he learned to do in his two years of intense training as a service dog. He was listening to the man's respiration. He was smelling whether the stranger was experiencing pain. Here Tuesday was, inside this huge and depressing veterans' hospital, staffed with hundreds of trained doctors, nurses, and cell-phone addicted aides. And the golden retriever was the one triaging the patient, checking this old man's vital signs—and making a new friend at the same time.

Dogs are amazing, aren't they?

With a little groan from the effort, the man's left hand came over Tuesday's head and started gently stroking. The man rested his right hand in the soft fur behind Tuesday's neck. This was exactly what Tuesday was reaching for, not because he wanted to be petted, though when he isn't working he does love that. Tuesday wanted the man to feel better. He wanted the man to smile. He wanted to shine some affection on someone who clearly needed attention. He wanted to deliver relief. Smack in the middle of this bustling VA hallway, he recognized that this man looked all alone and decided to remedy that.

<hr/>

I am used to this sort of thing.

Tuesday and I have been together for eight years now, and I am still amazed at how he can pierce these situations in ways humans can't. It no longer surprises me, but I am still in awe. As we travel the country, Tuesday keeps radiating that warm, loving light of his. And people are almost always unable to resist the power of that glow.

This time, Tuesday's life force started one man's engine and suddenly he was humming along. The difference was sufficiently striking that even the inattentive attendant couldn't help but notice. Suddenly, she was smiling. "I have to go," I heard her say into the phone, and then she too was bending over, petting Tuesday.

We've had thousands of encounters like that over the past eight years. Big ones. Small ones. Some I've totally forgotten. Others I never can. In connecting with Tuesday, countless lives have been changed.

The man's weathered face transformed as he smiled broadly. Behind the Coke-bottle glasses, I still couldn't see his eyes, but I'll bet they were sparkling. Unfortunately, it was time for our appointment and we had to go.

"It's been a real pleasure to meet you, Tuesday," the veteran announced, now speaking in a voice that hinted at the confident warrior he had once been. "My name's Harold. Most people call me Harry. You can call me whichever you like."

The man turned and looked up at me with pride, slowly straightening his frame until he sat taller in the chair. "I was a pilot in the Second World War. I flew with the 332nd Fighter Group. They called us the Tuskegee Airmen. We were something special, we were."

Just then, a nicely dressed woman walked up with a little girl who must have been seven or eight years old.

"There you are," the woman said to Harry, and then to me: "I'm his granddaughter. This is his great-granddaughter, Ella."

The little girl craned her neck to look up and told me, "Grampa Harry lives with us."

"So nice to meet you both," I said. "This great man was just saying hello to Tuesday, my service dog."

Harry took his eyes off Tuesday long enough to glance up at me. "What a wonderful dog you have," he said. "I am so glad the two of you decided to say hello."

I didn't have to utter another word.

A "Red Wing" was taking flight again. Lifted by the spirit of a special golden retriever, the man soared.

PART I

Road Warriors

CHAPTER 1

Tale of the Dog

Love never ends.

1 CORINTHIANS 13:8

WHEN TUESDAY FIRST CAME INTO MY LIFE, I WASN'T IN MUCH BETTER shape than the Airman in the wheelchair at the Manhattan VA, though I'm sure he had a good fifty years on me. I was at least as glum as he was before he met Tuesday. Life-or-death combat can do that to a person. I wasn't sleeping well. I had frequent headaches and panic attacks. I was drinking too much and gobbling pills. My marriage had been a casualty of war. It was a struggle to keep appointments, and all my friendships were strained. I walked with a limp and, even worse, I was too wracked with anxiety to really go anywhere. Day and night, I sat in my cramped Brooklyn apartment and phoned down to the local deli for food. This wasn't living. It was barely existing. I was back from Iraq and out of the army and more or less waiting around to die. I would not have called myself actively suicidal. Suicide takes initiative. Bummed out and distracted as I was, I didn't have the focus to end it all. But somewhere inside of me—thank God!—was a little voice that kept whispering, "You can do better than this. You can do better than this."

People who know me know this story. One day, I got an email from a veterans' organization about a nonprofit group called ECAD, which stood for Educated Canines Assisting with Disabilities. ECAD was looking to match disabled war veterans with service dogs. Even in the heavy darkness, I figured that might be worth a try.

I met a woman named Lu Picard, who ran the organization. She trained service dogs for people with physical disabilities—amputees, the visually impaired, people with muscular dystrophy and multiple sclerosis. But Lu didn't see why her work should stop there. She was convinced that a well-trained dog could be immensely helpful to someone who needed psychological assistance as well. Lu wasn't entirely alone in this belief, but she didn't have much company back then. Her timing couldn't have been more perfect, for me and for a whole generation of other men and women returning to America from Iraq and Afghanistan. Many of us—no one could say exactly how many, but hundreds of thousands for sure—were suffering from an array of conditions that experts lumped under the term post-traumatic stress disorder, or PTSD. After decades of misunderstanding, downplaying, and denying these "invisible wounds of war," military officials, veterans' advocates, psychologists, and even a few dog trainers were coming to recognize PTSD as the massive epidemic it was. "We have to do something about this," quite a few of them began to say, though not quite sure what that something was. Among the many approaches that seemed worth trying was the idea of partnering highly trained service dogs with men and women affected by the intense stresses of combat.

The dog Lu paired with me, an instinctively loving and exquisitely trained golden retriever with the mysterious name Tuesday, would help me change my life in dramatic and profound ways. But why should anyone be surprised by that? Dogs have been assisting human beings almost since the beginning of time.

The next time you hear someone say, "It's a dog's world," or "We're all going to the dogs," just agree. That's been true since the days when human beings were grunting instead of talking and still dragging each other around by the hair. Dogs aren't only our best friends. They are also some of our oldest and most talented companions.

There's a reason 40 percent of households in America now include at least one dog. Many reasons, actually. Dogs are our pets, our children, and our caregivers. They love us, teach us, entertain us, work with us, protect us, and help in more ways than most people imagine. Dogs are doing a whole lot more than fetching the newspaper from the front lawn and rolling over on command, though I certainly don't minimize either of those.

The close relationship between humans and canines goes back at least 40,000 years, well before history was written down. Modern genetic testing has proven that, at about that time, dogs diverged from an extinct wolflike canid in Eurasia, and they've been with us ever since. Yes, cave men and cave women had cave dogs, and I'm almost certain those cave dogs had their own names. Why wouldn't they? The cave people had to call them *something*.

Cats have been around a while too. House cats are clearly depicted in Egyptian paintings from 3,600 years ago. That's about the time Mesopotamians were busy inventing the wheel. And cat-loving archeologists were practically purring a decade or so ago when a Neolithic grave excavated in Cyprus contained two skeletons laid close together—a human and a cat. That ancient skeleton was no slinky feline. It more resembled a large African wildcat. But still. From that evidence we know that the feline-human relationship extends at least 9,500 years—about one-quarter as far back as humans and dogs.

Sorry, Fluffy! It's dogs over cats... *again!*

If it weren't for the dog, human civilization couldn't possibly have evolved the way it did. Early humans had very few tools and no developed language or writing. We were not the dominant beings we are today—the undisputed *alpha predators.* We were fighting against the elements and many other alpha predators for food, shelter, security, and all the basics needed to sustain human life. We often lost. Then, the dog came along. All of a sudden, we had a creature who could alert us to threats we couldn't detect ourselves—human threats, other animal threats, weather threats. Dogs enabled us to hunt better. They were uniquely able to help us track and kill for food. That is not surprising. Running with four legs beats running with two legs. Dogs could also smell things we couldn't. Their sense of smell, scientists now calculate, is 10,000 to 100,000 times more acute than ours.

There's a reason for this. Dog noses aren't like human noses, which have to inhale and exhale through the same narrow passages. Dog noses exhale through slits in the side, keeping those smells separate from the new smells that are coming in. Basically, they never stop sniffing new smells. Compared to dogs, we might as well be walking around with clothespins on our noses.

Dogs also enabled us to start keeping livestock. Have you ever tried to catch a chicken, a pig, or a sheep when it's running away from you? One trip to a livestock farm or a petting zoo will teach you that human beings are not very good herders. For eons, and still today, most of the livestock on the planet is herded by dogs. From Anatolian shepherds to Australian cattle dogs, from Belgian sheepdogs to Bernese mountain dogs, herding breeds are hard at work. There's no reason to believe they will ever be replaced.

Dogs have played a direct role in many other human endeavors— especially agriculture. For as long as we've grown our own food, dogs have protected our harvests against rodents, birds, rabbits, squirrels, chipmunks, and many other critters that could wreak havoc on a field of crops. Understanding all this, our forty-millennium relationship with canines makes perfect sense. Dogs have been essential to our becoming civilized.

Fast-forward to the present: Dogs are as vital to human beings today as they've ever been, if not more so. Canines work with the United States military in more than one hundred countries. We have dogs at our borders protecting our agriculture against insects and other pests, not to mention keeping illegal drugs and human threats out. Right now, wherever you are, dogs are patrolling in your community, helping the police. And don't forget the countless businesses and residences with "Beware of Dog" signs warning assorted human predators they'd better stay away.

And why stop there?

Dogs today are doing things to help people that canines have never done before, things cynologists have long suspected dogs to be capable of. *Cynologist* is not a word most people know, but it should be. Cynology is the study of things related to canines. These studies have proved that dogs are able to help humans in ways far beyond herding and hunting and protection. Everyone has seen dogs guiding the blind or the hearing impaired. They still do plenty of guide work, but the world is finally learning that their talents go far beyond that. Dogs are outsmarting high-priced medical machinery. Dogs are doing things that doctors can't. Dogs are helping people with diabetes by detecting whether their blood sugar is too high or too low and alerting them to take their medicine. We have dogs who prompt humans with epilepsy to the symptoms leading up to seizures. They do that by smelling the chemicals and minerals secreted through sweat, then warning their human companions to take medicine or to sit down so they don't fall and hurt themselves. It's said that one in sixty-eight children is born with autism, a condition that has isolated children from their peers and families. Today, dogs are improving the lives of those kids, teaching them to communicate and interact with the world. And other service dogs, dogs like Tuesday, are helping more and more people every day to mitigate disabilities of every sort. No one has a complete list of all the disabilities that dogs help with. No one ever will. Once compiled, it would have to be continually updated. Therapy dogs visit hospitals and schools and retirement facilities and nursing homes, bringing a cold, wet nose, and a furry spirit to comfort the sick, help the dying, and bring joy to children and adults from 3 to 103.

I can hardly believe how far I have come over the past eight years, and I can't give enough credit to that one special dog who remains at my side every step of the way. Those early cave dogs had nothing on Tuesday. He has proven himself over and over again to be a genius and the truest kind of friend. The change in me since Lu paired us could hardly have been any more dramatic. Instead of sitting inside a small apartment all day, an anxious prisoner of my own PTSD, I took to the road with Tuesday and never looked back. Not as occasional travelers. Not as two-week vacationers. Together, we became creatures who've traveled to many, many places but still have a long list of stops we are eager to get to. And though there are days and weeks that the road can feel like too much to handle—times I still struggle to cope with the lingering vestiges of my PTSD—we press ever onward, knowing we really can't afford to stop.

Given the darkness I was coming out of, who would have predicted how full our lives could be? Certainly not me. I could not have conceived any of it. That I would earn a master's degree from the Graduate School of Journalism at Columbia University. That my relationship with Tuesday would become a *New York Times* best seller (plus a pair of award-winning children's books) and a celebrated documentary film. That I would work with a U.S. senator to get service dogs some of the respect they deserve from the Department of Veterans Affairs. That Tuesday and I would appear together on

The Late Show with David Letterman. Do you have any idea how many people watched that show? I don't know exactly. But I know it's up in the millions. Dave is well known as an avid dog person. His own beloved dogs included Spinee, a yellow Labrador retriever. One of his show's longest-running segments was "Stupid Pet Tricks." He couldn't wait to call Tuesday into his arms for a nationally televised hug. Being such a people dog, Tuesday happily obliged.

Who would have believed that we would receive thousands of cards, letters, and emails from people across the country and around the world, sharing their own inspiring stories and sometimes seeking our help? Most of all, for myself and anyone who knew me during those darkest of times, who would have believed that Tuesday and I would leave our isolated lives in New York City and begin traveling full time as road warriors for the causes we believe in most? From Shut-Ins to Open-Roaders, from Inward Looking to Outward Bound. Going from city to city and town to town. Meeting people everywhere—and lots of dogs too. Traveling to forty-nine of the fifty U.S. states. Get ready, Hawaii! It won't be long! I can hardly explain how big a change this was for us. Advocating for disabled veterans, service members, and many others in need. Educating adults and children about the many wonders of service dogs.

I've never sat down and calculated the thousands and thousands of miles we've traveled together, but I do know this much: The longest journey of all was the one inside my head.

I'm not cured. But thanks to Tuesday, I'm permanently on my way. I am a profoundly different person as a result. Wasn't I the guy who once had trouble leaving his own apartment? Wasn't I the person who hated interacting with other people, even in the simplest ways? Sure, I was—but not anymore. I'm half of "Luis and Tuesday" now. It didn't happen overnight. In some ways, it's still a work in progress. But day by day, I've become the man who goes places and does things and has come to see what a glorious adventure living can be.

Until Tuesday told the story of my grueling battle to get here. *Tuesday's Promise* reveals the amazing world that Tuesday and I discovered once we arrived, a place I could hardly have imagined even existed. And none of this would have happened were it not for a certain rambunctious and furry creature with two golden floppy ears and a constantly wagging tail!

This wasn't a thought-out plan. It just sort of happened, an almost irresistible outgrowth of what Tuesday liberated in me. In hindsight, it all seems so obvious. Because of our special relationship, we wrote a book together. Because of that book, people want to meet Tuesday and me—Tuesday, especially. I don't kid myself about that. Then, bookstores and libraries started getting in touch with us, asking if we could do signings and talks. Media people wanted interviews. Educational institutions, veterans' groups, and mental health associations invited us to appear at their meetings and conventions. It is a whirlwind that keeps spinning at a pace that doesn't allow me to focus too long on being uncomfortable. Strangers approach us in hallways, in shopping malls, and in public parks. We spend a lot of time in parks. Tuesday loves to run around and he always has business to take care of.

"Get busy," I tell him, our special command for "do your business," and he does, wherever we are.

I couldn't have started any of this or kept on going if I had been alone. With the same encouragement he first used just to get me out of the apartment, Tuesday keeps herding me out onto the road.

"Come on, Luis," he constantly says to me with some combination of body language, physical nudging, and bright-eyed energy. "Let's go. It'll be fun. Come on. Let's go."

If you think it's easy to resist a barrage of that furry charm, all I can say is: You try it sometime! When Tuesday wants us to go somewhere, I shake my head and say to myself, "We're going—where?" I know I have no power to resist him.

A few days after Tuesday and I met the Tuskegee Airman at the VA in New York, we were in Tampa, Florida. We'd been invited to speak at the annual conference of the American Animal Hospital Association, the accrediting body for companion-animal hospitals in the United States and Canada. Two thousand veterinarians and other animal-care professionals were packed in a large hotel ballroom. These are good people. High-quality animal care is what they are all about. Every day, they and their colleagues care for sick and injured animals and work to prevent future health problems. It was an honor to be there. I'm a vet, but not that kind of vet. Tuesday and I were asked to share our experience and discuss the unique relationship between people and dogs. I wanted to let the vets know how appreciated they are and also leave them with something essential to think about.

That's what I did.

"You may be treating dogs, cats, horses, birds, or reptiles," I told the veterinarians as Tuesday stretched out on the stage beside me. "But that's not all you're treating.

"You are treating family members. These dogs, cats, horses, and other animals are someone's loved ones. They are cherished and beloved creatures who are essential to the health and welfare of the human beings who care for them at home."

I hoped the veterinary professionals knew this, but it still bore repeating. Regardless of what any of us do, it's easy to forget the big picture as we stay hyper-focused on the details of our daily routines. That's understandable. But we should never lose sight of the deeper impact we are having—the picture behind the picture of whatever it is we do.

"Let me speak about dogs," I said, as Tuesday glanced up at me, figuring I must be speaking about him. "Dogs are the animal I know best. It's incredible how many people, without even thinking twice, will tell you that their dog is 'like a member of the family.' It's a nice sentiment. It's meant affectionately. But I'm sorry. I have to disagree with part of that. For many, many, many people, dogs aren't *like* a member of the family. They *are* a member of the family. They are and deserve to be treated that way. That's who you are treating every day. Our family."

There are many ways to measure how important dogs are to people. One way is to add up the time people share with their animals, along with the amount of money many people spend on dog food, vet care, obedience lessons, grooming salons, walking services, kennel stays, spa visits, organic treats, and funny outfits—all of those things that have turned dog ownership into major engines of the world economy and human life.

"But time and money aren't the best measures," I told the veterinarians. "The best measure is one that can't be counted, itemized, or put on any spreadsheet. The best measure is how much our dogs mean to us."

That was something I could speak about personally.

"Tuesday saved my life," I told the animal professionals. "Were it not for Tuesday, I wouldn't be here today. I know something similar is true of hundreds of thousands of people, if not millions, in the United States alone. Tuesday and I have gotten tens of thousands of letters since our book came out, many from people saying much the same thing. 'I wasn't in the army, but I have to tell you, if it were not for my beloved Sophie'—or Jack—'I wouldn't have made it through that divorce'—or that cancer. I wouldn't have made it through being stood up at the altar, through domestic violence, through the biggest challenges life delivers to any of us.

"Your patients are not just animals," I told the veterinarians, and I think most of them understood exactly what I meant. "Not just pets. Not just *like* a member of the family. You are really treating, caring for, and saving essential relationships. You are caring for some of the most loved and helpful creatures on earth."

I paused a moment and looked down at Tuesday, who heard in my voice how strongly I believed everything I was saying. I nodded at him, smiled, and finished. "No one needed that love and that help more than I did. Thank you, all of you, for what you have chosen to do." ·

CHAPTER 2

Getting Here

Believe in a love that is being stored up for you like an inheritance,
and have faith that in this love there is a strength and a blessing so
large that you can travel as far as you wish.
RAINER MARIA RILKE

I WAS BORN TO BE A WARRIOR. THE BROKEN PART DIDN'T HAPPEN UNTIL much later, the healed part later still. If you've read *Until Tuesday,* you know a lot about how I got here. If not, let me get you quickly up to speed.

My parents were both big achievers who encouraged all three of their children to make something of their lives. My father, George, spent two decades in senior economist positions at the Organization of American States and another decade in a similar role at the Inter-American Development Bank. My mother, Patricia, was a top executive at a company called Westat, overseeing massive research and data-analysis projects for the federal government. Driven and intense—my father especially—they taught me to work hard always and expect nothing would be handed to me. As role models, they set the bar high. I always had plenty to live up to. Both my parents came from families with dual Latino and American roots. My mother's family came from Venezuela, Puerto Rico, and New York City. My father's family had a foot-in-both-worlds relationship with Cuba and northern Virginia. In 1960, when my father was eighteen, he, his mother, and his sister fled Fidel Castro's Communism to settle with relatives in Arlington. My parents met at George Washington University in Washington, D.C. They fell in love, married, and moved to the Maryland suburbs, joined soon enough by two boys and a girl. I was the middle child. Like so many families of that generation, the Montalváns—Papá, Mamá, Plinio, Luis, Cristina, and Max the dog, a giant schnauzer—got busy living the American dream.

I was a wiry, athletic boy who loved competitive sports. I played tennis, ran cross-country, and participated in track-and-field events. My teachers agreed I was plenty bright, though I didn't always live up to my academic potential. My grades fluctuated between stellar and average. Subjects that interested me like social studies and anthropology, I aced. Otherwise, I was distracted. The quality of teachers often dictated my interest and, consequently, my performance, something that seems to happen with a lot of kids. Too often, I'd rather be outside, looking for another race to run.

As my Papá's career flourished, we moved to nicer houses. I ended up switching schools several times, which meant I kept being the new kid in the class—never easy. I had an especially rough patch in junior high, when I was bullied almost every day—physical beat-downs by two or four boys on my way to the tennis courts. I didn't give up tennis or stay home. I always put up a fight. However, I almost always ended up on the losing end. I didn't report it to anyone at school, just taking my lumps and going on with my day. My parents, who were always busy working, barely noticed. Bullying just wasn't treated as seriously back then. At least I had Max, my faithful schnauzer, to console me. We spent most of our time together. He was always around. He was, for many years, my very best friend.

From my early teenage years, I wanted to join the military as soon as I possibly could. My parents weren't too keen on that idea. Why not go first to college? They both had advanced degrees and wanted their children to follow suit. My teachers weren't so thrilled either. Approximately zero percent of the graduating class at Winston Churchill High School in Potomac, Maryland, went somewhere other than straight to college. But I was adamant, and with my parents' grudging consent, I signed a U.S. Army enlistment contract on April 13, 1990, the day I turned seventeen.

The summer between junior and senior years, I skipped the beach and the summer tennis leagues and headed off to boot camp at Fort Dix, New Jersey.

It was a highly eventful summer, for me and the army.

On August 2, our drill sergeant posted a tiny newspaper clipping in his office window. It said that the Iraqi Army of Saddam Hussein had invaded the neighboring country of Kuwait. Suddenly, things got deadly serious around the fort. We weren't pretending anymore. We were heading to war. The 82nd Airborne Division promptly deployed to Saudi Arabia for Operation Desert Shield. Soon enough, my boot camp buddies at Charlie Company, 3-26 Infantry would be shipping out for additional training, then off to the Persian Gulf for the coming invasion of Iraq. Me? I got to cool my heels in English 401 and P.E. with the worst case of senioritis ever. I was eager for action, but army regulations had other ideas. I had to finish high school first.

The combat phase of Operation Desert Storm lasted exactly forty-three days, from January 17 to February 28, 1991—the start of my second semester senior year. By the time I tossed off my graduation cap and gown, the whole war was over and done.

My boot camp buddies were steeled combat veterans, if just barely, and I'd missed the largest deployment of American troops since Vietnam. I felt like I'd been benched for the Super Bowl, though even benchwarmers get flashy rings. Instead, I got a glossy piece of paper with fancy script that read: "Graduate, Winston Churchill High

School." I was sure our crusty British bulldog mascot could feel my pain!

When I finally reported for active duty, army life truly suited me. The physical challenges, the team spirit, meeting new people, learning new skills—this was exactly where I belonged. I didn't even mind the barking drill sergeants. I'm not saying they weren't intimidating. Some of them were. But I also thought they were hilarious. They swore just as richly as in *Full Metal Jacket,* and they seemed to think I was "squared away."

I could run two six-minute miles back to back and bang out as many push-ups and sit-ups as anyone ordered me to. And I didn't have the cluelessness or ghetto attitude that some of the other young soldiers did. I was happy to be part of the U.S. Army and up for whatever adventures might be ahead.

And so I spent the next decade as a communications specialist, a military police officer, and an infantryman, growing increasingly gung-ho about serving in the military. I attained the rank of sergeant and took community college courses at night. Eventually, I decided I wanted to become an officer. I signed up for ROTC classes at Georgetown University and the University of Maryland, College Park, and finally buckled down to complete my long-delayed bachelor's degree. My parents certainly approved of that part. When America was attacked on September 11, 2001, I witnessed part of it with my very own eyes. I was near the Pentagon when its western wall was struck. Like so many others did, I felt as though I had been attacked personally. The terrorists took aim at everything I believed in and stood for. I knew immediately we would soon be heading into battle. This time, I hoped I would get the chance to lead soldiers.

When I completed the Army Officer Basic Course at Fort Knox, Kentucky, the wars in Afghanistan and Iraq had just begun raging at full blast. I was sent to the 3d Armored Cavalry Regiment, then headquartered at Fort Carson, Colorado, and promptly deployed to

Iraq, where I would lead a tank and scout platoon in the western Al Anbar Province. My platoon was stationed at a forward operating base near the Syrian border. We patrolled the vast Iraqi desert and secured the Al-Waleed border crossing, one of the busiest and most treacherous ports of entry in Iraq.

At the time, I had no idea how all this might be affecting me and so many of the others I served with. But when you live in constant danger like that twenty-four hours a day, witnessing and experiencing trauma all around you—people dying, people almost dying, people lucky to be alive—you don't notice it, but it changes you. All that stress has a profound effect as the weeks and the months grind on. Your senses are heightened. You never let your guard down. You become pro-grammed to danger. You are constantly on alert. You never fully relax. After a while, you are wired differently than you were before. This has psychological *and* physical effects. You can see it on a CAT scan. Pro-longed exposure to a highly tense environment actually changes the shape of the human brain. And it isn't a temporary change. The amyg-dalae are permanently altered. These are two almond-shaped groups of nuclei, located deep inside the brain's temporal lobes, that perform a primary role in the processing of memory, decision making, and emo-tional response.

Therefore, the amygdalae are where our emotional memories are stored. You've heard of the fight-or-flight response, which is the body's instant physiological reaction in the face of an attack or a threat. All that happens inside the amygdalae. I know that my reac-tions were forever changed during my time in Iraq. People may scoff, "It's all in your head." I guess that's true in a way.

Four nights before Christmas of 2003, elements of our unit—Grim Troop, 2nd Squadron, 3d Armored Cavalry Regiment—were manning a border crossing outside the Iraqi town of Al-Waleed, a busy transit point in and out of Syria. Private First Class David Page and I were clearing an area of truckers who had been using the crossing as a rest stop. That was an obvious security threat to soldiers quartered at Forward Operating Base Latham, which was only a few hundred feet away.

Some of the truckers refused to move. One got out of his vehicle and slammed me from behind into a metal trailer hitch. Just then, another man came running at me with a long knife held overhead, which he stabbed downward toward my neck. The knife pierced the body armor at my left shoulder, tearing into my uniform and left arm. I pulled my pistol from my right thigh holster and started shooting. A few moments later, Pfc. Page reacted and started shooting at the attackers as well. As I fell toward the ground, the man with the knife was on top of me, stabbing downward. I fired two more shots before my spine hit the concrete and my head snapped backward. Suddenly, everything went black.

I was medevacked in a Blackhawk helicopter to a field surgical hospital outside of Ar-Rutbah, where I received immediate treatment for blunt-force trauma to my head and spine. This was austere battlefield medical care. There were no CAT scans or X-rays or careful neurological workups. The personnel did what they could, concluding that I had sustained trauma to vertebrae. The word "concussion" was used. Swelling was noted along my spine. So were various bruises and stab wounds. But no one said "traumatic brain injury." I'm not even sure that was a common medical term at the time. After three days of convalescing at the field hospital, they wanted to transfer me to a full-service combat-support hospital in Baghdad. If I got sent to Baghdad, I was sure I'd be sent on to Germany and then back home. In hindsight, I should have gone. But I wanted to return to duty. I was in charge of that border crossing. I wanted to be with my men. We were already shorthanded. I hadn't waited all those years to reach the battlefield, only to be sent out prematurely. How could I have known the full extent of my injuries? I was pounding through Motrin. I didn't want to leave Iraq, the war, the mission, the Iraqis, my guys. I wanted to do my part to help my country win. Warriors don't quit, I told myself. Warriors shake things off. Warriors go back into the fire.

And so I did, pressing ahead with the mission until the deployment ended in March of 2004 and I was shipped back to Fort Carson, Colorado.

I was proud of my service. I had done what I was sent over there to do: defend my country and lead my men into war. It had been challenging. I'd gotten banged around. Like far too many others, by the time I got back home, I knew I was messed up, physically and psychologically—but not as bad as some people, I kept reminding myself. I was jumpy and anxious, but I could still get through the day. I had two arms and two legs, ten fingers and ten toes. "Snap out of it," I kept saying. "You'll be okay." But I wasn't sure I'd be staying in the military and going back to the war zone. I was thinking about putting in my discharge papers, going to law school, then maybe returning later to serve in the JAG Corps.

In June of 2004, we had a regimental change of command within the 3d Cavalry. Our new commander was Colonel H. R. McMaster, a legendary soldier known for his charismatic leadership style and his fearlessness in questioning authority. His battlefield legend was solidified in the fabled "Battle of 73 Easting" during the Desert Storm campaign. A captain at the time, McMaster's company of M1 Abrams tanks happened upon a large Iraqi Republican Guard armor unit on February 26, 1991. Though badly outnumbered, his company destroyed more than eighty enemy tanks, while American forces lost zero. His exploits were glowingly recounted in Tom Clancy's 1994 nonfiction bestseller, *Armored Cav.* As a major, McMaster made a further impression with his own 1997 book *Dereliction of Duty,* a scathing critique of the Joint Chiefs of Staff for failing to stand up to President Lyndon Johnson during the Vietnam War.

I was struck by his eloquence and obvious intelligence. Not only was he a dynamic person, he had vast knowledge of military history as well as the ability, it seemed, to motivate almost anyone. To me, that's what command is about!

Soon after McMaster arrived, we got word that the 3d Cavalry would be heading back to Iraq in 2005 for a second year-long deployment. This was an especially difficult time. After the first deployment, the regiment suffered high attrition as soldiers departed the service or transferred out, badly shaken by the many stresses of the war. For those of us still there, that would mean extra pressure and extra burdens, as we tried to pick up the slack. All that just solidified my intention to leave the battlefield and move on to law school.

Then, Colonel McMaster spoke to us.

"Listen," he said. "As you know, the regiment is going back to Iraq. And when we do, we are going there to win!"

We are going there to win.

It was strange, but no one had ever quite said that during my first deployment. We were there. We were doing what we were told to do, our duty. But no one had ever quite asserted we were going to win.

The way McMaster said it, it was almost impossible not to believe him. If I believed in him, then I knew I could believe in myself. I couldn't imagine not being part of his team. I had just experienced the ultimate locker-room halftime pep talk. I reversed my plans and re-upped for another deployment.

Returning to Iraq in March of 2005, I was quickly thrust into Operation Squeeze Play South, led by the 2nd Brigade Combat Team, 10th Mountain Division, in what became the largest combined military operation up to that date. I faced the special challenges of urban combat, leading a Military Transition Team in the volatile Triangle of Death south of Baghdad. House-to-house combat. Mosque and market bombings. Trips along pockmarked Main Supply Route Tampa, the highway in and out of Iraq we all called IED Alley. Improvised explosive devises kept killing and maiming civilians, Iraqi Security Forces, and Coalition Forces. Bodies and body parts were strewn about. The level of suffering was difficult to absorb. On May 23, a car bomb exploded outside a Shiite mosque killing ten civilians and injuring thirty more. On June 5, a complex IED vaporized one of our heavily armored Bradley Fighting Vehicles, killing three of our cavalrymen. That sort of devastation is not something you can prepare for.

One day, just as our convoy headed out on patrol, an eight-year-old boy waved us down with a swollen and bloody right hand.

"Please help!" he pleaded.

Usually, when kids approached us, they wanted candy or money. Commanding the lead vehicle of our patrol, I could see that this boy's needs were more urgent. I stopped, got out, and radioed Sgt. First Class Michael Hanaway, who was commanding the vehicle behind mine and who was an experienced army medic. He got out to have a look.

"You know it's not life, limb, or eyesight, Sir."

Of course, he was right, and I knew that. Those were the only three circumstances that permitted us to take any Iraqi—soldier or civilian—to an American hospital. The boy's shrapnel wounds, horrible as they were, didn't fall into any of those three categories. But we had to do something. How could we not do anything? The boy was wailing, and we were right there.

Mike looked at me. I looked at him. We knew we had to help. "I'll get my bag," he said.

I held the boy's hand while Mike went to work, skillfully plucking hot metal chunks out of this eight-year-old's hand. Right there on the road, with rudimentary tools and no anesthesia, we did what we could that day. I was really proud of Sgt. First Class Hanaway when he finished.

The boy smiled. "Allah ma'ak," I said before he walked away. *Go with God.*

Many times since then I have thought of that boy. How's he doing? Is he still alive? How does he feel about America and its military? Does he appreciate the assistance we gave him? Does he hate us for being there in the first place? I saw much worse in Iraq, but that memory has stuck with me. I have never forgotten that boy and I never will.

I rejoined the 3d ACR in western Nineveh Province, where I led Regimental Iraqi Security Forces on "clear and hold" missions in the city of Tal Afar, establishing Joint Coordination Centers throughout the western Nineveh Province. It was brutal duty, more danger and bursts of close combat. Like many American service members, I was never quite sure what the overall strategy was—I kept hearing we were liberating the Iraqi people—but I took great pride in my dedication to the mission and to the extraordinary men I had sworn to lead. And I always had Colonel McMaster in my head: "We are going there to win."

That mission culminated in September with Operation Restoring Rights and the defeat of the city's insurgent strongholds. Colonel McMaster's strategy was to deploy his cavalry troops into Tal Afar around the clock. Once the local population grew confident that we wouldn't withdraw when darkness fell, they began providing information on the insurgents, enabling U.S. forces to target and defeat them. President George W. Bush praised our success, and we got kudos from CBS's *60 Minutes,* PBS's *Frontline,* and *The New Yorker* magazine, whose writer said our pioneering tactics led to the first success in overcoming the Iraqi insurgency.

We returned home, and they pinned medals on our chests. I ended up with two Bronze Stars, the Purple Heart, the Army Commendation Medal for Valor, and the Combat Action Badge, among others.

So what was wrong with me? Clearly something was. Back at Fort Carson, I felt like I was just going through the motions of life. I was jumpy and irritable. I was glad to be off the battlefield and also missing it terribly. I wondered what I was going to do with the rest of my life. Sleeping became increasingly troublesome. I wasn't sure what was coming next. I was in the throes of what I now recognize as a worsening case of PTSD.

Then, I suffered another blow. Literally.

On June 26, 2006, Colonel McMaster would head off to a new assignment. A change-of-command ceremony was planned at Fort Carson to mark that important transition.

During a rehearsal the day prior to the ceremony, I was sprinting across the parade field in front of a few thousand soldiers, executing the Regimental Adjutant's portion of the ceremony, when I tripped on something, I'm not sure what. My traumatic brain injury and worsening neuropathy may have been contributing factors. But I fell and ruptured the patellar tendon in my right leg.

That's a very painful injury and a game-changing one for most. It's not an ACL. It's the major tendon of the leg. I was whisked to Evans Army Hospital for surgery, where the doctors did what they could. But my tumble at Fort Carson exacerbated my injuries from Iraq, further compromising my spine, worsening my traumatic brain injury, and advancing the neuropathy that was already suppressing my circulation and stiffening my joints. Compared to the physical injuries that some others experience in Iraq and Afghanistan, I still counted myself lucky. But after seventeen years in the army, I knew that even after leaving the military I'd be dealing with the physical *and* psychological traumas of war, and I knew my recovery would be a long and challenging one.

I had no idea where I would find the help I needed. Actually, it was worse than that: I didn't even understand how badly I needed it.

That is, until Tuesday came along.

CHAPTER 3

Direct Action

—◦◦⟪●⟫◦◦—

*The better I get to know men, the more I find
myself loving dogs.*
CHARLES DE GAULLE

WITH TUESDAY AT MY SIDE, I NEVER HAD TO BE ALONE AGAIN.
When I was sad, he would nuzzle up against me. When I was
cooped up inside too long, he would shoot me one of his looks that
said, "Come on, Luis! Let's go outside and play!" That look was similar but not exactly the same as the look that said, "Come on, Luis.
Let's go outside. I really need to pee!" I learned to heed both pleas,
which got me off the couch and into the great outdoors, a therapeutic
maneuver all by itself. When I felt anxious, Tuesday would march
beside me wherever we had to go. When my mind wandered, Tuesday would refocus me squarely on the issue at hand. Wherever we
were, whatever time of the day or night, Tuesday was always tuned
into me. Even when I was sleeping, he was still on the job. Just from
the rhythm of my breathing in bed, he could tell when I was having
a nightmare. He knew to nudge me awake with his cold, wet nose.

Over time, I came to see that this brilliant animal was capable of
just about anything, small or large. He could fetch my sneakers when

I needed them even before I knew I did. He could make friends with almost anyone. With his smarts, his cuteness, and his relentless jocularity, he could—and did—turn my life around. After being with Tuesday a while, it was almost impossible to tally up all the ways that he helped me—and even more important, all the ways he helped me help myself and helped me help others. He wasn't just doing. He was teaching. Even today, I still struggle. PTSD doesn't ever just vanish. But with Tuesday around, I got better and better at life. And we were ready to get on with the business of healing others in need.

———— ◦◉◦ ————

We heard from Amee Gilbert on Facebook, one of the reasons Tuesday and I always try to stay accessible via social media. Amee had a son, U.S. Army Specialist Cole Vickery, who was an infantryman and recent Iraq War veteran, currently stationed at Fort Carson, Colorado. I didn't know Cole. But I knew Fort Carson. I had been stationed there with the 3d Cavalry Regiment.

As is often the case when Tuesday and I hear from military families, Cole's mother was heartbroken and didn't know where else to turn. She hoped that, somehow, given our own experiences, we might be able to help.

Her son had served with valor and distinction in Iraq with the 4th Infantry Division. He had sustained a traumatic brain injury when his Bradley Fighting Vehicle was almost obliterated by an IED. He'd been awarded the coveted Combat Infantryman Badge, meaning he and his unit had seen plenty of action in the war zone. But like so many other combat veterans, Cole Vickery returned stateside and almost immediately began displaying symptoms of PTSD. The first time I spoke on the phone with his mother, she ticked them off for me, though I'd heard the litany often enough I probably could have ticked them off for her. Anxiety. Nightmares. Lethargy. Difficulty connecting with comrades. Depression. Her son's post-combat mental state was undeniably affecting his daily performance. He missed formation a couple of times, which is not a trivial infraction in the army. Soldiers are expected to muster on time.

His superiors noticed that something wasn't right. How could they not? He wasn't the Cole he'd been before Iraq or even the Cole he was in the war zone. Things got so bad, Amee told me, her once-gregarious, twenty-two-year-old son tried to kill himself with an overdose of pills.

"I cannot take it, Mom," he said in what he thought would be his last call home. "I am done. I am sorry." Thankfully, the suicide attempt failed.

"I don't know how else to put it," Amee told me. "It was the ultimate, desperate cry for help."

But instead of reaching out to this obviously troubled service member, Cole's superiors turned their backs instead. It didn't seem to be any one superior officer. The hostile reaction was institutional, running straight up the chain of command. Which, of course, only made things worse, as anyone would have predicted. These warriors come home with a chest full of medals. They start to experience adjustment problems and emotional pain. Rather than being given the chance to deal with their issues in a decent, supportive environment, they get an old-fashioned army beat-down.

"My son loved the army, and he served the army valiantly," his mother told me. "But then when he needed the army most, it paid back his loyalty like a cold, hard machine."

After more than seventeen years in the army, I knew exactly what Amee was talking about. Though I left with an honorable discharge, my exit from the army was under far less than ideal circumstances. To get the help I needed—which included *canine therapy*—I had to leave the army I had served for my entire adult life.

The fact that Cole was at Fort Carson, my former home—well, that made it even easier to put myself in his boots. And the fact that

Cole was a junior enlisted soldier, I knew, made things that much worse for him. I was an officer, a captain! Far too often, junior enlisted personnel are treated as if they are expendable, just another replaceable cog in the big army machine. If one causes trouble, get rid of it, and slap in a new one.

Once that course is set in motion, it is very difficult to change. Good luck trying to get the army to reverse itself. But I knew Amee and I had to try.

The army was already moving quickly to kick Cole out—or, to use the army slang, to "chapter" him with a less-than-honorable discharge. "Chaptering" refers to a section in the Uniform Code of Military Justice, and it's happened hundreds of thousands of times to America's sons and daughters in the decades between Vietnam and today. In some cases, it is, no doubt, warranted. But in my experience, it's employed far more often than is justified, a convenient way to dispose of anyone who has become inconvenient to the army. As in Cole's case, PTSD often figures in.

A less-than-honorable discharge can create a lifetime of chaos. It's hard enough for the average veteran to find productive, post-military employment. Imagine if you had to explain on every job application how you were kicked out of the army because you didn't behave in a manner that the military considered quite right. How many jobs do you think you'd be offered? It's almost like being a convicted felon. In some ways even worse, and it never goes away. It's hard to think of a betrayal worse than saddling an undeserving service member with *that*. Working together, Amee and I came up with a multifaceted strategic plan.

I helped her draft a letter—then a series of letters—to her son's superiors at Fort Carson and the Pentagon, insisting that they take another look at the injustice that was about to be done. If you can reach these people on a human level, I have found, sometimes you can make progress. At the same time, we made efforts to generate media publicity. I thought maybe we could embarrass the army into doing the right thing. I helped Amee draft an op-ed piece and we got it published in Amee's hometown newspaper, *The Seattle Times*. It highlighted Cole's situation and pointed out how common this kind of treatment of soldiers had become.

"After returning home from an intense combat tour in Iraq," Amee wrote, "Cole realized he needed help. He began to have nightmares, anxiety, and rage for no apparent reason. Then he courageously asked for help from the army's mental-health office. But, instead of getting help, he was ridiculed, threatened by his chain of command, drugged by the medical providers, isolated as a form of 'corrective action' for sleeping in, and left with no hope."

And where were his superior officers? Where was the army he had been so loyal to?

"Either because of a lack of education or total disregard from his superior officers," Amee wrote, "his calls for help were dismissed."

The letters, the phone calls, and the op-ed were impactful. We heard from a caring medical official at Fort Carson, who sounded appalled at what was being done. And damned if the stubborn army bureaucracy didn't start to bend! But despite the seeming change in tone, I was still concerned. Were we just getting lip service? Were they just ducking bad publicity? I needed to see for myself that Cole was getting the treatment and understanding that he and so many others truly deserve.

Tuesday and I got on a plane and flew to Colorado. It was my first time back at Fort Carson since I'd gotten out. When we arrived, Cole was being held at Fort Carson's so-called Warrior Transition Unit. These Warrior Transition Units were supposed to be a compassionate, healing environment, the type of supportive environment where soldiers returning from the war zone could get the help they needed. I had reason to be wary, even beyond Amee's disturbing reports. There had been some media publicity at the time, from NPR and others, describing these transition units across the country as "warehouses of despair." It was said that soldiers were being kept there with little or no treatment until they could be discharged, honorably or not, back into the outside world.

I didn't know what to expect. But as soon as we got to Colorado Springs, Tuesday and I went directly to see Cole at Fort Carson.

To our great relief, Cole's therapist, Robert Gren, was exceptionally welcoming. He'd read Amee's op-ed piece. He knew who Tuesday and I were. He seemed genuinely concerned about Cole's well-being. Tuesday, of course, bonded with the therapist immediately. A few minutes after we arrived, Cole walked into the office.

He was a nice-looking kid, broad-shouldered and calm.

I gave him a huge hug. Tuesday leaned up against the soldier's right leg, and Cole reached down to pet him. Cole was friendly and looked healthier than I expected him to.

"My mom told me you'd be coming," he said. He seemed glad to see us.

He gave us a brief situational report. His superior officers had been treating him with concern, not disdain. "They've pretty much done a one-eighty," he said with a smile.

I was pleased he seemed so relaxed given everything he had endured. We each took a seat to talk some more. I noticed as we spoke, Cole kept glancing down at Tuesday. Tuesday kept bumping his head against Cole's leg and his chair. At one point, Cole knelt down and gave Tuesday a loving embrace. I noticed his eyes watering as he did that.

After we spoke a few more minutes, Cole and Robert invited Tuesday and me to walk around the inpatient clinic. This was definitely something I hadn't expected. Such facilities are usually off-limits to outsiders. Maybe they didn't consider us outsiders.

I didn't get an exact count, but there were probably fifty men and women, mostly young people, all veterans of Iraq and Afghanistan. I let Tuesday off his leash, knowing he was in a contained environment and trusting that he knew how to behave. You could feel the energy shift when the soldiers spotted a friendly golden retriever in the hallway. That change was palpable. Even though the unit was billed as a supportive environment, it still had a sterile look, white walls, government furniture, other standard-issue stuff. Tuesday was an unexpected, furry ambassador. It's amazing how much difference one dog can make. It was like he was painting the walls with tail-wagging, loving goodness.

Soldiers started coming over to him, giving a pat or a pet or just saying hello. He went from person to person, from soldier to soldier, not in an uncontrolled or excited way—just warmly. I watched from a short distance, the extraordinary calming effect he had on everyone, like a four-legged Dalai Lama had just arrived. I don't think the staff or the patients had seen anything like that before.

Cole's therapist, Robert, led us into a conference room, where a group therapy session was about to begin. There were two dozen chairs in a large circle, people sitting in all but three of them. Cole, his therapist, and I joined the circle. Tuesday started at my feet.

I say *started* because he did not remain there.

As the discussion began, I was struck by how open everybody was. These hardened combat veterans were telling each other about their night sweats and their quick irritability and the frustration at how they felt after returning home. They weren't feeling sorry for themselves. But they were acknowledging—to each other at least— that the transition off the battlefield had been far more challenging than they ever thought it would be.

It was a very soulful therapy session. People were talking and crying and sharing their experiences. Some were angry. Some were upset. Some were asking for advice. All of them were facing difficult issues in what was, finally, a helpful environment.

And like the four-legged ambassador he was, Tuesday went from man to woman, soldier to soldier, chair to chair, nuzzling each individual, leaning into them, burying his head in their legs and their laps. He seemed to provide enormous comfort.

At the therapist's invitation, I spoke for a few minutes about my own experiences coming home from war. I reminded the enlisted soldiers that these issues affect officers as well. I don't think many of them had heard an army captain talk like that. Not as a superior but as one of the many who has suffered the effects of war. I am certain none of them had heard an officer extol the therapeutic benefits of a service dog.

For a captain to say, "Listen, this shit almost did me in"—they seemed gripped by my own confession.

Almost as much as they were charmed by Tuesday.

Cole was honorably discharged from the army. He was thrilled, his mother even more so. I felt a great sense of satisfaction. And, of course, I told Tuesday. He could tell how excited I was—my voice, my smile, my body language. His wagging tail and perked-up ears told me he was every bit as psyched as I was.

A few months later, after his discharge, Cole decided he could benefit from having a service dog. I connected him and Amee with a terrific agency, whose staff paired Cole with an impeccably trained and absolutely adorable St. Bernard named Cylis. It was tremendously fitting that this story had a beautiful furry ending.

CHAPTER 4

Marine Mom

⟾⟪◉⟫⟾

To describe my mother would be to write about a hurricane in its
perfect power. Or the climbing, falling colors of a rainbow.
MAYA ANGELOU

TUESDAY AND I WERE AT HOME IN NEW YORK CITY WHEN I GOT AN
email from a woman in Connecticut named Karin Marinaro. She
had a son she was worried sick about.

"Hi, Luis," she wrote. "I think your book was put into my hands
by divine intervention. My son, Rob, has been suffering from severe
PTSD since his return from Afghanistan. He is a 1st Lt. in the Marine
Corps and is a Human Intel officer."

Many of the emails we get start off very much like this one. They're
written by moms and dads, wives and girlfriends, husbands and boy-
friends, children, friends and, of course, veterans themselves. Someone
has an issue. They are frustrated and don't know where to turn. Somewhere between confused and desperate, they reach out to Tuesday and
me, not quite sure how we can help but hoping that we can.

Some days, it feels like I never left the military. I'm taking care of
soldiers, taking care of families, taking care of people with disabilities. It's like being an officer, just without the commission I used to

hold. I'm still leading people. I'm still trying to influence them in a positive way. The main difference is now I have a trusted and formidable ally at my side.

In the best cases, we don't only address their individual issues. We also make a dent on macro issues that affect thousands or millions of other people. What Karin Marinaro told me about her son was both familiar and outrageous. Rob could so easily have been me. "He went through a similar situation like you, where he was ambushed and almost died," his mother wrote. "One of the young infantry Marines died in his arms."

As anxious as she was when Rob was sent to Afghanistan, that's how relieved she was when his deployment ended and he returned to American soil, to Marine Corps Base Camp Pendleton in California. "I have to tell you, Luis, I was so happy to have my son back," she said. "But as the year progressed after his return, I knew the beautiful, pure child I raised was gone. He's had a few issues in the last year: a DUI and an unauthorized visit to Mexico. One of his Marines committed suicide. Rob was so distraught he didn't care if he lived or died and went to Mexico because he wanted to be in danger."

Rob knew he could no longer serve in the military, his mother said. He just wanted to leave with an honorable discharge and get on with his life. Unfortunately, he got caught in a dispute between two three-star generals. "The three-star general at Camp Pendleton said that due to his incredible service and PTSD stress, he should be discharged honorably and be let out in April," Mrs. Marinaro explained. But what should have flown through without question had been unexpectedly blocked. "Long story short, my son received notice that when his paperwork hit the Pentagon, another three-star general wanted to Administratively Separate him," a less-than-honorable discharge. "Upon hearing the news, my son lost the will to live. He tried to commit suicide and has been in the hospital twice and is now in a rehab program. Rob's doctors know that the best thing for him is to be out of the Marine Corps, but the bureaucracy is holding him hostage." Karin had been told it might be many months, or even longer, before he got out. "I cannot watch my son slowly die. I am reaching out to you to see if you know of anyone that will help me."

How could we not help?

Karin and I spoke on the phone and agreed to come up with a plan. She didn't seem at all reluctant to confront the military establishment, if that's what it took. We agreed we would find a time to meet in person in the not-too-distant future and sort through what came next. Tuesday and I would be on the road for the next week or so, I told Karin. We had several appearances, one at a senior-citizens' community near the Aberdeen Proving Ground, home of the U.S. Army Ordnance Corps, where much of the bombs and ammo are made. But I looked forward to speaking with her after I got back to New York.

—————◆—————

Tuesday and I arrived an hour early at the Glen Meadows Retirement Community in Glen Arm, Maryland. This is open farm country. Before we went inside the meeting room, I parked the car, began pulling my things together, and let Tuesday out to run off his leash in a nearby field. The corn had already been harvested. Spread into the distance in three directions were acres of open fields dotted with piles of cow manure. We'd been in the car for more than three hours. I knew Tuesday was eager to do his business and work off some of that pent-up energy of his.

I pulled on my jacket, tightened my tie, and collected my papers and my business cards. I could see out the car window, about one hundred yards away, that Tuesday seemed to be romping happily in the field. He was almost dancing out there. He was flopping his shoulders and his back against the ground, while he held his hind legs up normally. He was doing little half-somersaults and rolling in the grass. Watching him I couldn't help but smile. I was glad he was getting some exercise. I knew we'd be inside for three hours at least.

Then, it hit me.

"Oh, no," I mumbled to myself. So that's what Tuesday was so giddy about? He was doing more than dancing away the long car ride.

He'd found a pile of cow manure and was rubbing the poop all over his body. What I took to be somersaults I now realized were his way of smearing the cow manure all over his coat. If this was really a dance, it was his manure dance. He was literally rolling in it and sliding through it and pressing into it and having the time of his life, right before we had to go inside for this event with the nice people of the Glen Meadows Retirement Community.

"Jesus, Tuesday!" I yelled at the top of my lungs. *"Stop that!"*

He definitely heard me and came running back to the car. I could see right away what a horrible mess he was. He had three huge splotches of manure on his back and God knows what else buried in his fur. And he smelled awful. Of course, I hadn't brought much in the way of cleaning products in the car. I did have his brush and a container of baby wipes, but this was a dog who desperately needed a head-to-tail bath. I couldn't imagine how I would make him present-able to the people inside who were eager to meet him. And pet him. And hug him. And get up-close-and-personal with my well-behaved service dog, as audiences so often like to do.

I did what I could with the brush and the baby wipes. I got the stuff off his vest the best I could, but the mess was everywhere—places a simple wipe couldn't reach, in the seams of his vest and where the straps connected to the nylon. I stepped back and looked at him as objectively as possible. I was relieved, at least, that he looked vaguely passable. The smell was evaporating and a lot less offensive. I didn't yell at him. I understood. He'd been in the car for hours. I'd seen how much fun he was having out there. This is what dogs do. They like rolling in smelly things. And, anyone with a dog understands: Surprises like this one invariably hit at the worst possible moment.

I let out one, last, exasperated, *"Tuesday!"* and we went inside.

———

Tuesday's roll in cow manure, I'd soon learn, wasn't the only surprise of the day. Tuesday and I said hello to the organizers. A good-size crowd was already waiting for us—quite a few vets included, from Vietnam and Korea and a full row up front from World War II. That's one of the pleasures of events with older audiences. We get to meet members of that Greatest Generation, whose number is dwindling fast. The place could have been a Norman Rockwell painting. It was that American and that pure. Everyone stood for the Pledge of Allegiance. The women's choir sang the National Anthem. Many of the veterans had on caps and other military gear. No one said anything about Tuesday's questionable hygiene, though I'm not sure if no one noticed or they were just too polite to bring it up.

We had a great event. I told about the day I got Tuesday and how I never stopped learning from him and about him. I spoke about the invisible wounds of war and how easy it is for many people to overlook them. People asked a lot of questions—about Tuesday's favorite places and favorite foods, about the sprawling and maddening Veterans Administration bureaucracy, about our lobbying efforts in Washington and across the nation. I told stories about our many adventures and all the many surprises we'd experienced as we traveled around and the one particular surprise we'd encountered in a field right outside. Hopefully, that answered any unasked questions about Tuesday's slightly musky odor. I signed several dozen books. And just as things were winding down, I got my second surprise of the day. A friendly, blond woman came over to say hello.

"Karin Marinaro," she said, holding out her hand. I was suddenly face to face with the concerned mother who had written to me about her Marine son.

"When I saw on your website you'd be speaking in Maryland," she said, "I figured I might as well drive down from Connecticut. It's not *that* far." A quick mental calculation and I realized she'd driven almost 300 miles. Just as I had expected. This was a woman who was focused on getting things done.

Karin and I grabbed some coffee and found a table in a quiet corner where we could sit down and talk. We spent the next three hours figuring out how we could best help her son. Thankfully, this had been an afternoon program and we didn't keep our Glen Meadows' hosts up all night.

As Karin and I spoke, I could see Tuesday reacting to her many strong emotions. He could feel her sadness, her stress, and her pain. He naturally gravitated to her. He stood there, nuzzling her and snuggling her underneath the table. She pet him, and she didn't stop. He became her *de facto* service dog. It was gratifying to watch him help this woman he'd only just met. For one thing, he's so good at it. For another, she needed it so badly. And of course, I wanted her to feel relief from the grieving it was obvious she was experiencing. I could do what I could do. But Tuesday, he had an entirely different set of tools. He was bringing Karin into the circle. He's trained to support, but he also has an intuitive understanding of how to comfort and connect in ways that very few humans, myself included, ever can. He goes to people, as he went to the Tuskegee Airman and now Karin, out of a pure heart filled with pure love.

There is an innocence about the way Tuesday feels a person's needs and then acts on his instincts. It's magical. Or more accurately, I could use the world *divine*. What Tuesday does is so much more than most humans do for so many reasons. Maybe it's because they don't know how to or they don't want to. Maybe it's because they don't feel it's appropriate or they don't believe they have the skills.

Here, Karin and I were, having a conversation that evoked high emotions. It wasn't inconceivable that I might reach out and hold her hand or give a quick, gentle hug. But as humans, we are socialized to do that only in the most highly restrained ways. We don't want to make the other person uncomfortable. We don't want to violate anyone's personal space.

Dogs aren't saddled with all that. A dog, especially a highly trained dog, has none of that baggage. A less well-trained dog might invade a stranger's space, possibly frightening that person with a gregarious welcome, ultimately creating a wall of suspicion between them. A well-trained dog can pierce our human aura to get to the core. A dog can help a person take a deep breath, to really be raw, to be herself.

With Tuesday easing the emotionally difficult parts of Karin's story, we kept talking. "We have to be smart about this," I told her. "We have to find the techniques that will be effective."

She explained to me that Rob's honorable discharge was formally approved by Lt. Gen. Thomas Waldhauser, the three-star commanding general of the 1st Marine Expeditionary Force at Camp Pendleton and the Marine Corps Forces Central Command. And that should have been that. But General Waldhauser's decision was promptly overturned by another three-star general in the Pentagon, someone who didn't know a damn thing about Rob and his case.

"Frankly," I said to Karin, "this is horse shit."

"You're telling me!" she said, shaking her head.

"I have zero qualms going out to Camp Pendleton with you and meeting with the commanding general," I told her. "I'll happily go eyeball-to-eyeball with him. But that might not be enough," I cautioned. "We may need to take this to the Secretary of the Navy. And honestly, a little pressure from Congress and some media publicity wouldn't hurt."

These weren't empty suggestions. I knew I could deliver here.

"Never kid yourself," I told Karin. "The U.S. military is a highly political organization. A decorated army-captain-turned-advocate-turned-*New-York-Times*-bestselling-author has some leverage to make people pay attention, even at the highest ranks."

Even as I said the words, I was struck by the sad realization that common sense and decency sometimes have to be prodded. "None of this means the Pentagon will immediately snap to attention," I warned Karin. "But I do know that the Pentagon brass like avoiding trouble as much as every other bureaucrat. They can't be sure what we might do. We might call NPR or CNN. They don't like any of that."

We finally agreed we'd take a two-pronged approach. Karin would fly to Camp Pendleton and see her son. We agreed we would work together to respond in writing to the Marine Corps and the navy. I would help her and Rob put things in ways that might be clearer or could be expressed in the military's preferred lingo, which is another way of saying *ridiculous legalese*. I would also interpret whatever it is they said back.

At the same time, we agreed to launch our second prong of attack. We decided we would work together writing a column for the biggest paper in her home state of Connecticut, the *Hartford Courant*, explaining exactly what was going on from the clear-eyed perspective of the loving mother of an honored and suffering Marine.

That would get noticed. I was sure of it.

———— ◦❖◦ ————

Karin went to be with her son in California. Initially, she stayed several weeks at Camp Pendleton and then returned as often as she could after that. When you are in a situation like this one—and believe me, I know—it feels like it's you against the Marine Corps or the navy or the army or whatever branch of service it is. It's a lonely place to be. Any kind of support is comforting. You feel small, unappreciated, misunderstood, inconsequential, in danger. You feel like an ant about to be crushed by a giant shoe. I was glad Karin had the means and desire to be with her son as much as possible.

Karin and I got into long back-and-forths with various military lawyers, commanders, and other officials. It's amazing how many people get involved in a case like this. She was a great natural advocate for her son—firm, focused, reasonable-sounding, and utterly dogged. She didn't seem to be scared of anyone.

Meanwhile, we began working on that newspaper column. I helped her focus on the details of her son's battle with the bureaucracy, while she wrote the words that only a mother could. "To lose a child is one of the worst tragedies in life," she wrote from her heart. "I have almost lost my son, Marine 1st Lt. Robert Marinaro, 26, twice—once in Afghanistan and once here—by suicide."

The column we came up with was pretty moving, I thought. It was written in a clear, mother's voice.

"My son was raised with strong morals," her piece began. "He received a Navy ROTC scholarship to Carnegie Mellon University and excelled. Rob was commissioned at the top in his ROTC class, received honors from Carnegie Mellon in 2008, and graduated with distinction from the Marine Corps' Basic and Intelligence schools."

She went on to describe his deployment in Afghanistan, his excellent leadership skills, and the firefight where one of his Marines was lost. She told about his return to Camp Pendleton and the issues that began to appear.

"I watched my beautiful, bright, loving son wrestle with his mental demons and implored him to get help," she wrote. "Sadly, Rob did not receive the help he needed until it was too late." She held nothing back, describing the alcohol, the drugs, the suicide attempt, and the run-ins with the law. She asked why a clueless military bureaucracy could not grasp the causes of this, preferring to turn a hero into a pariah.

"I will do everything in my power to save my son and others like him," the mother wrote. "They are not 'worthless,' as one of the colonels at Camp Pendleton referred to Rob, but human beings who need help. As the mother of a Marine, I stand true to the Marine Corps motto, 'Semper Fidelis.' It is sad that there are those in the Marine Corps who do not."

At the end of the column was a simple author's description:

"Karin Klarides Marinaro lives in Cheshire," it said.

The editors, I thought, might have added one more line to that. "She is a mother who helped save her son's life."

※

Our one-two punch sparked immediate momentum for Rob's case! It's amazing what media publicity and motherly pressure can achieve. Almost overnight, rational people inside the Pentagon took a second look at Rob's situation and, without anyone admitting error, things just changed.

Rob received that honorable Marine Corps discharge he so patently deserved. He moved back east to get on with the rest of his life. He seems to be doing well. He still doesn't like to relive the final parts of his military experience. But he gets well-deserved satisfaction knowing how honorably he served on the battlefield. His mother, Karin, is glad to have her son back and glad their ordeal is over. That's exactly what Tuesday and I are traveling the country for.

CHAPTER 5

Happiest Spirit

━━━━━━━━━━ ꞉«◉»꞉ ━━━━━━━━━━

The Way is in the Heart.
ATTRIBUTED TO BUDDHA

TUESDAY IS THE HAPPIEST SPIRIT I KNOW—OF ANY SPECIES. HE HAS A nearly miraculous way of making people smile. He does it through his facial expressions, his body language, and, of course, that golden coat of his. I don't want to say blondes have more fun, but maybe blondes do have more fun.

It's much more than that, though. There is a certain glow about Tuesday that isn't just from his natural good looks. It comes from his illuminating personality.

It doesn't matter where we are in the world, we are asked a lot of questions. When I say "we," I mean the royal, furry *we*, Tuesday and me. The questions really are to both of us. And often, Tuesday's the one who knows the answers best.

People ask: "So what is Tuesday's favorite place to go?"

When I was first asked that, I had to think hard. At first, I wasn't sure how to answer. I went over in my mind some of the amazing places he and I have been blessed to visit: The Arizona desert in spring-time. The misty seaside cliffs of the northern California coast. The sugar-white beaches of the Florida panhandle. New York City during the holidays. Various farms and ranches we've been to, where Tuesday got to breathe in two scents that always seem to delight him: the smell of dead things and poop. But as I kept thinking, I was having trouble settling on any one place.

Then, it hit me.

"You know," I finally said, "Tuesday's favorite place is his next place. Wherever the next place we're going—that's his favorite place."

What a precious gift it is to feel that way! If only all of us could live our lives with an attitude like that. Having such an exuberant zest for life, wherever we are, whatever we're doing, that *next* is our favorite thing. He's happy everywhere, but he never stops believing there is more joy to come. There is a lesson in that, one of many that Tuesday has taught me, infecting my spirit with this open attitude of his. Day after day, it can't help but affect you, being around such an optimistic creature. That energy gets into your head and your heart and your bloodstream. It is a tremendous blessing. There is no other way to put it.

It doesn't matter if we are going to Naples or getting in or out of a car or stepping into the next room. Whatever the next place is, that's his favorite. You can see it and feel it right away, just being in his presence. It isn't just sort of. It's not a subtle thing at all. I'd say it's impossible to miss.

Some people who believe they have a deep connection with animals tend to anthropomorphize them, placing too many humanistic characteristics onto dogs, cats, and, I suppose, snakes and birds too. It is possible to exaggerate these things. But by and large, I find that it is more interesting to examine the differences in our characteristics. Dogs—and Tuesday is certainly this way—have a special way of being excited over the now. Of course, we are all striving for that in our lives, to be fully present where we are right now. But as humans, we are constantly trying to center ourselves, to find some balance, some peace, whether that's through medication, yoga, exercise, drugs, relationships, hobbies, or prayer. It is hard. As humans, we tend to vacillate between the past and future. It is difficult for us to focus on the now. Our busy lives, our intrusive technology, our constant multitasking, the many things that need to be done—all of it can stand in the way of being focused and excited about where we are right this very minute and what is about to happen next. Dogs just aren't wired like that. They are far better at living in the moment. They have that kind of Zen, a sort of Jedi mind-set, that begets positive feelings and harnesses a state of peace—positive feelings that lead to positive actions. Tuesday is that way and not just with me. With other people. With other dogs. With other species. It's remarkable to watch and valuable to learn from.

Even people who are afraid of animals say to me: "You know, I had a terrible experience with a dog who bit me. But this dog, I am comfortable being around." Tuesday has this energy, this openness, this enthusiasm. Children, adults, it affects everyone.

Since Tuesday came to me in November of 2008, I have given a lot of thought to how he achieves this. It sure would be nice to harness that spirit, learn from it, and be more like him. A big part of it, I am convinced, comes from how extraordinarily deferential he is toward others. In his mind and through his actions, he is always trying to put somebody at ease, from ancient Airmen in VA hospitals to mothers with struggling sons. Not standoffish. Not feeling fear or stress or discomfort. Fully at ease. Tuesday is not possessive. He will not violate a person's space or a dog's space or a cat's space. He won't play with another being's toy if he senses any hint that the dog or cat or person feels "this is my territory" or "this is my domain." And he always lets other dogs and cats smell him first.

You know how it is when most dogs meet. They naturally go to each other. One smells the other's rear and vice versa. They take a measure of each other that way. But Tuesday approaches that first encounter in a noticeably different way. He will let the other dog, big or small, smell him thoroughly before he takes his first sniff. That's his way of being deferential to that being. He instinctively knows that the other dog may need a calm approach. And believe me, it's noticed, by creatures large and small. Most dogs approach interactions with other dogs the same way people interact, burdened or buoyed by past experience. They carry dog memories of their own past interactions. That dog may have had a traumatic experience, being beaten by a human or lunged at by another dog. Those memories can linger for years. Tuesday allows the other dog he encounters, or the person he meets, to work through those feelings without unnecessary interference or pressure from him.

It is really something, Tuesday's situational awareness and self-control. He has this natural ability to be humble and gracious and respectful toward other beings from the very moment of contact. It sets the tone. It begets comfort. It says right from the start: "I am here to connect with you, not to threaten you in any way." This is especially true in how he interacts with people.

We humans walk around with so many layers of anxiety. We have so many inhibitions and fears and walls, it can be difficult to be genuine. It's even harder, I think, to be perceived as being genuine. Tuesday's approach is the opposite. He seems to be saying all the time: "Be kind to everyone. Everyone is fighting battles of some sort." Tuesday understands that intuitively. With all the many ways he's helped me in my battle with the symptoms of PTSD, this has been especially valuable for me to try to emulate. His spirit has—partially—invaded mine! It's a spirit Tuesday and I would like to spread everywhere. The world would be a much better place to live if all of us were more that way.

I see proof of his unique ability to interact positively nearly every day. One day when Tuesday and I were getting coffee, a man came up to us. I could tell he liked dogs. He had his cup of coffee. I had mine. Tuesday was sitting with me. As the stranger approached us, Tuesday reacted in a way that suspicious humans, and even some of the best-trained dogs, would never do. Tuesday stood up from his seated position, started wagging his tail, telling the world with his body language that meeting someone new was special and great. "Oh, boy! This is wonderful! I get to meet someone new! Say hello! Connect with this new person!"

Sure enough, that is exactly what the man wanted. "I have a dog," he said as he got closer, "and I lost a dog two years ago, a dog I loved very much."

"It's a love affair, isn't it?" I said.

"Yeah," he said. "It is."

He glanced over at Tuesday, who was wagging his tail and smiling. "I didn't want to approach your dog," the man said. "I've always thought the dog should approach the person."

"That is very wise," I answered. "A lot of people don't understand that. Quite a number get bitten by dogs they don't know."

"Yeah," he said. "As a matter of fact, I had a very bad incident with a dog. The dog nearly tore my hand off and pierced my tendons. I'm grateful I didn't have nerve damage."

I nodded. I'd heard those stories before, often from people who, for one reason or another, were deathly afraid of dogs but recognized something in Tuesday that is kind and approachable. "Tuesday," I said, smiling, "Go say hi."

That's one of the commands Tuesday instantly recognizes. "Go say hi." He walks from wherever he is—usually next to me—to wherever I am pointing, whether it's to a dog or to another person, and he launches into his let's-be-friends moves: His tail starts wagging. His butt begins to wiggle. His head bobs up and down and from side to side. It really is Tuesday's love dance. *I see you. I am paying attention to you. I love you.*

How can anyone not respond positively to that?

These are just the first little actions that clearly show he is happy and wants to connect. And he takes it from there. He's always determined to make himself clearer still. He'll nudge the person. He'll brush against their thigh, touch their arm in such a way that tells the person, "Please pet me." This isn't about the enjoyment a dog gets from the physical act of a hand rubbing his fur. It's deeper than that. This is the way dogs communicate. This is the way Tuesday talks.

"I want to connect with you," he is saying. "I want to embrace you."

Most people crave this type of interaction—a warm, friendly embrace—even if they don't realize how much. But it's when they get the chance to actually experience a hello from Tuesday, they find that they really like the way it makes them feel. They recognize instantly that, unlike with humans, with this special dog it's a true embrace. There is no hidden agenda. No ulterior motive. With this being, what you see is what you get. It's "Hello, I am Tuesday, and I would just love to meet with you and snuggle with you." At its very core, it's what everyone wants—maybe not literally, but we all want to be embraced, respected, connected with, and loved. For a long time, PTSD robbed me of the ability to experience any of this. But being with Tuesday and watching him, I am constantly reminded of what many people take for granted and also how others are suffering or hiding inside their own shells in some way. Life would be very boring without relationships. Not just human relationships, relationships with all kinds of beings.

Not a day or hour goes by when I don't think about Tuesday and what he is doing in relation to what I am doing. It is a deep and genuine relationship we've forged. I use him as a touchstone, a role model to emulate, telling me when I should go out and have a nice walk and when it's time to play. Striving to be like Tuesday, I find myself thinking that I should engage with more people. I should not be so introspective. That is not who I really want to be. And I see in his infectious behavior the things I want to be better at. He is this omnipresent reminder to be true to thyself, which is a blessing of immeasurable value.

———◈———

For Tuesday and me, wherever we are, I begin most days sitting up in bed, looking out the window and drinking a cup of coffee. Tuesday has his butt and side pressed up against my right thigh. It is nice. It's a cozy way to begin the day.

When I first got Tuesday, I learned that dogs fall into two categories: dogs that are leaners and those that do not lean. The leaners want to touch you, paw you, snout you. Leaners always want some part of their body in contact with some part of yours. They love to be connected.

Not all dogs are like that. Some dogs like to be off by themselves. They will come and connect with you for a while, but the rest of the time they very much like to sit in their own special places alone. It could be a favorite chair, a quiet corner of a room, a sunny window—maybe a beloved doggy bed. That is fine. But I am, I have discovered, the type of person who likes the leaners. Luckily, my service dog seems to feel the same way I do. Tuesday—sometimes subtly, sometimes not so subtly—wants to have his side touching mine. To me and to a lot of animal owners, this touching has a powerful effect. It is a subconscious form of love that seems to promote confidence. It is a sign of support.

The ancient Chinese philosopher Lao Tzu put it like this: "Being deeply loved by someone gives you strength, while loving someone deeply gives you courage." I have found that to be 100 percent true.

As human beings, we experience this by holding the hand of someone we love, by silently resting our head on the shoulder of someone we trust. People sleeping with or sitting next to their animals—it's a genuine reflection of a bond that is deep, pure, and fulfilling. It may give you peace of mind. It may offer relief if you are stressed. Day to day, it is life enabling.

Serious studies have been done showing that looking into a dog's eyes or petting a dog for twenty seconds releases oxytocin in the human body, which is beneficial. This is the same hormone that is shown to spike in mothers' brains when they interact with their newborns and strengthens the mother-child bond. Oxytocin diminishes stress and cortisol and increases endorphins. There is a physical component to this sort of connection that is certainly true for me. What I've learned is that it goes both ways. Tuesday needs that same connection that he's supplying me with. Not just Tuesday, lots of animals, especially dogs, need that. They are pack animals. Have you ever passed by a pet shop with a litter of puppies, all smooshed in there on top of each other in the window, adorably cute, and nearly impossible to tell where one ends and the next one begins? Is that her tail, his paws, and where did that one's head go? You wonder, "How on earth can that be comfortable? How can that puppy on the bottom not feel crushed?"

The reality is this snuggling, this cuddling, this warmth is comforting and nurturing to them. Pack animals need their packs. That's how they thrive—on the connection of the pack. Likewise, it gives them strength and peace and a sense of nurturing that is essential to their being. Without question, Tuesday and I are a pack.

CHAPTER 6

Dirty Water

—«○»—

. . . the Spirit of God was hovering over the waters.
GENESIS 1:2

A CAREER IN THE MILITARY COMES WITH CERTAIN DANGERS. ANYONE who's ever worn a uniform understands that. But the water at a U.S. military base on American soil? No, that should not be one of the deadlier threats.

Too bad no one warned Sgt. David Metzler.

Even before he and I talked, I knew I was going to like him. "Not as lean—not as mean—still a Marine," he wrote in the subject line of his first email to me. This was a guy who stood for something and could also laugh at himself.

"I've lost my inner-ear balance and most of my hearing," the former Marine Corps sergeant told me the first time we spoke. "I have macular degeneration. So I don't see too well. All my teeth have been pulled out. I have total nerve damage in both knees, lower legs, ankles, and feet," which makes it impossible for him to walk. "I was prescribed Vicodin twenty-five years ago, and Oxycodone during the last fifteen years. The local doctors treat me like a street junkie, although I still take the original dosage, and I live with a lot of pain. I also wear an oxygen unit twenty-four-seven due to lung scarring."

"All that," he added, "because of the water at Camp Lejeune. If it weren't for my daughter and my service dog, I don't know what I would do."

David Metzler wasn't reaching for sympathy. He was just getting me up to speed on where things stood with him. Since leaving the Marine Corps honorably in 1959, he'd been on a long and frustrating journey through the veterans' health-care system, and I was shaking my head at nearly every word.

A retired auto worker and always a 6th Battalion Marine, he could barely see or hear. His walking days were mostly behind him. He'd found himself largely confined to a wheelchair. But he hadn't lost his gung-ho spirit or the willpower that got him through the day. His daughter, Patty, a registered nurse-practitioner, had been hugely helpful, as had his constantly alert service dog, a twelve-year-old Scottish terrier named Shannon.

"I am blessed to have them both," he told me.

David's avalanche of ailments, it turned out, weren't the result of bombs or bullets. He spent most of his four-year tour at Camp Lejeune, North Carolina, with a shorter stint at Guantánamo Bay, Cuba, nowhere near a battle zone. America wasn't even at war at the time. His main assignment was manning Lejeune's Wallace Creek Boat House, where his duties included signing the watercraft in and out and washing them down with high-pressure hoses. I remembered as a young soldier being assigned to wash down seventy-ton armored vehicles that had been out on training exercises. They were caked with dirt, sand, mud, grease, and grime. We used high-pressure hoses and other equipment similar to those used by boat washers at Camp Lejeune. We had tightly fitting rain gear, and, when the day was done, we were still dripping wet from head to toe.

I never considered equipment washing hazardous duty. Neither did David Metzler. But there was a problem with the water at Camp Lejeune.

A major problem.

And it put hundreds of thousands, perhaps as many as a million U.S. service members and their families, at terrible risk.

I had heard talk about the toxic water at Camp Lejeune. But until I met David, Patty, and Shannon, I had no idea how much human devastation that poisoned water had caused or how poorly our government has responded to the crisis. For a thirty-year period from 1957 to 1987, a variety of solvents and other industrial chemicals were dumped or buried near the wells feeding Camp Lejeune's water supply. These chemicals, more than seventy in all, included some very nasty stuff: a degreaser called trichloroethylene, a dry-cleaning solvent called perchloroethylene, and a highly flammable, colorless liquid called benzene. Believe me, you do not want to drink, bathe in, brush your teeth with, or be anywhere near water as polluted as that. For all those years and for decades after, no one paid much attention until doctors started noticing unexpectedly high rates of cancer, leukemia, miscarriages, and birth defects among people who'd been stationed there—or had lived or worked nearby. At first, government officials reacted the way government officials often do, by ignoring, denying, obstructing, and downplaying the problem. But in 2007, a retired master sergeant named Jerry Ensminger, whose nine-year-old daughter, Janey, had died of cancer in 1985, found an official 1981 document describing a radioactive dump site near a Lejeune rifle range. Finally, the Departments of Defense and Veterans Affairs were pressured into action. On March 8, 2010, Paul Buckley of Hanover, Massachusetts, who'd been stationed at Camp Lejeune, received a 100 percent service-connected disability for multiple myeloma. It was the first time Washington admitted a link to toxic water exposure at

Camp Lejeune. In the months and years that followed, claims poured in, including one from an increasingly disabled former sergeant by the name of David Metzler.

Congress finally took a vote in 2012, and President Barack Obama signed the Janey Ensminger Act, named in honor of the master sergeant's daughter, authorizing full medical care for some military personnel who had been at Camp Lejeune between 1957 and 1987 and developed health problems caused by the water contamination.

This was certainly a step in the right direction—but just a baby step. The new law applied to Camp Lejeune personnel suffering from only fifteen specific ailments including leukemia, multiple myeloma, myelodysplastic syndromes, renal toxicity, non-Hodgkin's lymphoma, and cancer of the esophagus, lung, breast, bladder, or kidney. Unfortunately for Sgt. Metzler, and for hundreds of thousands of others who had served at Camp Lejeune, his many medical conditions were nowhere on the list.

———※———

What has happened and is continuing to happen to these men and women who served at Camp Lejeune is an enormous blight of national significance. Yet the situation has never been elevated in the national consciousness. It is one of a startlingly large number of issues faced by our nation's warriors that fall into the category I refer to as "the War after the War." Ironically, that's often the toughest war of all.

Tuesday and I have been inspired by the many thousands of people who've contacted us about their ongoing battles, as well as our own experiences, to join in and sometimes lead these campaigns. Of course, the sheer number of issues and sufferers means no one person can do it alone. The good news is we have some phenomenal allies on our side, men and women who care deeply and are armed with a real fighting spirit. This is often true of those who are or have been in the military. They have the training, the temperament, and the experience that leaves them ready to take on life-or-death challenges, and they hate nothing more than surrendering.

———◆———

As with many people in his situation, David's medical issues had pushed him to the edge of bankruptcy. "My wife, Jane, and I are deep in medical debt," he told me. "Two mortgages and fifty-five thousand in credit cards over the passing years. Our oldest daughter is taking over our debts, our home, furnishings, and a small storage business we opened after my retirement to meet rising costs."

The first thing I wanted to help David with was something very close to my heart. He and his wife had decided to move to a furnished apartment in Punta Gorda on the Gulf Coast of Florida, where life would be less expensive and the winters less harsh. But almost immediately the move had gotten complicated. The manager of the rental condo was objecting to his service dog. "Although we mailed them all of the necessary and notarized papers about a service dog," he told me soon after he arrived in Florida, "they are insisting I also sign documents stating I do not own a dog, which I have refused to do."

He couldn't imagine living without Shannon, and he certainly didn't want to lie.

This made my blood boil. Tuesday is my service dog and my family and no one had better try to test my loyalty. I knew David felt the same way about his service dog. And he needed Shannon, who listens for any adverse changes in David's breathing during the night and quickly nuzzles him whenever the oxygen unit stops or the hose moves from his nose.

I reminded David that refusing to rent to someone because of a service dog was a clear violation of the Fair Housing Act. There was no way a major complex in Florida would get away with banning service dogs. I was confident that, after receiving a strongly worded letter, the management company would fold immediately.

Done and done.

The United States military was a tougher fight.

David put me in touch with his daughter, Patty, and I learned more about his terrible journey through this health-care nightmare. Within a year of being honorably discharged in April 1959, he began to develop neurological problems. In 1963, he was first diagnosed with inner-ear nerve damage. The damage caused chronic dizziness, falling, and hearing loss. By the late 1960s and into the early 1970s, he developed degenerative eye disease and muscle atrophy with progressive loss of function in his lower extremities. His muscles and nerve cells degenerated. "Bilateral lower-extremity muscular myopathy" and "neuropathy," the doctors called it. David's growing list of unexplained ailments included Ménière's disease, sensorineural hearing loss, depression, congestive heart failure, and bilateral macular degeneration. He'd been fine before he reached Camp Lejeune and a medical mess thereafter. For many years, he had no idea what was causing any of this. Despite countless tests and medical exams, specialists at the Cleveland Clinic and the Ohio State University couldn't figure it out either.

With her nursing background, Patty had her own ideas. With a push from her, doctors concluded in May of 2000 that his long-term neurological decline was related to mitochondrial abnormalities, just the kind of thing that repeated exposure to toxic water could cause. But this was 2000, a full eight years before anyone was paying attention to the water at Camp Lejeune. The VA was still in deny-and-minimize mode, nearly two decades after discovering the toxic-water problem. So David got no help. It wasn't until May of 2013, after he heard about the Janey Ensminger Act, that David applied to the U.S. Department of Veterans Affairs for compensation for his extensive medical care. Sadly, in June of 2014 he got a rote denial. The VA ruled that his medical conditions were not service-connected since none of his many ailments were on the limited list of just fifteen linked conditions. In desperation, Patty sent a letter to USMC headquarters, asking for help. She got the coldest of brush-offs.

"It would be inappropriate for us to interfere or comment on the VA's independent decision-making responsibilities related to health care," A. R. Wright, Chief of Staff, USMC Installation Command, responded.

The few, the proud, the forgotten.

———◦◉◦———

Sadly, David's case is still stuck in the purgatory that is the Veterans Affairs appeals system. But we refuse to give up. On a visit to Ohio, Patty showed me piles of missing documents she's been gathering. Together, she and I are reanalyzing old reports. And we are bringing in top medical experts to assess David's case. They include Dr. Zarife Sahenk, one of the nation's top neuromuscular pathologists whose specialties include genetic testing and nerve and muscle biopsies. In February of 2016, the doctor saw David and wrote in his report words that give us all big hope: "the possibility of exposure to TCE and PCE may have contributed to his disease process is a valid one and cannot be dismissed."

Just like David and Patty have been saying all along.

That doesn't settle things. But it's another step closer to getting David the medical help he deserves for putting his flesh on the line. And with perseverance, there is much more to come.

We have gotten the media involved, often a good way to force the bureaucracy to pay attention. That's often an important part of the dynamic advocacy strategies that Tuesday and I develop with people. After David and Jane moved to the Tampa area, a journalist at the *Tampa Tribune* put together a great piece about local Camp Lejeune veterans in that area who had ailments like David Metzler's. As I did with Amee Gilbert and her son Cole at Fort Carson, we worked with Patty to write a powerful op-ed piece, hers published in the *Tampa Bay Times*. It recounted her father's long and difficult fight. "At 78 years old," she wrote, "my father can hardly walk, see, or hear. He suffers from chronic pain. He has a history of depression. In one desperate moment, he attempted suicide to try to end his suffering. No human being, especially a veteran, should ever have to endure this."

This wasn't easy to write, of course. But Patty believed it was important that people knew.

"The Marine Corps motto, 'Semper Fidelis,' means 'Always Faithful,'" she wrote. "However, the USMC has failed to uphold this principle. For decades, our military has proclaimed, 'No one will be left behind, no matter the cost.' Americans enlist believing that they will be protected under this admirable principle. It breaks my heart knowing they lay their lives on the line for each other and their country yet, once they complete their duty, they become 'fallen comrades' left alone on 'the battlefield.'"

Shortly after the piece was published, a television reporter in Youngstown, Ohio, interviewed Patty for a segment about the fight. Her story and that of her father are certainly of local and national importance.

Patty, Tuesday, and I vow not to stop until we get David the justice he deserves. I've spent many hours researching everything I could find about toxic water in Camp Lejeune, then asking myself, "Okay, where can Patty and I and Tuesday gain traction? Who is the Marine Corps general ultimately responsible for Camp Lejeune? Who in Congress would be interested in this? Who do we lean on at the VA?" All of this takes dogged advocacy. It takes a thick skin and a refusal to fold even when doors slam and requests are repeatedly declined.

We keep making progress, but we don't have a second to waste. Mortality is a clock that ticks loudly for David Metzler. The idea of waiting another couple of years for the VA to decide his appeal is almost unthinkable. What a hollow victory it would be if we receive it after he was gone.

CHAPTER 7

Father and Son

⸺ «◆» ⸺

*Not only so, but we also glory in our sufferings, because we
know that suffering produces perseverance; perseverance,
character; and character, hope.*

ROMANS 5:3–4

"ARE THERE ANY MARINES IN THE ROOM?"

When I talk to groups, that's one of the questions I sometimes ask. At other events, I'll call the roll of other branches of service—the army, navy, air force, and Coast Guard. But when I mention the Marine Corps, I usually get a spirited *Oorah!* or two in return—sometimes more, depending on the audience. I got several on this particular evening at the Waterloo Public Library in Iowa.

"Who is the most decorated Marine in U.S. history?" I asked.

"Chesty Puller," two or three voices called out in unison. And they are right.

Lewis "Chesty" Burwell Puller was awarded five Navy Crosses. When it comes to valor in battle, the Navy Cross is just below the Medal of Honor—and Chesty Puller was awarded five of them plus an Army Distinguished Service Cross. He tangled with Caco rebels in Haiti and mountain guerrillas in Nicaragua, leaving that nation with a 5,000-peso reward on his head. He led Marines in some of the most treacherous battles of World War II and the Korean War, rising eventually to the rank of lieutenant general. Somewhere along the line, people started calling him Chesty because of his short and stocky build. Folks insisted he looked and also growled like a bulldog.

Although the Marines in the room seemed to know, I was pretty sure there were other people in the library crowd who didn't know anything about Chesty. The librarian had been kind enough to bring me a chair to sit in while I talked. So I set aside my cane, invited Tuesday to sit nearby, and settled down to share the incredible story of an amazing American warrior.

"Announcing 'I want to go where the guns are,' young Chesty dropped out of Virginia Military Academy and enlisted as a private in the Marine Corps," I began. Across a thirty-seven-year career, Chesty was never far from the action for long. On the Pacific Island of Guadalcanal in World War II, he commanded the 1st Battalion, 7th Marines on an amphibious assault near the Matanikau River. But when they hit the beaches, they collided almost immediately with a massive force of Japanese infantry. The Marines were quickly cut off and surrounded. Another company of Marines tried to break through the Japanese flank and rescue Chesty's stranded men, but the enemy resistance was too powerful. The situation was hopeless, the operation commander announced. Chesty didn't like the sound of that. He stormed out of camp and beat a path to the beach, where he flagged down a U.S. Navy destroyer that happened to be sailing off the coast. With absolutely no authority to do so, he boarded the vessel, ordered support fire, and organized a second amphibious assault. The shelling, coupled with the second landing, punched a hole through the enemy blockade and cleared a path for the stranded Marines to escape.

That was pure Chesty. "Hit hard, hit fast, hit often," he liked to say.

He commanded the "Frozen Chosin" in Korea's Battle of Chosin Reservoir. Chesty and his men found themselves holed up in the town of Koto-ri, surrounded this time by ten full divisions of Chinese infantry. Heavily outnumbered and the temperature sinking below zero degrees, they broke the Chinese lines, smashed through seven enemy divisions, then stayed behind as the rear guard against a brutal Chinese onslaught so that the rest of the Marines could get the hell out of there.

If the expression applies to anyone, it applies to Chesty Puller: This was a Marine's Marine.

When I finished telling the story of this celebrated American warrior, I put another question to the audience: "How many of you know about Chesty's son?"

This one almost always stumps an audience. And this night wasn't any different. I looked around and saw nothing but blank stares in Waterloo.

"He was named for his father," I started. "And what happened to Lewis Puller Jr. is every bit as important for people to know. It's the closest thing we have to an American Shakespearean tragedy. It's every bit as revealing—and even more instructive—as his father's battlefield exploits."

This wasn't just a lesson from history. It happens that my father knew Chesty and his son in the 1950s as he spent time between Cuba and northern Virginia. Chesty, back then, enjoyed passing many summer afternoons watching tennis matches involving his Episcopal Diocese. Tennis is often known as the gentleman's sport, but Chesty being Chesty Puller, was taken by my dad's super-aggressive style of play. I suppose it reminded him of his own approach on the battlefield.

Lewis Jr., I explained to the library crowd in Iowa, graduated from Virginia's prestigious College of William and Mary, then followed his father into the Marine Corps. He arrived in Vietnam in July of 1968 with the 2nd Battalion, 1st Marines as the commander of a rifle platoon. You can imagine what it must have been like for the young second lieutenant, arriving in the war zone as Chesty Puller's son. Talk about big boots to fill!

During a jungle engagement with North Vietnamese regulars on October 11, Lewis tripped a "Bouncing Betty," a booby-trapped, World War II–era howitzer round. When tripped, the makeshift land mine was designed to bounce up to hip level, before exploding. That's exactly what happened. In the devastating blast, the young lieutenant lost his right leg at the hip, his left leg below the knee, his left hand entirely, and most of the fingers on his right hand. His body was riddled with shrapnel.

As he lay there gravely injured, drifting in and out of consciousness, he turned over command of his unit to another young officer then ordered those helping him not to frighten his pregnant wife with the terrible news. Corpsman in the field quickly patched Lewis up. He was medevacked to a military hospital in Saigon, where he lingered near death for days, his body weight plummeting to a skeletal fifty-five pounds.

Ol' Chesty flew into Vietnam. He rushed to his only son's bedside. There, the most decorated Marine in U.S. history looked at his boy in that hospital bed, then broke down and wept uncontrollably. He was the toughest son-of-a-gun imaginable. Yet when he looked at his son, he cried.

———◦———

Doctors didn't think Lewis Jr. had a chance. But almost miraculously, the young Marine survived. He must have inherited his

father's bulldog stamina and stubborn refusal to surrender. He was
a triple-amputee, likely to spend his life in a wheelchair. But his grit
and his spirit and some fine medical attention managed to keep him
alive. After spending nearly two years in a hospital, he was medically
discharged with a chest full of medals of his own: the Silver Star, the
Navy and Marine Corps Commendation Medals, two Purple Hearts,
and a Gallantry Cross from the Republic of Vietnam. He retired as
a captain and, despite the battering he had taken, he bravely got on
with his life.

In the early 1970s, Lewis Jr. went back to the College of William
and Mary and put himself through law school. He took a job as an
attorney in Washington, D.C., with the U.S. Department of Veterans Affairs. He was appointed to President Gerald Ford's clemency
board. He and his wife, Toddy, who'd been together since college,
had a daughter, Maggie, and a son, Lewis III. On the outside, he
seemed to be making the best of things—but, as I told the library
audience, the story was more complicated than that.

Lewis Jr. suffered from terrible depression. He drank far too
much. He ran for Congress from his wheelchair and was beaten
badly. In 1981, he checked himself into an alcohol rehab program and
stayed off the booze for a while. But he continued to battle depression
and relapsed several times.

That year, Lewis Puller Jr. published his autobiography, *Fortunate
Son: The Healing of a Vietnam Vet.*

The Waterloo librarian, who'd been sitting nearby in rapt attention, interrupted excitedly: "We have a copy of that book, if anyone
wants to read it." Several people in the audience nodded that they'd
be interested. When everyone's eyes were back on me and Tuesday, I
continued.

In *Fortunate Son,* I explained, the son gave a gripping account
of that terrible day in the jungle leading his platoon on a mission.
He recounted when he stepped on the mine. "I felt as if I had been

airborne forever," he wrote. "I had no idea that the pink mist that engulfed me had been caused by the vaporization of most of my right and left legs." In frank and vivid detail, Lewis Jr. chronicled his fight with despair and alcoholism. He spoke of his journey toward reconciliation with the nation that had sent him to war. The book, I explained, ended on a hopeful, almost triumphant note, the wounded Marine learning to deal with his profound disabilities, finally seeming at peace with himself. The following year, *Fortunate Son* won one of literature's highest honors, the Pulitzer Prize.

But despite the book's success, things were still unraveling for Lewis Puller Jr. He quit his job at Veterans Affairs. He struggled with his old addiction, alcohol, and a new one too, painkillers, to fight the lingering effects of his long-ago injuries. He separated from his wife of twenty-six years. The darkness kept closing in. On May 11, 1994, he shot himself to death at his home in Mount Vernon, Virginia. He was forty-eight years old.

His wife, who'd been through so much with him over the years, said the following on the night he died: "To the list of names of victims of the Vietnam War, add the name of Lewis Puller. He suffered terrible wounds that never really healed."

It wasn't the missing appendages she was talking about.

Chesty's son didn't die because a land mine blew his legs off. He didn't end it all because of the physical wounds he experienced. He didn't put a gun to his head over missing his legs and hands. He killed himself because of the darkness that had settled inside his head. That Bouncing Betty battered his body, but post-traumatic stress disorder is what did him in.

The way Lewis Puller Jr. died—that's the real story of the effects these wars are having on many of the men and women who've been asked to fight for all of us. It's an iconic story and a real American tragedy. And yes, the way it's ignored, misunderstood, and mischaracterized makes me furious.

What happened to the Pullers, senior and junior, is an epic drama of the modern age.

‎‧‧‧—⟨◉⟩—‧‧‧

After allowing the library group to process what they'd just heard, I wanted to ask a follow-up question.

"I want you to give me what we in the military call a SWAG," I said. "A scientific wild-ass guess."

People chuckled at that acronym. The audience seemed game.

"Okay," I said. "Two-point-seven million Americans have served in the wars in Afghanistan and Iraq. How many amputees do you think there are?"

The SWAGs were all over the map.

"Two hundred thousand," someone seated to the side shouted.

"Fifty thousand."

"Three hundred thousand."

A woman up front must have been a math major in college. She did the long division in her head. "If it's 20 percent of those who served, that would be 540,000. Is that about right?"

Actually, no. All the SWAGs were way, way high, as they almost always are when I ask that question to an audience.

"The correct number is about two thousand men and women," I said. "That's how many amputees we have from Afghanistan and Iraq. If you prefer percentages, it comes out to less than point-zero-zero-one of those who have served over there."

I am utterly respectful of their sacrifice, which is a profound one. I wanted to make that clear. "God bless these men and women," I said. "They have sacrificed for our country." I have friends who are amputees. Good friends. Lots of them. All over the nation. Mary and Andrew are amputees who received dogs when I received Tuesday. But the real number, low as it might seem, is approximately two thousand from the wars in Afghanistan and Iraq combined.

I know that most people expect a number much larger than that. Americans have been fed the perception that to be wounded in war is to be visibly wounded, to have a missing appendage or to be on crutches or to be suffering from some other physical disability that can be easily seen. The media feeds this misperception. So do Veterans officials and politicians and, worst of all, some of our most prominent nonprofit veteran service organizations.

Most people just assume that most of the wounds of war are the visible kind. The exact opposite is the case. The vast majority of those who are seriously affected by war have invisible scars. Hundreds and hundreds of thousands of men and women—make that millions—are affected with traumatic brain injuries, with anxiety, with debilitating pain, with PTSD, with a whole range of maladies that people walking down the street can't see.

Just like me. I had walked into that Waterloo library with the aid of a cane. But the injuries that had almost buried me alive were not the physical ones. That beautiful, well-behaved golden retriever at my side wasn't with me because of a limp or the leg pain I experienced every day.

The veteran with his leg blown off won't hesitate to go to rehab or get fitted for a prosthetic leg. A veteran suffering from crippling anxiety will often think: "Oh, I'm not really injured. I don't need help. Save it for my brother who walks on crutches or uses a wheelchair."

Wrong!

And dangerous!

This narrow focus on the visibly wounded—this war-porn fixation on amputees—strongly discourages our warriors from getting emotional and mental help. And as bad as physical and visible injuries are, it's too often true that the worst off remain as invisible as their wounds.

They suck it up. They try to deal alone. They buy into and deject-edly accept the outmoded line that if they weren't treated at Landstuhl or Walter Reed, how bad could their injuries be? They commit sui-cide like Lewis Puller Jr. did.

No one ever commits suicide for just one reason. It starts with a small shadow and spreads out from there. By the end, everything is shrouded in darkness. But still I wonder whether writing his book contributed to Lewis Jr.'s suicide. Could that have been what trig-gered his final act of desperation?

Writing *Until Tuesday* was the hardest thing I've ever achieved in my life. I'm in a better place now. But when I think of Lewis Puller Jr. and I think of the autobiography he wrote and the difficult truths he tried to tell, I suspect the experience had to have been excruci-ating for him, like it was for me. Just a hell of a painful experience. He had to relive his worst experiences ever, over and over and over again.

"After tonight," I told the people at the library. "I hope you'll think of Lewis Puller Jr. and his invisible wounds. Maybe one day our country will learn something from him."

———◦———

The military today has slowly become more open-minded. There are public service announcements and barracks pep talks warning about the seriousness of PTSD. Politicians weave the term into their speeches. But still, the false narrative of how we define a wounded warrior is everywhere.

That's one of the reasons we were in Iowa that night and why we'd be in another town the day after and many others in the weeks after that. The enduring lack of consistent and proper diagnosis has left us with a genuine pandemic of untreated mental illness—at the very least, it has severely exacerbated the problem. And the misinformation does not stop. The wild stereotypes of PTSD sufferers. The notion of who gets injured in war is skewed completely wrong. The treatments that need to be funded aren't. The rehabilitation that works needs to be expanded while failed methods of treatment need to be eliminated.

I battle PTSD, just as many, many others do. But I'm not a Hollywood PTSD victim. I'm not John Goodman in *The Big Lebowski* waving a .45, getting into fights with German neo-Nazis, constantly ready to blow. Few of us are. But that caricature of hair-trigger eruption is now a widely accepted archetype of veterans with PTSD. It's an insultingly exaggerated, cartoonish way to portray sufferers of a serious condition. These are not the classic symptoms of PTSD. So, yes, I cringe every time another crazed-vet character turns up on yet another TV, movie, or video screen. I can't say there's never been a veteran like that. But I can say that cartoon is contradicted by the reality of PTSD. Those dim-witted portrayals are not remotely the truth. Real PTSD sufferers are far more likely to be introverted, depressed, and detached than violent or out of control.

Just look at the fund-raising juggernaut that is the Wounded Warrior Project. Launched in 2003 with a mission of sending socks and backpacks to service members deployed abroad, the group rode the visibly wounded narrative to $372 million in revenues in 2015. Its TV ads, with amputees as constant poster children, are blasted across national TV.

Representatives know the truth, but choose easy emotion over the complex realities of war. Imagine the good the Wounded Warrior Project might have done if they used all those donations and all that publicity to focus on the wounds that warriors really have.

How deep does this misconception go?

Here's a telling comparison: When the Vietnam Veterans Memorial Wall was completed in 1983, there were 58,191 names etched in the stone. By Memorial Day 2015, the number had risen to 58,307. New names are inscribed as military personnel who were wounded in Vietnam between 1957 and 1975 die of their wounds.

The visible, physical kind.

What most people don't know—and there is no wall to memorialize this—is that two to three times that number of Vietnam veterans have committed suicide. Of course, it's not a tragedy that belongs to just those who fought in Vietnam. It's the untold story of millions of America's sons and daughters who have served in conflicts from World War II to today and have killed themselves by their own hands.

The struggle is to see that by the time someone gets around to building a wall for Afghanistan and Iraq vets, this terrible phenomenon has changed. But it's far from any sort of certainty. Only for the past few years have top military officials even been willing to acknowledge the pandemic of military and veteran suicides. In early 2013, the official website of the U.S. Department of Defense published a sobering statistic: The number of military suicides in the previous year had exceeded the total of those killed in battle—an average of nearly one a day.

A month after the first statistic was published came an even more startling number from the U.S. Department of Veterans Affairs: Suicides among military veterans were running at 22 a day—one every 65 minutes, about 8,000 a year.

For combat veterans, there's a deadly combination. They have the motivation. They have the methods. They avoid seeking help.

"Listen," I told the folks in Waterloo that night, "these are men and women who were at one point in their lives the toughest our country had. Right? Before Iraq and Afghanistan, they fought in Vietnam, Korea, and World War II. Before there was anything classified as post-traumatic stress disorder, they came home 'shell-shocked.' They suffered from 'soldier's heart' and 'battle fatigue.' Before PTSD was a diagnosis, they were just screwed."

I continued. "Well," I said, "if the toughest that our nation has have fallen victim to trauma, to anguish, to mental pain, so can any of you."

CHAPTER 8

Grooming Tuesday

—⫸«⬦»⫷—

nur•ture

/ˈnər-chər/

verb

to care for and encourage the growth or development of

OXFORD ENGLISH DICTIONARY

AS TUESDAY AND I TRAVEL AROUND, DIVING INTO ALL THESE challenging situations, people often ask us how it is we remain so tight. What these people are also asking, I think, is how they can deepen the connection with their own animals, what they can do to enhance that special human–canine bond. Part of it, certainly, is all the time we spend together. Part of it is the important mission that we share. But there is another aspect that few people fully appreciate, even lifelong animal lovers. It the special bonding opportunity that occurs when it's time to groom Tuesday. That's right, our grooming sessions are some of the most powerful and intimate experiences that he and I share.

I understand why people pay for grooming services at pet stores and salons. There's the convenience of letting a professional take care of it all—the fur-cutting, the nail-trimming, the bathing, to name just a few of the many services these places provide. However, Tuesday and I—both of us—get a great deal out of our grooming rituals.

And that's what these are—rituals. The way we approach Tuesday's grooming and the time and energy we devote—it really does qualify as a spiritual event. Skipping this time we spend together would be a loss, a profound loss for us both.

Tuesday and I turn what could be an ordeal, something that many animals and their owners consider stressful, into one of our favorite activities together. And over time, we have established our own individual approaches and techniques.

Dogs and children are a lot alike when it comes to grooming. The more often you do it, the less likely you'll hear whining or crying. In one form or another, I am grooming Tuesday constantly. I brush his coat twice a day. I brush his teeth every night. Chicken-flavored canine toothpaste, of course. We cut his nails once a month and trim back his toe tuffs, the hair around his toe pads. Once every month or two, I give him a bath.

Then, comes the real fun. Twice a year, we do a full snout-to-tail grooming. We can do this as a day-long marathon, or we can do it in forty-minute bursts over seven or eight days. Either way, it's a powerful experience with innumerable benefits—physical, psychological, and practical. He feels better, looks better, and, when we are finished, goes out into the world with a new spring in his step. Dogs are a lot like humans in that way.

"Come here, Toopy" I say, and we get started. Toopy is a special nickname I've given him, a combination of Tuesday and Snoopy.

We always begin together on the floor. It's crucial that I be on Tuesday's level. Not above him. And never standing beside one of those elevated grooming tables you see at full-service pet salons. I understand why some professional dog groomers use them. They want to control the animal's movement. Dogs who don't know the groomer can be frightened and act unpredictably. Groomers have figured out that if they put the dog way up in the air on this metal table, he or she won't move around so much. That much is true. Most dogs won't jump around if they are on a table three feet off the ground. That's an unnatural altitude for an animal. It can also be a scary one.

I don't want to imply that professionals are only interested in control. If you are grooming animals for an eight-hour shift, your back gets sore after a while. Those elevated grooming tables are great for alleviating some of that discomfort. I get it. That said, however ideal it is for the human groomer, it's far from ideal for the canine.

I never miss a chance to suggest to owners that they consider grooming their own dogs, at least a lot of the time. This isn't brain surgery. It doesn't have to be done by pedigreed professionals. Truly, any caring person can learn.

But the less conducive conditions for the dogs aren't the biggest reason to consider doing it yourself. The most important reason is that a loving owner will do a better job—a much better job. And if you begin when your pup is young or new to your home, it's never a job. It's a special treat and an unparalleled bonding, nurturing experience.

We start with a long, slow brushing.

Tuesday is seated. I sit beside him, brushing his coat, not actually giving him a haircut. Just running a nice wire brush through his coat. Not too hard. Not too soft. Just smooth, long strokes flowing in the direction his coat lays. One look at that face and there's no doubt that the gentle strokes are relaxing to him.

Twice a year, in spring and in autumn, he blows his coat. It's a natural thing. As his new hair grows out, his older hairs loosen and this leads to heavy shedding. Around that time, I do shear his coat. I don't shave him. It's not a close cut. But with a pair of shearing scissors, I cut some of the volume off, close enough to make him feel more comfortable.

A nice, soft brushing is me saying, "I love you" and, "You can trust me." That's a much better way to get started than him feeling, "Oh, my God. This is really gonna hurt." Consequently, Tuesday looks forward to being groomed.

No wonder when I say, "Tuesday, I'm going to brush you," he starts wagging his tail—not running in the other direction, which is what a lot of dogs do.

As the brushing winds down, I do something that is good for his circulation and joints: I add some evenly applied hand massage. But it's not only good for his health, it also connects us in yet another way. Lots of people hug their dogs. It is similar to that but it's also a part of our grooming ritual. I start by massaging his hind legs. It builds the trust between us. He can't see me behind him, but he knows I am there and I am doing something that makes him feel secure and comfortable. Loved. It removes any tension from the air.

Next, I run my fingers through the fur on the top of his back. From front to back. Down the opposite sides of his spinal cord. Often, I mix in some brushstrokes. It's a comb/pet/massage on his spine that is very soothing to him. I spend some time on that, not rushing. Just connecting with him. Telling him what a good boy he is.

"You are such a good dog, Tuesday! You are such a handsome and beautiful boy. I love you."

I'm grooming and massaging, but it's Tuesday who is setting the pace. At some point, when he is ready, he turns around. He wants me to stroke his mane—his neck area, front, back, and sides. The nerve endings are very sensitive. When I stroke around his neck, it releases endorphins, similar to what happens in humans. It's hard not to smile when I see him enjoying this back rub. Of course, I want him to feel good. I love him. It's tremendously important to me that he feels and knows that he's loved.

If you have dogs, you know that special joy they feel when you stroke their faces. Tuesday is highly trained, but in this way he isn't any different from any other dog. I can see in his eyes that he enjoys it. Tuesday has a unique way of showing this. If he really likes what you are doing, he will drop his head and burrow the front of his body into you, leaning in on you. The message is nonverbal but crystal clear, "This feels good."

I refer to it as the "massage table position."

"Please rub my neck and shoulders," Tuesday says with exacting body language. It's almost precisely the way humans position ourselves on a massage table with our head in that hole toward the end of the bed.

It is also a sign of deference, like a bow in eastern cultures, a sign of respect and humility. In humans, it is an ancient, physical, and spiritual ritual. I can't prove this. But I firmly believe that dogs do it with the same type of message in mind, a sign of submission. A sign of respect.

Dogs are natural predators. Humans too. Both our species have that instinct and that capacity. By burrowing his head into my chest, he is placing himself in a vulnerable position. If I wanted to, I could do him harm, which of course I don't and never will. But by placing himself in a vulnerable position and doing it willfully, he is offering a sign of trust in my good intentions, in the fact that I love him and care for him and the knowledge that I will never hurt him, no matter the circumstances.

It is amazing—isn't it?—how sophisticated canine communication can be, especially in quiet moments like this one. If only humans could learn to communicate so warmly and clearly. We have highly advanced linguistic abilities, and we still have trouble saying, "I love you." How can we not admire the talents of dogs?

It's interesting how we interact with canines, similar to the way we do with our children. I give Tuesday some kisses on his cheeks. Around his eyes. He is as calm as he will ever be.

Slowly, gently, calmly, I lift his left paw with my hand.

"Good boy," I say.

Then, I clear the feathers around that paw.

Golden retrievers have unique feathers around their front and hind legs. They need to be shortened so they don't pick up dirt from the ground when they walk. I use a special shearing tool, a brush with a razor embedded in it. The blade isn't very sharp so I am confident I am not in any way hurting him, not even accidentally. When I run that tool through Tuesday's feathers, it doesn't cut them off entirely. It just cleans them up a bit.

After I am finished with the left front paw feathers, I do the same with the right front paw.

Some dog owners think of dog hair as if it is human hair. It isn't. It grows differently and needs to be treated differently. Most often, it has to be cleared rather than cut, which is why that shearing tool is far more useful than a pair of barber scissors. To do the job right, you need the right tools.

Again, I turn Tuesday around so his backside is facing toward me. I shear down his tail feathers, just as I did in the front. As with collies and other long-haired dogs, golden retrievers have longish hair back there. Their backsides need regular shearing. Not just so the feathers don't drag in the dirt. As you can imagine, long-haired dogs need this done to clear a path for their eliminations. It's a matter of basic hygiene. The alternative is no fun for them and no fun for us. Far better to keep his backside neat and clean. This takes a while because those feathers grow long and the area is a little delicate. Slowly and carefully, and don't wait for a yelp to know you've been careless. It's definitely worth being careful with the shearing tool. That is something Tuesday does not need to tell me.

You don't need a lesson book. Some of this is just instinctive. Early on, I figured out a special technique to use back there. I wouldn't say

Tuesday likes this part, but he seems to understand it's important and he has gotten used to it. I grab his tail like a mother would grasp her daughter's hair, as close to the scalp as I can, which eases the pain if the hairs get pulled. Essentially, Tuesday's tail becomes a ponytail with my hand closed around the base. That way, he doesn't feel like I am pulling his tail while I am shearing his tail feathers. It also controls his movement, which allows me to groom him evenly.

This isn't just a method to calm him. It is also allows me to remain calm and steady. The bonding experience would be totally lost if we weren't both calm.

It wouldn't be relaxing if he were squirming and flinching like a lot of dogs tend to do. What I'm doing is as nurturing as a mother brushing her child's hair, a teaching and bonding moment. But, just like with a mom who chooses to use force and harsh words to hold a hyperactive child down, there's a better way.

It's all very primal. I try to make Tuesday feel good. I groom his hair and skin, massaging him to make him feel better. Just like we feel better when we get a massage or a haircut. So do they.

Once we are done with the longer feathers, I go around his thighs with the shearing tool. Gently, I remove some of the hair on the backs of his legs near his hind paws. These feathers can grow long too if we let them. It's amazing how unkempt an ungroomed retriever can appear. The change from before to after is profound. The hairs come off in little clumps. Admittedly, I'm a bit of a neat freak. So I collect them with my hand and toss them into the garbage. The hair I remove from Tuesday's lustrous coat can quickly fill a good-size wastebasket.

Next, I groom the feathers along Tuesday's stomach. Go watch an ungroomed long-haired dog run in the park. It's fairly easy to see why this part is especially important. I don't want those long hairs to get too close to the ground. Even with frequent shearings, he accumulates things in that stomach fur. He picks up dirt and God knows what else. This is just a reality for creatures who walk so close to the earth.

And even if I weren't worried about finding something new and unusual during his next belly rub, I want him to look good.

Tuesday is not a house pet. He is out in public all the time, everywhere that I go. He represents his breed. He represents service dogs. He represents me. We are in restaurants together and grocery stores and hotel lobbies. We are invited into schools and libraries and people's homes. I want to make sure he not only meets the standard, but exceeds it. I don't want people thinking he is dirty. It's important to me that they recognize immediately that his hygiene is superb. One look at Tuesday, and they have no reason to say, "Oh, my God, there is a dog in here. He might have fleas." I want people to say, "Wow, that is a beautiful golden retriever." Not because I want him to be a super model or because I get ego gratification from having a handsome dog. I want people to recognize he is very well cared for and is capable of extraordinary things. Most importantly, he is my service dog—a dog with special responsibilities that take him to places where many people and most dogs never go. And at those times, no one can be the least bit concerned about their own safety or comfort or hygiene.

This is an attitude and a standard I was taught by Lu Picard and the team at ECAD and one that I embraced wholeheartedly. All these years later, I still embrace it.

Beyond helping me, Tuesday is an ambassador. He is a public dog. It would be terrible if people thought he was not being taken care of. It would be contrary to what he and I stand for, contrary to what we talk about and fight for and believe in. It's a central part of our human-canine bond. We have standards and we live up to them. Everything about his appearance should convey the seriousness of how we go about the business of changing the world.

Before we go any further in the grooming ritual, we take a break.

I pet his head. I keep affirming what a good dog he is. "Such a good boy, what a good boy."

Then, it's time to turn my attention to his ears. We're wandering into delicate territory here.

For this job, the gentle shearing tool won't do. I open a pair of small scissors. With one blade in my hand, I gingerly scape around the top of one of his ears, lightly shearing back some of the hair. Then, I do the same on the other ear. Not cutting. Not shaving. Shearing, just to shorten the hairs. If those hairs grow too long, falling past the ear flap, they knot. They get kinky. Such hair growth can facilitate bacterial growth inside and around the ear canal which, in turn, can become infected. That's painful as it irritates the skin. He would scratch incessantly. That would likely break the skin and cause greater infection. The whole thing would be really uncomfortable for him, not to mention bad for his overall health. Grooming is about so much more than looking nice, not that there's anything wrong with that.

Next, I clean his paws.

I start with the toe pads, the black paw area of his hind legs. I clean the dirt and other gook that has accumulated there. He really likes that. He feels the same way humans do when we wash our hands after a long day of work. It's refreshing and nice. I also want to make sure there aren't any rocks, sticks, bugs, or specs of dirt in his toe pads. The same with his nails. Any dirt there, I brush out.

At the same time, I search around his paws and on his skin for what is referred to as hot spots, areas that might be agitated or turn pink. They aren't really hot per se. But the rosy color can give that impression and can cause tenderness that might make him limp. Those spots can be painful, and they tip us off to possible skin issues.

After all the shearing we have done, there is inevitably some hair that has been sheared but hasn't been removed. It's just sitting there, hiding in one of his crevices or stuck to his coat.

That's a job for a fine-bristle metal brush, going over his entire body this time to remove the lingering hairs. For him, it's like one last luxuriating massage.

One thing we don't do much of is bathing. Frequent bathing really isn't the best way to keep a dog fresh and clean. Or healthy. For Tuesday, baths are comparatively rare, perhaps every four to six weeks, unless he has made an unusually large mess of himself. Daily or even weekly bathing isn't good for his skin or his coat. It dries him out. The natural oils in his skin would become affected. A lot of people bathe their dogs way too often, I believe. As a general principle, a brush is far superior to a bathtub.

Of course, this isn't so for humans, where soap and water is still the way to go. But brushing really is Tuesday's routine form of bathing. It's better all the way around. It keeps him clean. It relaxes him. He very much enjoys it. I do too. There are no negative consequences. And something I learned when I've taken Tuesday to warmer climates: Dogs don't need bathing to cool down. Dogs are like bears, deer, and other furry mammals in this way. They regulate body temperature differently than humans do. They have a different physiology than we do. We sweat. They pant. For the most part, it is through panting that dogs circulate the necessary air through their bodies to cool down.

When we are finally done, I use baby wipes to clean the brushes and the other grooming instruments. I treat them the way I was taught to treat my weapons and equipment in the Army, according to careful and predictable routine. The same way we wanted our machine guns and vehicles to operate properly when needed, I don't want bacteria and other toxins growing on our grooming tools. I want to be sure everything is ready for me in perfect order when we return for our next grooming session.

Recognizing our grooming session is over as I finish cleaning the tools, Tuesday hops on the bed and looks down at me from above. I know what he is thinking because I am thinking the same thing.

With an expression of affection and contentment, he is saying, "I love you."

CHAPTER 9

Under Arrest

>«◉»<

¡Madre mía!

I'M NOT SURE WHY VETERANS AFFAIRS HOSPITALS IN NEW YORK CITY need such hair-trigger security. Are these institutions trying to serve veterans and their families or keep them out? Some days, it's hard to tell. When Tuesday and I travel, we visit VA medical facilities all over the country—Michigan, Wisconsin, Florida, California, you name it. Only New York City's VA hospitals are locked down like forward operating bases in Afghanistan or Iraq—not even the sprawling medical center in Washington, D.C., which is in a very tough section of southeast D.C., feels as forbidding. When Tuesday and I pulled into the parking lot of the VA hospital in Long Beach, outside Los Angeles, we were met by a friendly veteran in a golf cart, who whisked us to the main entrance and directed us exactly where we needed to go. That was a nice touch, I thought. At the VA hospitals in Manhattan, Brooklyn, and the Bronx, it's more like they've laid out the un-welcome mat!

Just to get inside, you have to show your ID, empty your pockets, clear an airport-style metal detector, and—if it rings, which it almost always does—wait while a uniformed security guard passes an electronic wand up and down your body. How many other hospitals in the U.S. treat their patients like that? Not too many, I'll bet. These are veterans. They've served our nation. They have come for medical care. Do they deserve to be treated like suspected terrorists?

Let me tell you what happened on the afternoon of August 10, 2011, when Tuesday and I arrived at what is officially known as the Manhattan campus of the VA New York Harbor Healthcare System on East 23rd Street. This was our regular hospital, where we'd been countless times before. Tuesday and I weren't strangers there. Quite a few of the staff members told me they'd read *Until Tuesday,* which had come out a couple of months earlier and was still on the *New York Times* bestseller list. Tuesday and I had already been on *The Late Show with David Letterman.*

I wasn't there that day for a doctor visit. I just needed to have my prescriptions refilled. Under VA rules, you can't do that at Walgreens or CVS. You have to go to the VA hospital pharmacy, then wait anywhere from thirty minutes to two-and-a-half hours. Yes, there's a reason many veterans don't like going to the VA. The littlest thing can easily take half a day.

At the main entrance that afternoon, I followed the usual drill. I showed my VA identification card. Emptied my pockets. Placed my cell phone, my cane, and my other stuff on the conveyor belt. Submitted to a thorough wanding by a contracted security officer. Tuesday was at my side in his black-yellow-and-orange service-dog harness, calm as always. He knew the routine as well as I did.

Then, a uniformed VA police officer spoke up. "Okay," she said, "where's your ID card for the dog?"

"Pardon me?" I answered. No one had ever asked for that before.

"Your ID for the dog," she repeated. "Where is it?"

"I'm not sure what you're talking about," I told her. "There is no government identification for a service dog."

"Yes, there is," the officer insisted.

Tuesday was registered with the VA as my service dog. I knew he was in the VA computer system. In fact, he'd been the first service dog not assigned to a blind vet ever approved by the Department of Veterans Affairs. In 2010, we'd successfully lobbied for that in our nation's capital. I'd never been asked to show ID for Tuesday. Not at any VA facility. And certainly never here, at *my* hospital where I'd already presented my own official ID.

The guard at the hospital security checkpoint was already sounding agitated. But I stayed calm, figuring if there was any confusion about canine ID cards, she could certainly check with the administrative office.

"With all due respect," I repeated evenly, "there is no such thing as an official government ID card for a service dog. My dog is harnessed. He is highly trained. He is registered upstairs as my service dog. We're here all the time."

She had to be new and maybe confused. So I added: "And no one else has ever asked for an ID card."

Tuesday's nylon harness could hardly be any more obvious. It has large orange-and-black ID patches on both sides and across the front. "SERVICE K-9," the placards read. Two smaller patches say, "DO NOT PET." Tuesday also has on a two-inch, orange-and-black nylon collar that says, "SERVICE K-9." I'm not kidding: In that harness and collar, the only thing Tuesday could have been mistaken for was a four-legged billboard.

The VA police officer said nothing else to us, though I did notice she picked up a telephone. At that point, the security guard with the wand motioned Tuesday and me inside.

"Let's go, Tuesday," I said.

I wasn't expecting an apology or even a friendly nod from the officer who'd been quizzing us. But I was grateful the security guard stepped in and let us through. We made our way, as we had so many times before, to the first-floor pharmacy waiting room. There, I took a number, we found a seat, and waited to speak with the tech. Tuesday settled in at my feet as he was trained to do. We didn't wait for long. Perhaps three minutes later, an armed VA police officer, huffing and puffing, sprinted up to Tuesday and me.

"What are you doing?" he demanded.

"What do you mean?" I asked. I'd been here so many times before, the question seemed odd. But this was already turning out to be a day of odd encounters. "I am sitting here, waiting for my number to be called."

"What are you doing?" he said again. "Where is your dog's ID card? The dog needs an ID or you have to leave the hospital. You can't stay here."

Oh! The officer at the entrance who'd been asking for non-existent ID must have called for reinforcements! "I will leave," I said calmly, "as soon as I get my prescriptions refilled. As I told the officer out front, there is no such thing as an official government ID card for a service dog."

He shot me one of those "you're-being-argumentative" looks. Then, he stepped back a few paces and muttered something into his radio. I couldn't hear what. But in another couple of minutes, three fresh Veterans Affairs police officers rushed into the waiting room, also armed and breathing heavily. I was still in the chair with my cane and pharmacy number in hand and Tuesday at my feet. The four officers formed a semi-circle around us, as if they were staring down a major security threat.

I was really having trouble understanding what was happening here. I'd shown the officer my VA identification card. They knew who I was. Tuesday was registered upstairs. I hadn't busted past security. A guard had waved me through. I had cleared the metal detector. I had no weapons on me. I had a cane and service dog and a cell phone, and I was sitting in a chair.

One of the four, who had sergeant stripes on his sleeves, spoke up next.

"What are you doing?" he asked.

"I'm waiting to see the tech so I can refill my medication."

"I'm talking about your service dog," he snapped.

"Yes," I said. "He is my service dog."

"Well," the sergeant continued, "how do I know that's a real service dog? Anybody could buy a vest online."

"Maybe," I said. "But I am a veteran. I showed my ID. My dog has a harness on his back that clearly indicates he is my service dog. Tuesday is registered in the VA system. Furthermore, there is no such thing as an official VA ID for a service dog—or any other type of governmental service-dog identification card. So what ID card are you talking about?"

I don't think he liked that answer. It must have made too much sense.

The sergeant got on his radio. A couple of minutes later, a higher-ranking supervisor—a chief maybe—appeared. Clearly, the incident was being kicked upstairs. The chief was in civilian clothes with P-O-L-I-C-E written on his jacket. Now, five armed men were standing over Tuesday and me.

"What are you doing?" the chief asked. They must teach that question at the VA police academy. All their people kept asking it.

I gave the same answer as before: "I am here with my service dog waiting for my medication."

"Listen, why don't you come with me?" the chief said.

That seemed unwise to me. I've been a military police officer. I recognize the technique of asking a question as if it is a command. Such questions are not orders. "I'm sorry," I said, "but if I come with you, I am going to lose my place in line. My number will be called. I will have to wait much longer. Why don't you have a seat? We can talk right here."

"Why don't you come with me?" he asked again.

No sooner were those words out of his mouth than the chief turned to his subordinates and said: "You know what you have to do." He didn't have to ask twice. Two of the officers grabbed me by the arms. They yanked me out of the chair and onto the floor, facedown. I still had one hand on Tuesday's collar.

As they pulled me to the ground, I gripped Tuesday's collar to prevent him from lunging at the police officers. In the violence of the moment, I feared for his safety and theirs. How strange that when others are harming you and someone you love, you think of their safety before your own. I could see one of these idiots unholstering his sidearm and shooting Tuesday. Their cowardice was that evident.

"Get off me," I shouted. Tuesday immediately tensed up. His eyes narrowed. His neck muscles tightened. He was staring at me. I knew exactly what he was thinking: *Luis is in trouble. I have to act.*

By that point, a heavyset officer, the largest of the five, was kneeling on my back. I felt a sharp pain in the same area where I'd injured my spinal cord in Iraq. Mainly though, I was worried about Tuesday. My hand was still cinched on his collar. But here I was, getting manhandled by armed police officers. He is constantly focused on my well-being, always concerned about me. But what was he supposed to do? I certainly didn't want him biting one of the VA police officers. Certainly, that would make a bad situation worse. I'd seen the news. I knew how often dogs get shot by police officers in situations exactly like this.

"Stop resisting," one of the cops said to me.

Ever since the Rodney King case in 1991, police have been saying, "Stop resisting" when someone is being arrested in public, whether the person is resisting or not. It shifts the public perception of what is happening, especially in this era of camera phones. It makes people think maybe the individual is resisting, even if there's no resistance at all.

"I am not resisting—*I am disabled!*" I called out. "I can't get up."

I could feel the cold metal of a handcuff slapping around my left wrist and squeezing tight. That arm was pulled behind me. My right hand was still holding Tuesday's collar. One of the officers reached over and grabbed it too before pulling my hand away and squeezing the cuff around my right wrist. Now, both my hands were behind my back. The officer had Tuesday's collar. I could feel my legs being folded at the knees and my heels digging into my back. Finally, three or four of the officers yanked me off the ground, hard enough and high enough that my feet dangled in the air for a second. The handcuffs were really ripping into my wrists.

Tuesday was whimpering, looking like he wanted to pounce, but not quite sure what to do. I wanted to reach out and hug him or at least rub the fingers of my cuffed hands through his coat. But I couldn't do any of that.

The five VA cops marched me out of the waiting room and down the hall with Tuesday a couple of paces behind. People were looking and trying to figure out what was happening. The whole thing was extraordinarily embarrassing, and I was in physical pain. The pain in my back was bad. But the leg pain I felt from walking without my cane was worse. And I was really mad: *This is a betrayal of the highest order. I come to my VA hospital, the place I go to for care. Instead of getting my prescriptions filled, I get questioned, scuffed up, and then I get arrested for no good reason.* It felt infuriating, too stupid for words.

They paraded me upstairs to their office on the second floor. Then, they locked me in a holding cell. But that wasn't enough. They handcuffed me to a wall inside of the locked cell and they left Tuesday outside.

The cell had a heavy wood door with a Plexiglas window. There was a second window beside it as long as the door. Through the window, I could see that one of the officers had tied Tuesday's leash to a metal locker. When I saw that, I started to cry. I could see Tuesday watching me through the Plexiglas, and I know he could see I was crying. I'm not a big crier. Tuesday had rarely seen me cry.

I was really losing it.

You idiots, I thought to myself. *There is no such thing as an official ID card for a service dog. Is this really how you treat the people you are supposed to serve?* I kept replaying the scenes in my head. How quickly and ridiculously it had escalated! The checkpoint. The waiting room. Now, the cell.

I could see one of the officers going through my wallet and hear him say: "Holy shit. He's a Purple Heart recipient."

"I've been trying to tell you," I called out through the door. "This is a big mistake you're making here. This is 100 percent outrageous. Shameful. Dishonorable."

I am not sure how much of that they heard or cared about. No one answered. But I could feel what was left of my composure slipping away.

I could tell I was banged up pretty badly. Bruises were forming on my wrists and my arms. My back was killing me. The muscles in my leg were throbbing. I was still cuffed to the wall. I just felt terrible for Tuesday. My constant companion, the being who always looked after me and made it safe for me to go outside, was breathing hard. He was wailing. He looked so innocent and helpless. He looked like he wanted to leap through the Plexiglas to comfort me. I certainly wanted to comfort him. He was straining at the leash and howling and whimpering and writhing to get inside.

I looked over and saw the police chief speaking to the other officers. By this point, he actually looked concerned. "Why exactly is he here?" the chief was asking the sergeant. Were second thoughts building on the other side of the door?

With the firmest voice I could muster, I shouted to them, "I demand you contact Dr. Mary Belmont and Dr. Brown."

Dr. Belmont was the VA nurse practitioner who for nearly two years had been my primary-care provider at the VA. She knew all about my physical and mental health and the reasons I went everywhere with my beloved service dog. She was also a retired U.S. Army colonel and a very formidable woman. Dr. Brown was the physician she worked closely with. "You call them immediately."

And someone actually did. In what felt like an eternity yet was probably only a few minutes later, Dr. Belmont and Dr. Brown were both standing outside my cell. Thank God they were working that day. I hadn't come to the hospital to see either of them. They could easily have had the day off.

I should say that Dr. Belmont still carries a big load of command presence like the retired army colonel she is. When she asks questions, she expects answers—from me or anyone. She marched into the cell and asked me what on earth had happened. She certainly wasn't used to seeing me like this. As I gave her a quick rundown— the grilling at the security checkpoint, the nonexistent service-dog ID, the five cops in the waiting room, the manhandling, the cuffs, and arrest—Dr. Belmont looked increasingly concerned.

"This doesn't make any sense," she said. "Why?"

"I don't know," I told her, shaking my head. "Maybe these 'gentlemen' can explain."

She exited the cell and went to find answers from the police chief.

I couldn't hear what she was saying, but from her facial expressions— and, especially, from his—I got the distinct impression that Dr. Belmont wasn't holding back. The more she spoke, the more worried the chief appeared.

As they were still talking, one of the other officers came into the cell with a citation for me.

"Disorderly conduct," the citation read.

I, frankly, didn't see how I was the one who'd been disorderly.

Maybe they should have handed the citation to themselves. But with my doctors on the case now, there wasn't any need for me to argue the point.

Whatever Dr. Belmont said to the officer, it seemed to be working. She was allowed to unleash Tuesday from the locker and walk him to me in the cell. As soon as he got close, his mood changed. He was wagging his tail. He was grinning. He was doing his little butt dance. I leaned over and gave him an excited, warm one-armed hug.

A few minutes later, the VA police chief shuffled back into the cell, looking far more sheepish now. He didn't say, *"Uh-oh"* or *"I'm sorry,"* but he might as well have. He picked up the citation and said to me: "Listen, this really isn't necessary. If you will just come to my office when you get out of here, I'm sure we can take care of this."

I just nodded in his direction. Then, I looked downward because I didn't want him to see the seething expression to follow. I could hardly imagine sitting down and having a friendly conversation with him. I wasn't in any state of mind for a calm discussion of what had just occurred.

The whole thing was just so outrageous. Utterly shameful from stem to stern. I was already thinking about filing a grievance with the director of the hospital, literally drafting the complaint letter in my head. "You and your people are entrusted with protecting the peace. Where do these thugs in uniform get off responding with five police officers, pouncing on a disabled veteran, affecting an unlawful arrest, causing physical and psychological pain—over an ID card for a dog? An ID card that doesn't even exist? Handcuffing me to a wall in the cell as though I were a rabid dog, biting patients and foaming at the mouth?" I was quietly sitting in a chair with a cane and a service dog. My spirit was on a tear. All those thoughts were racing through my head.

Finally, one of the officers opened the cell door, uncuffed me, and announced that I was free to go. Just like that, an unceremonious end to my latest misadventure in veterans' health care.

"It's okay, Toopy," I said quietly. "We're leaving now. I'll try and explain to you what just happened. But we're leaving. Everything will be okay."

I could tell he was thrilled our immediate ordeal was ending— dogs are so much freer with their body language than humans are— but I don't think he could have been any more thrilled than I was.

Dr. Belmont and Dr. Brown walked us through the hospital to the emergency room, where my scrapes and bruises were treated immediately and I was fully checked out. No waiting this time. We went to the pharmacy and the prescription refills we'd come for were ready for me. Again, there was no waiting. Suddenly, the whole VA bureaucracy was springing into action on our behalf.

After all that, Dr. Belmont brought us back to her office. A VA psychiatrist checked in with me, making sure I was sufficiently together to get on with my day. Both Tuesday and I were finally able to calm down. Tuesday, who hadn't been checked out in the ER or questioned by a psychiatrist, was finally catching his breath. I had rarely seen him quite so agitated. Just when I'd needed him most, he couldn't help me. I hated that, and I knew he hated it even more. He's not used to feeling helpless when I am in need. He wanted to comfort me, and I wanted to comfort him. The leash, I kept discovering, goes both ways.

The next morning, I sent an email to my dad. There'd been years I could not have been certain he'd be on my side. Thankfully, this time, when I needed my family's support, I knew I could turn to him.

"Hi, Papá," I wrote. "I'm in bed today—pretty sore from five (no exaggeration) idiot VA 'Police' officers piling on top of me. I really don't know what to do. It's just disgusting. I sent a letter to John Donnellan, the hospital director, a short while ago.

"Love, Luis & Tuesday"

My dad wrote back right away.

"Hi Luis," he said. "So what will happen to the police officers—anything?? Maybe Senators Franken and Isakson can send a letter to the VA Secretary." (Democrat Al Franken and Republican Johnny Isakson had been very helpful in getting the VA to recognize service dogs for sighted vets.)

"I hope you're over your aches and pains by now.

"Love, Papá."

The aches and pains got better in a few days, though the sense of distrust and violation did not ease quite so quickly. Not surprisingly, Tuesday recovered far more rapidly than I did. I never heard anything else about the disorderly conduct citation. It just seemed to disappear into the bureaucratic ether. But for a long time, my memories of the encounter and its aftermath haunted me.

For months, I didn't want to go back to the VA hospital. The whole thing still felt like a terrible betrayal to me. This was a place I went to get treatment. It was my safe place. What should you do when your safe place becomes an unsafe place, when those in charge who are entrusted to protect have abused their authority and have caused you pain? Those are not easy questions, but I knew I had to face them.

The whole situation could so easily have been avoided. The guard at the front door or the officers in the waiting room—any of them could have called upstairs. They'd have been told Tuesday was registered as my service dog. That would have taken five or seven minutes. Instead, the question consumed hours and hours of staff time and resulted in a huge amount of hassle and pain. My personal rights were violated. In a larger sense, human rights were trampled on. An ugly incident occurred in a main public area of a hospital that treats our military veterans. The institution opened itself to a lawsuit. People who should have been professionals behaved in a way that I assume even they came to regret.

In the days that followed, we would make progress on the issue. Police would be educated. Consistent regulations would be put in place for all VA facilities. Today, outside that hospital and at most other VA hospitals across the country, you will find a bright red sign that says, "As per 33 CFR 1.218(a)(11), service dogs are permitted in this facility."

CHAPTER 10

Health Scare

――――― »《●》« ―――――

A voice within me is sobbing.
ANNE FRANK

TUESDAY AND I HARDLY EVER LEFT THE ROAD. DRIVING AND FLYING, sleeping in hotel rooms and short-stay apartments, keeping focused on our mission at hand—that was the life we had chosen. Our stops in New York City, where we supposedly lived, were short visits on our way to somewhere else. Both of us were spent, me more than Tuesday. But even Tuesday was ready to chill.

Where better than the breezy city of Naples on the sunny southwest coast of Florida?

We had friends in the area and some upcoming commitments—a couple of speeches, a handful of book signings, some veterans' advocacy cases to follow up on—but this, I promised Tuesday, was going to be more vacation than work. Mostly, we came to relax, catch our breath, and recharge—and maybe sit for a while. My right leg was really bothering me. Walking and balancing had become a growing challenge. The pain rarely subsided. Nothing the doctors had suggested—braces, physical therapy, and a whole assortment of blood thinners, pain relievers, and other medications—seemed to do much good. By this point, I wasn't just a vet with a service dog who'd mostly gotten on top of his PTSD. I was a vet with a service dog who'd mostly gotten on top of his PTSD and now could hardly go anywhere without a cane.

I was proud that, up to now, we hadn't let any of this slow us down. We'd been keeping our breakneck schedule, hitting every region of the country, making real progress on the issues we cared about. I was also more than ready to turn it all off for a short while. As things turned out, a stress-free breather wasn't exactly in the cards.

Just after we arrived in Naples and got settled in our short-term rental, I got a scare I was completely unprepared for. It made me forget my bum leg in about five seconds flat.

I felt a lump on Tuesday's belly.

I had no idea what it was.

My knowledge and experience told me not to jump to conclusions. I jumped immediately.

Tuesday had cancer! That stuff's lethal!

Then, I caught my breath. What good would panicking do?

Tuesday's belly is normally as smooth and soft as a warm pat of butter, his nap all running in one direction, his golden coat beautifully groomed. But on this particular bright Florida morning, as I was brushing him, I felt something. I was certain it had never been there before. The lump was unmistakable.

"What's this, Toopy?" I asked.

With Tuesday facing me, the bump was just behind his front left leg on his belly. Of course, it could be anything, although I had no clue what. Maybe it was just a bug bite. Or maybe something a little worse. Did he jab himself? Or maybe it was nothing at all. Was it just some unexplained swelling? Maybe it would be gone if I touched that same spot again.

I ran my hand through his fur, and nothing had changed. It wasn't a cut or a bruise or a bone poking out of a socket. On closer inspection, I could tell it wasn't some foreign object caught in his fur. It didn't feel like a pimple or a cyst. It was definitely a mass, about the size of a pencil eraser. There was no squeezing it. It wasn't coming to a head. It was something beneath the skin but not too deep. It felt different from anything I had ever felt on him.

I didn't have any experience with lumps. I'd brushed and petted and rubbed Tuesday's fur enough times over the years to know for sure that this was the first lump he'd ever had. That's not to say my fingers hadn't discovered a few other things when I groomed him. He'd had a couple of blisters and cysts and other random eruptions. But those were different. They'd always been visible, and I knew immediately what they were. I'd never discovered something underneath the skin. Even Max, my dog growing up, had had a couple of abscesses, but never any lumps.

Anyone who has ever been through a health scare with an animal knows the mad collision of feelings I felt and just how rattling such a discovery can be.

My first sustained thought after the knee-jerk cancer thought was: *It's nothing. I'm sure it's nothing. Maybe I'm imagining it. Maybe there isn't a lump there at all. Maybe it will be gone if we take a walk outside for a few minutes and come back in.* We took the walk. We came back in. The lump was still lumpy, and it was still there.

My second thought was, *Tuesday's definitely going to die. It will be slow and painful and horrible, and I won't be able to help him, and I will be totally lost without him, and my life will quickly descend into depression and chaos.*

Thankfully, I shook that off in a hurry. Tuesday looked up at me with those piercing eyes of his, and I was able to get a grip on myself. He needed me. I *had* to get a grip on myself.

My third thought was to wait. I figured I'd keep an eye on the lump and give it some time and see if it went away. Tuesday seemed fine with that. He could tell I was anxious, but I don't think he knew why. He didn't seem weak or ill. At least the timing was good. We were off the road.

For two weeks, I tried not to think about the lump. That was easier said than done. I have to admit I did check it from time to time—make that *constantly*—trying to remember how it felt before and whether it felt any different now. I was pretty sure the lump wasn't going down. In fact, although it made me nervous to admit, that damned lump was growing—from a pencil eraser to the size of a large pea to the circumference of a dime. Larger, higher, fatter. I couldn't deny any of that.

We had waited long enough. "Okay," I said to Tuesday, "we need to get this thing checked out."

The good news, if you can call it that, is that a lump is a physical issue. There is an objective answer to the question, "What is this?" You may not like the answer, but with professional assistance, that answer can be found. And I aimed to find it, which would mean taking Tuesday to a full-service animal hospital where he could get examined and we could figure out what the hell we were dealing with. I needed to know. He needed to know. There was no other choice. This was a Sunday afternoon.

"We will go see a doctor in the morning," I announced to Tuesday.

By then, I felt like I almost had a degree in *canine lumpology.* Sure, I'd been trying not to check every second, and I'd kept things as normal as I could. But the truth was, with so much downtime, I had spent many hours doing what I bet any panicked dog owner would do under the circumstances. I went on the Internet, pulled up Google, and typed in the words "lump" and "dog." From WebMD, I learned the "classic signs" of cancer in dogs are very similar to those in people: "A lump or a bump, a wound that doesn't heal, any kind of swelling, enlarged lymph nodes, a lameness or swelling in the bone, abnormal bleeding."

I looked up from my computer screen and saw Tuesday studying my face. Did he know what I was researching? The last thing I wanted was for him to pick up on my growing concerns. I quickly turned back to my reading, deciding not to mention WebMD's doomsday symptoms to Tuesday. But it did rattle me that "a lump" was the first sign on the list.

I found a study from the University of Georgia College of Veterinary Medicine called "Mortality in North American Dogs." It did not make me feel better at all. Actually, I felt a little sick. The researchers had studied thousands of dog deaths, and here is what they found: "Young dogs (two years or younger) died most commonly of trauma, congenital disease, and infectious causes." Got it. And for older dogs? "Older dogs, on the other hand, died overwhelmingly of cancer."

Ugh!

I didn't mention that study to Tuesday either, who had turned nine two months earlier. Clearly, nine was different than five, six, seven, and eight, let alone one or two. When a dog turns nine, it's a wake-up call. Ten is right around the corner. You're getting into double digits there. Definitely an "older dog."

It didn't get better. I saw another article that said that certain breeds—golden retrievers among them—have a disproportionately high incidence of cancer.

I also kept that one to myself.

It was already late on Sunday, but I didn't want to put this off another moment. I called a couple of people whose judgment I trusted. One was Jeannie Bates, who lives in Naples and is the founding director of PAWS Assistance Dogs. Jeannie knows and loves dogs as much as anyone on earth—and recognizes how talented and precious they are. She has devoted her life to that cause. I didn't have to explain to her how much Tuesday means to me—or how devastated I would be by losing him before his time.

"Listen," I said to her, "I need a veterinarian. What's the absolute best animal hospital in southwest Florida?"

I figure there had to be good ones nearby, Naples being a resort town—a fairly ritzy one at that. Wealthy people don't love their dogs any more than poor people do—but they are often able to get higher-quality veterinary care. I didn't care about the cost. I just wanted the best.

"Animal Oasis," Jeannie said without hesitation.

She went on to tell me why this place was the best. For one thing, Dr. Lien d'Hespeel ran the place and was a truly excellent vet. Another was that the Animal Oasis Veterinary Hospital had better facilities, greater specialization, fancier equipment, and a better-trained staff than any other such places in and around Naples. "I trust them with the health of our service dogs in training," Jeannie said. "They treat all the PAWS dogs."

I couldn't think of a better reference than that.

While preparing to speak at the American Animal Hospital Association conference, I had learned that there is a huge difference between an animal hospital and a veterinary clinic. It's like the difference between Memorial Sloan Kettering Cancer Center and a street corner Doc-in-the-Box. There are doctors at both of them, but there's a world's worth of difference between the two. For Tuesday, I wanted the animal equivalent of big-league medicine.

So that night, I sent an email through the Animal Oasis website and also left a voice mail, dropping Jeannie's name and asking for a callback as soon as possible. Monday morning, we were up early, eager to go. But when I hadn't heard anything by 10:00 A.M., I got Jeannie back on the phone. This time, she called the animal hospital directly. A few minutes later, she sent me an email. "You have an appointment at noon. I would love to pick up you and Tuesday and go with you, if that is something you want."

Now, *that's* a friend! Given the purpose of our appointment, I sure needed one.

"Yes!" I emailed back.

Jeannie didn't say much on the drive over in her white minivan. She left me to my thoughts and Tuesday with his. Her van was a classic dog-mobile. Two seats in front. The whole back section a rolling dog domain. There were dog scents everywhere. Tuesday snooped around, exploring the space. I was grateful for his diversions.

I was also cognizant that I was getting crazy anxious. That was the last thing I wanted Tuesday to sense. I did my best to control my impulses. Normally, I'd be open with him. For years, that was one of the things I most treasured and expected from our relationship. Soothing me in times of trouble is what Tuesday does best. But in this case, it was weird. I wasn't worried about something else. I wasn't affected by memories of the battlefield or some social issue that pissed me off. My anxiety was all about him. And it didn't feel right to expect him to fix that.

When we arrived and the three of us went inside, I could see immediately why Jeannie liked the hospital. This was no chilly medical practice. Everything was modern, sunny, and bright with a Florida décor of pastels, pink and light-blue walls and some darker accent colors. The techs wore dark-blue scrubs. Everyone seemed to know Jeannie.

Without delay, one of the techs led us into an examining room and took some biographical information about Tuesday—his age, his shots, any long-standing health issues. Then she asked: "So what's going on?"

"He has a lump on his belly," I told her. "I noticed it about two weeks ago. I thought it might go away, but it's only gotten larger." Two weeks must have seemed like a long time to wait. But in my defense, I had spent that time boning up on worst-case scenarios. "I'm pretty sure it needs to be aspirated," I said.

In all those articles I'd been reading on the Internet, everyone kept talking about aspirating lumps, jabbing the lump with a hollow needle and extracting some tissue to test. I had no doubt Tuesday's lump should be aspirated.

She repeated back to me everything I had said in a way that made me confident she was listening carefully. "Lump on his belly... larger...aspirate." In the military, we call that technique a "brief back." I can tell you it's a good technique for reassuring someone, even in civilian life.

She ran her hand over Tuesday's belly, lingering just a moment on the spot I directed her to. Tuesday was totally cooperative, standing still when she asked him to, then wagging his tail, putting his head down in a very nice-to-meet-you way, giving off his usual friendly vibe. I was the one who was tense. Not Tuesday. He was still providing comfort to me.

"Can I take him into the back?" the tech asked.

I didn't like the sound of that. A lot of veterinary personnel—heck, a lot of human doctors—like to separate the patients from their loved one, taking them to the back for testing or whatever it is. It was the old separate-to-conquer idea. The animal might start crying. Separation gives the medical professionals more control. It's also a law enforcement tactic we employed when I was a military police officer. Separate the parties in any tense situation.

Luis does not play that game, certainly not with Tuesday.

Dogs are pack animals, and this one had been at my side constantly. Tuesday wouldn't react well. Separation wasn't familiar to him. It would be extremely atypical. Plus, there was no good reason that he should be alone at a time like this. There was no good reason for me to be left alone, either. More importantly, I told myself, there was no chance I would get in the way. My being there could only help the staff if any issue arose. I know him, and he knows me. Believe me, he would be 200 percent easier to deal with knowing that I was there. I'm not saying our bond is utterly unique or stronger than what other handlers have with their dogs. Then again, it might be and it sure feels that way to me.

But I didn't say any of that to the tech. "I would prefer we stay together, and he be aspirated right here," I said.

She didn't argue. She didn't discuss. She didn't debate. "Okay" was all she said.

A couple of minutes later, the tech came into the examining room. Dr. d'Hespeel was with her this time. She was also very nice. She greeted Jeannie and me. But there was someone else in the room who needed to be introduced. "This is Tuesday," I said. "He is my service dog. He's a very happy boy and I love him very much," I said making it clear that this guy meant everything to me. Remembering the questionable medical outlook for older dogs, I added: "He's nine years old."

Tuesday looked at Dr. d'Hespeel then back at me, prompting me with his eyes to go on. "We have something we'd like you to look at."

Tuesday loves being introduced that way. It's amazing. A few humans gathered in a room speaking to each other, but he somehow knows that he is part of the conversation.

"Nice to meet you," she said, addressing Tuesday directly. Clearly, these were animal people. They spoke dog.

Just about then, I began to feel concern that I might be making Tuesday nervous. We'd been to vets before, lots of times. He doesn't have a doggy version of white-coat syndrome. But with so many concerned faces in the room, this was different, and I think he knew it. "Oh, he's okay," I said, more for Tuesday's benefit than the doctor's with the same smile you'd hope would fool a wary child. Then, I added, "Really, he's all right."

As good as I am at reading his mind, I still didn't know exactly what Tuesday thought about the lump. He understood, I knew, that it was some kind of issue. I'd been assessing it for two weeks and now others were, too. But I'm not sure he fully grasped what the issue was or what we were trying to answer or why I was so upset. Try as I did to hide it, I knew my highly intuitive dog was picking up on at least some of this. My best guess was that, to Tuesday, the lump was something less than a real distraction—like a mole would be for us. He knew it was there. He knew it was something. He knew I knew about it. But he'd never been to medical school, and I don't think he connected the dots. That's what the doctor was for.

Dr. d'Hespeel explained what she'd be doing and how I could help.

As I held a hand on Tuesday's back, keeping him calm and still, the doctor reached around and probed the mass with a needle, extracting a small sample before she pulled the needle out. I held my breath, ready for a small yelp.

Tuesday hardly seemed to feel it.

Very gently, the doctor placed the sample on a glass microscope slide and, holding it carefully by the edges, excused herself. She and the tech headed back to the laboratory, leaving Jeannie, Tuesday, and me in the examining room.

If you've ever waited in a doctor's office for results of any serious test, you know what this was like. It was one of the longest half hours of my life. That much time leads to a lot of soulful thinking, worrying, and imagining.

Why was this taking so long?

Was there a problem?

What were they seeing in their microscopes?

I didn't say any of this. Jeannie didn't bother to make small talk. Neither did I. Tuesday hung out, happily. I mostly just stared blankly at Tuesday, at the floor, at the ceiling, at the signs on the wall. I tried, every now and then, to smile for Jeannie and Tuesday's sake. But my mind was reeling, I promise you that.

After a short eternity, Dr. d'Hespeel came back into the room.

I watched her for signs, but thankfully she didn't make us wait a single extra second. "Well, it is not cancerous," she said. "It's just a benign mass of fatty tissue. I can see why it was so concerning. But it's nothing to worry about."

Whew!

I let out an enormous sigh of relief.

"Oh, that's good!" Jeannie blurted out. She didn't show it, but I think she'd been as nervous as I'd been. She jumped up and gave me a hug, sharing in my own relief and delight.

Tuesday, no slouch when it comes to detecting mood shifts, immediately sensed the black cloud dissipating and the sunny burst of brighter energy.

I pet him on his side, on his back, and on his head. He knew I was happy. I kept hugging him, telling how very much I love him.

Tuesday's a sucker for warm attention, even when there's no precise reason.

But this time, he knew it was something special.

His ears went back.

His tail was wagging vigorously.

His butt went down, and he dropped into a low wag. That low wag, for Tuesday, is a very tender gesture. Tender was exactly what I wanted to convey to him, and he was sending it back in my direction.

It was such a huge relief, hearing the news from the doctor. I swear, if I hadn't wanted to get Tuesday out of that hospital as quickly as possible, I could have fallen into the corner of the examining room and gone to sleep. Yes, sleep. That's a very military inclination, being so mentally and physically exhausted you just flop down wherever you happen to be and rest. It reminded me how on edge I was.

As long and agonizing as the wait had seemed, it was over. Really over. We thanked the doctor and the tech. I gave Tuesday one last hug, and we got out of there.

Walking out to Jeannie's dog van, I was already thinking back on it all. This was an experience I had never quite been through before. Even though it turned out well, I hoped never to experience it again.

I'm not someone who's ever thought a lot about death, mine or anyone else's. Not when my father had heart problems and had a mechanical valve put in. Not when I was in combat with my guys and we faced danger every day. I really love my father. I really loved my guys. Dying was a possibility in both of those circumstances. But I hadn't dwelled on either of those like I had with the prospect of losing Tuesday. Tuesday is a member of my family and more. He is my caretaker, my confidant, and my best friend. He is all of those things wrapped into one. He pulled me through stuff that no one ever had.

"We should go to Norman Love," I announced. "We need to celebrate."

"That's a great idea," Jeannie agreed.

Norman Love Confections is a Naples institution, a decadent coffee and dessert salon run by the former global pastry chef for Ritz-Carlton Hotels. Tuesday and I had been there only once before, and not only because I wanted to try everything on the menu. They also offer a small line of super-tasty baked doggie treats. Tuesday remembered and recognized the name immediately.

He was game.

The place was just as sin-sational as the last time we'd visited. Jeannie ordered a high-octane hot chocolate. I got myself a chocolate coffee. Tuesday could have had anything he wanted. He had a *Puppuccino.*

As Jeannie and I slumped into our chairs and Tuesday curled around my legs, I have to say I was still a little lost in my thoughts. I raised my cup and whispered a quiet hope that we would never go through anything like this again.

CHAPTER 11

Rapt in Paws

The most beautiful thing we can experience is the mysterious. It is the source of all true art and science. He to whom this emotion is a stranger, who can no longer pause to wonder and stand rapt in awe, is as good as dead: his eyes are closed.

ALBERT EINSTEIN

NO ROAD GOES CONSTANTLY UPWARD, INCLUDING THE ONE TUESDAY and I are on. We hit peaks and valleys and some potholes, too. Some days are better than others, even though Tuesday never loses his good cheer.

This day started out as a downer and ended with a nice surprise. My head was killing me. If you've ever had a migraine, you know the kind of pain I am talking about. My temples were pulsing. My eyes were watering. My neck was stiff. My skull was a supernova about to explode.

People with traumatic brain injuries get more than their share of migraine headaches. I know I do. And this time I'd already exhausted my first line of defense—turning out the lights in my apartment, laying a cold washcloth against my forehead, lying silently on the couch, and, for good measure, moaning out loud. When I gingerly opened my eyes around 7 P.M., I could see in the semi-darkness that

Tuesday was conducting his own assessment of me. He studied my face. He observed my body language, listened to my breathing, and then started gently nudging me.

"Let's get out of here," he was saying. "You need some fresh air at least."

Talk about a role reversal! Now, my dog would be walking me!

I didn't want to leave the apartment. It was barely 10 degrees outside, the coldest day of the year so far in New York City. The wind was snapping across Morningside Heights. The sidewalks were still slushy with leftover snow. But twenty-four hours into this headache, even I could see Tuesday had a point. Maybe I could find an over-the-counter headache remedy at the drugstore that would actually be effective. At the very least, some soup would probably do me some good. After hitting the Duane Reade pharmacy on 111th Street, I told Tuesday we could go across Broadway to our favorite little café, Le Monde. He loves their medium-rare beef burgers, at least as much as I like their steamy, soothing chicken soup.

As he led me up the block, I had to admit the biting wind actually felt good against my sweaty face. Inside the drugstore, I grabbed a bottle of juice and a box of Kleenex, and then I went to the colds-and-headaches aisle, where the many options packed four full shelves. Regular Strength, Extra-Strength, Advil, Tylenol, Excedrin, daytime, nighttime, 8-hour, 12-hour, 24-hour, blue pack, red pack, white pack, with herbs, without herbs: How could anyone possibly choose? There were enough choices to give me a headache all by themselves. The only thing the store didn't have was a product that guaranteed: "Take this one. Your migraine will go away."

As I stared at the packed shelves, feeling totally overwhelmed, Tuesday gave me one of his thigh hugs, nuzzling his snout against the upper part of my leg and sharing the warmth of his fur. "It's okay, Luis. You'll be better soon. These headaches don't last forever. It just seems that way."

That's when I noticed a woman staring at me.

She was dark-haired and middle-aged and wearing a heavy wool coat. I looked away, but when I looked over again she was still staring at me. I felt bad enough from the throbbing in my head and the rapidly increasing nausea. Now we had a stalker? I shot her a scowl, and that made her turn away.

Hypervigilance is frequently a symptom of PTSD, especially for people who've been in law enforcement or the military, fields that already encourage situational awareness. But I wasn't imagining this woman's stares. I grabbed a box of something that seemed like it might be helpful and moved to the front of the store. As we waited in the checkout line, she was eyeballing us again.

There is no point in having a confrontation, I told myself. *I'll be out of the store in a minute.* I opened the pill bottle, shook out two and washed them down with a swig of juice as Tuesday and I headed out to the sidewalk. The wind, now at my back, didn't feel so biting anymore. It was so damn cold. Clearly, I wasn't dressed warmly enough. But I knew we wouldn't be outside for long. Le Monde was just across Broadway. Once inside, we'd both warm up. While Tuesday wolfed down his burger, I'd be diving into that bowl of brothy chicken soup.

As we waited at the light, straight-up freezing, I noticed two people—a man and a woman—walking a large gold-colored dog. They were coming toward us up Broadway from the south, but not quickly, stepping carefully across the ice patches and the slush. Tuesday noticed, too. He's always aware of other dogs. *That could be a playmate,* he was thinking. *Maybe, I can meet someone new,* he wagged. Even from that distance, I was pretty certain that the dog was a golden retriever. You don't see that many golden retrievers in New York City. They are big for small spaces. This is a city of Westies and Malteses and chihuahuas, dogs that don't take up half a studio apartment and don't seem to miss having their own backyards.

At first that's all I noticed, a couple and a dog that could have been Tuesday's distant kin. But as I kept watching them, something seemed off. The retriever was trotting funny, and, from that distance, I couldn't quite say why. Hop-bouncing up the sidewalk. That's how I would describe the gait.

Just then, the woman from the drugstore walked up.

Her, I mumbled to myself.

"Excuse me," she said tentatively. "I am very sorry for staring at you in the store. But by chance is that Tuesday?"

There was something about her tone—her politeness, her timidity. And the way she said "Tuesday," it was like she was talking about a beloved celebrity, which of course he is to me—but I still like hearing others say so. I'm unabashedly proud of Tuesday. All of a sudden, my eyebrows unfurled, and I was looking at this woman in a whole different light. In ten seconds flat, I went from *oh, great, here's the psycho-stalker lady* to *oh, hello!*

I believe I can explain the sudden change. I like to think of Tuesday as a reflection of the best in me. Now, instead of a stalker, here was someone who was inquiring politely about the best of me.

"Yes, this is Tuesday," I said.

"Oh my God," she said. "I knew it."

"It's Tuesday," I nodded, assuring her.

She wasn't a stalker, but she did know a lot about us. "I have been hoping I would see you and Tuesday," she said. "I knew from your book that we were neighbors. When I read your book, all I could think of was my daughter. She is eighteen. She has severe anxiety—about everything. She doesn't like to meet people. She doesn't even like to go outside. We have been thinking about getting a service dog for her."

When people approach Tuesday and me, they often feel comfortable opening up about the most intimate details of their lives. They'll share whatever they are feeling or going though. I do think dogs encourage honesty in humans. Dogs are so naturally open and accepting, they make us drop our human defenses and our usual fears.

Here was a woman I had never met, a woman I moments ago believed could be a crazy person, now conveying the deepest pain in her life. The emotion was flowing out of her. Her eyes filled with tears, and for a moment she lost her composure. She was obviously deeply concerned for her daughter. What she might not have realized was that it was because I had Tuesday in my life that I was able to listen to her story. I was more comfortable doing that than I ever would have thought possible. None of it scared me anymore. This woman had just met her hero—Tuesday—and she was reacting without artifice or restraint.

She spoke and I listened, and the light changed to green and then red again. As the three of us stood there, completely unaware of the elements, I did notice the couple with the golden retriever were finally approaching, just a few storefronts away. As the distance narrowed, I could see that something more than the slush was causing the dog to hobble. This beautiful golden retriever had only one front leg.

The minute I realized that, my mind raced back to Angel, a wonderful woman who lives in Grand Rapids, Michigan, and to Benjamin, my God-dog. Like this dog on the frigid Manhattan sidewalk, Benjamin is a golden retriever missing his right front leg.

Angel is a total sweetie-pie. She is what we call in the dog world a "foster failure." She was working with an animal rescue organization, helping to place unwanted and abandoned dogs in loving "fur-ever homes." When Angel met Benjamin, an eight-week-old golden retriever puppy, the tenth in a joyful and rambunctious litter of ten—she couldn't bear to pass him on. Benjamin stood out from his furry brothers and sisters. He was smaller than the other puppies, and he had a congenitally deformed right front leg. Angel already had seven other dogs at home, all different breeds. But little Benjamin totally stole her heart. She had to make him hers. She consulted with several veterinarians, and they all agreed on this: Benjamin's best hope for the future was a full amputation of his badly deformed leg, which is how he became a tri-ped.

Like the woman in the drugstore and so many others, Angel had been moved by Tuesday's story and, several years after welcoming this special dog into her home, she had reached out to me.

"Benjamin is 4 years old this year," she said in an email. "His body is strong and his spirit is incredible, but the wear and tear has begun to take a toll on him. His frustrations get the better of him on occasion. But he is still in charge of this pack of dogs, and he is still the one who knows when my head hurts, when I am happiest, or saddest. He is so in tune to my emotional state that I have to check myself often because if I'm unstable, he will challenge our environment until he feels the harmony come back into our world."

Echoes of Tuesday! Benjamin may not be an *official* service dog, I thought—but he was certainly performing like one. I love that story.

Angel and I traded a few emails. A few months later, she and Benjamin drove four hours to Chicago to a fund-raiser Tuesday and I were doing for Elana Morgan's War Dogs, a wonderful not-for-profit group that places service dogs with veterans suffering from PTSD. It didn't take long—both Tuesday and I also fell in love with Benjamin that day. Angel told me more about his frustrations and how the missing leg seemed to affect his mood and his basic ability to get around. When a dog is off balance, especially because of a missing front leg, the consequences can be dire. It isn't only a balance issue. The spine is pressured. The organs are strained. Most of a dog's locomotion comes from the front.

Hating to hear how Benjamin had been suffering, I told her I would do what I could to help. From that day forward, I considered him my God-dog.

My first thought was a prosthetic leg. But after doing some online research, I realized sadly that Benjamin's condition—he had no stump, or "residual leg"—didn't make him a promising candidate for that. His entire limb was gone. There wasn't even a socket to support a prosthetic. I kept looking online and, determined to help Benjamin, I also spoke with several experts. Finally, I came across a group in Colorado called OrthoPets that creates custom braces to strengthen the "good leg" of tri-ped dogs. I loved their slogan: "Endless Paw-sibilities." One of these custom braces, I learned, can support a dog's gait and the rest of his body. It can also reduce the strain on the spine and organs. Working with the OrthoPets people, we had Benjamin's vet carefully measure the precise dimensions of his leg for the brace, which was made just for him, sliding over the good leg like a tight-fitting sleeve. Angel was thrilled at the huge difference it made. So was Benjamin, maybe even more so, as he started bounding around Grand Rapids better than before.

His gait was smoother. His spine was less stressed. His overall health improved. His vet couldn't get over how well Benjamin was doing. He is a wonderful creature. I was thrilled to be his God-human.

I smiled and thought of Benjamin's journey as I saw that three-legged golden retriever hopping awkwardly toward us on Broadway. Tuesday was wagging away. At first, he might have thought that it was his old friend Benjamin coming up the sidewalk.

"Excuse me," I interrupted the drugstore lady, "I've got to meet these people."

I introduced myself to the couple with the dog.

"I noticed your beautiful dog is a tri-ped," I said. "It so happens that my God-dog Benjamin is also a tri-ped and a golden retriever."

That might have raised some suspicion. A New York City stranger who just happened to have a tri-ped golden retriever God-dog? Really? But these lovely people smiled, and I told them more.

I told them about Benjamin's mobility issues and what a difference the custom brace made. The woman expressed great interest, completely understanding what I was saying. "That's amazing," she said. She said that she too was growing concerned about how her dog was walking. She said she was eager to do anything that would be helpful. But the brace, she told me, wasn't something they were familiar with.

I wasn't surprised. Until I'd done the research I, too, had no idea that any of this was possible. "A lot of people don't know this exists," I told her. "But it's becoming more common."

I thought I saw a hopeful spark in her eyes. "That's very intriguing," she said looking down at her dog.

We exchanged cards, and I promised to send her some detailed information.

"I'd really appreciate that," she said, tucking the card into her warm coat pocket.

It hadn't gotten any warmer on the sidewalk. Now, six of us—two dogs and four humans—were standing on the wind-whipped corner in below-freezing temperatures talking about amputee dogs, the drugstore lady's daughter, all this heavy stuff, right in the middle of my migraine. And suddenly I realized that I wasn't thinking about the pain in my forehead. I was feeling immensely grateful that Tuesday had dragged me out of my apartment for a walk.

We all talked a while longer until the couple with the golden retriever said they had to get going. They said their goodbyes to Tuesday and then reached out to shake my hand. The man was wearing gloves. The woman was wearing mittens.

As the woman shook my hand, I could feel that she was missing several if not all of her fingers. There was no doubt about it. The front part of her mitten was empty. Her right hand was shaped more like a stump.

I had no idea how that might have happened or what could have caused it, any more than I knew whether her own condition played any role in her having adopted a disabled dog. I didn't ask, and she didn't offer. We just said our warm goodbyes and wished each other well.

But I had to admit, the handshake affected me, knowing that this particular woman was caring for this particular dog. It seemed like something out of the Bible. I couldn't help it. It made me like her more.

To shake this woman's mitten and to feel that, I thought to myself, *Oh, man, that's the stuff that saints are made out of.*

Like I said, dogs have an incredible way of helping people connect.

The drugstore lady lingered just another minute.

"Would you and Tuesday please consider meeting my daughter?" she asked. "A personal visit from both of you would be a tremendous help to her. I'm sure it would be."

I told the mother, of course, we would visit her daughter. We would be happy to. "I don't have a daughter," I told her, "but I have other people in my family, and I have Tuesday. I know how tough this must be. I can only imagine what it would be to have someone you love suffering like that."

I gave her my card. "Please email me," I said. "We'll set something up."

There was one thing I was thinking that I did not say: My own family certainly knows something about that...

———————◦◉◦———————

After I told the drugstore woman goodbye for now, Tuesday and I finally crossed at the light. By that point, both of us were exhausted and almost numb from the cold. My migraine, which I'd momentarily forgotten, was pounding back again, and my nose was running now. On top of all that, the pain in my leg seemed to have been sharpened by the cold. I was more than ready for the warmth of Le Monde and my steaming bowl of soup, though perhaps not as ready as Tuesday was for his burger. So much had happened in the past twenty minutes.

After we sat and ordered, I called Angel in Michigan. I had to tell someone about this chance encounter. Who better than Angel?

As I sat there in the café with Tuesday at my feet, nuzzling against my legs, both of us warming each other and waiting for our food, I started telling Angel everything. About the woman in the drugstore with the anxious daughter. About the couple on the street with the tri-ped retriever. About the woman's hand. About my rush of Benjamin memories. As I spoke softly, the beauty and emotion of it all came gushing forward. I'm not a big crier. And maybe I can partly blame what happened next on the migraine and frigid temperature. But all that feeling just overwhelmed me.

Amid the buzz of the busy restaurant, I erupted in tears. I reached down, grabbed my napkin, and cried at the beauty of it all.

And it was all because of Tuesday. That drugstore lady saw us because of Tuesday. I noticed that golden retriever tri-ped because of Tuesday. Were it not for Tuesday, I would never have gotten the email from Angel or become Benjamin's God-human.

I am so lucky, I thought. So blessed. The tears flowed, and I let them.

PART II

Will and Desire

CHAPTER 12

New Year's Resolution

*If you would attain to what you are not yet, you must always be
displeased by what you are. For where you are pleased with yourself
there you have remained. . . . Keep adding, keep walking,
keep advancing . . .*
SAINT AUGUSTINE

I BELIEVE IN NEW YEAR'S RESOLUTIONS.

Oh, I know. They can be trite devices of self-delusion. Lots of
people, myself included, have made sacred vows in late December
that are already long forgotten by January 15.

*Did I really say I was going to lose fifteen pounds? I think I'll have
another slice of* Tres Leches *holiday cake instead!* But still, as each year
comes to a close, I do find myself reflecting on how things have gone,
how they're going, and how I might make improvements.

And so it was this year. On Christmas Day, I had a nice phone call
with my parents. They were in Miami, where they had moved to enjoy
their retirement. I was on the opposite coast of Florida with Tuesday.

Mamá and Papá had resolved never to live in snowy environs
again. Looking out the window at palm trees and sunny skies, I didn't
see any reason for them to break that resolution. I'd also escaped the

cold, but weather wasn't the main thing on my mind. "One of my biggest resolutions for the new year," I told them in that phone call, "is to regain control of my physical health."

It was about time. Over the past decade, I had spent an enormous amount of energy getting my head together. It would forever be a work in progress, but I had undeniably made huge progress. My life was so much better. The worst of my full-blown PTSD was securely in the past. Gradually, with Tuesday's help, I had dug myself out of that very deep hole. Our lives were living proof of that progress. My mind, on most days, was truly mine again.

But what about my body?

The truth was that I had worked so hard getting my head together, I really had neglected the rest of me. I had a feeling of now-or-never. I had to devote some serious energy to regaining control of the physical me. Partly, this meant an honest commitment to losing weight and working out again. I'd been an athlete for most of my life. My career was that of a warrior. But it had been a while since I'd stepped foot in a gym or on a battlefield. And did I really have what it took anymore? There was no excuse for me to spend the next couple of decades sitting around and deteriorating. That sounded almost as depressing as being paralyzed with PTSD. I didn't want either of those conditions to define me.

There was no pretending anymore.

I'd been living with pain for several years already. My bones were as creaky as an old man's. My nerves were shot. My spine was getting stiffer. My walking was labored. My posture was off. I couldn't imagine leaving the house without a cane. How could I? My right leg was constantly killing me.

I didn't publicly complain much about any of this. When it came to my physical ailments, I did what the army had taught all of us to do, a message reinforced at home, by my father especially: *Suck it up and drive on!* That's what warriors do! That's what Montalváns do!

Strangely, the frankness and openness I brought to my struggle with the invisible wounds of war were severely lacking when it came to these more visible ones. In that way, I was precisely the opposite of many military veterans. For several years, I had been talking openly and publicly about my mental anguish. I hardly ever got around to mentioning the physical wounds.

I had seen many doctors, in and out of the VA system. The doctors seemed to agree that much of my condition could be traced to the ambush on the Iraqi-Syrian border and the tumble I took on the parade grounds at Fort Carson in Colorado. Whatever the causes were, the doctors all agreed on one other thing: My condition wasn't getting better. It was getting worse.

I still believe in the old Greco-Roman adage: Sound mind and sound body lead to sound spirit. But what was I doing about it? I was sorely lacking some soundness here. I needed to put some oomph in my efforts. I couldn't just feel sorry for myself and suffer in silence. That wouldn't do any good.

But what could I do? Whatever it was, I knew, it had to be something dramatic if I was going to see real results. This had to be a genuine transformation. Not changing a few bad habits or losing a few pounds. Real transformation. Demolition and reconstruction. A wrecking ball followed by bricks and mortar. Something real.

"I'm gonna do this," I told my parents in that holiday phone call. "I'm not quite sure what *it* is yet. But I promise you. I am going to figure that out and give it my all."

I just had the sense I couldn't wait any longer, like I was at some kind of crucial decision point. It was now or never, and I didn't like the way that never sounded. Looking back, I can see that Tuesday's cancer scare played a role in my thinking—or at least its urgency. Life can be shorter than we ever imagined, for dogs and people, too. There is no excuse for not living fully, making whatever bold moves there are to be made. That didn't just mean deciding. It meant acting too. Once I had diagnosed the problem, I knew I had to find the cure.

What was I made of? Was getting out from under PTSD going to be my biggest achievement in life? What could I learn from the distance I had traveled so far?

Those were the questions bouncing around in my head as one year was ending and a new one lay just days ahead. Everyone on television, online, and in the Fort Myers Starbucks seemed to be nailing down resolutions meant to improve their lives. I figured I should probably take a basic assessment of my own.

I was tired of hobbling.

I was tired of aching.

I wanted to run.

I wanted to play happily with Tuesday.

I wanted to be the man I had been, the man I knew I could be again.

I already knew I had someone on my side. I had been there for Tuesday when we discovered what could have been a life-threatening illness. Would you be surprised to hear that, this time, Tuesday would be there for me? Of course not.

None of what I resolved to do was as easy as joining Weight Watchers or signing up at Gold's Gym. That I knew.

"Tuesday, how would you like it if we could go to the beach much more often?"

Tuesday ran to the door, smiling, tail wagging. His movement reflected a resounding "Yes!"

Now all we had to do was navigate the health-care system of the U.S. Department of Veterans Affairs. How hard could that be?

Being a patient with the VA is like having a difficult job. I have certainly learned that the hard way. You have to work at it if you are ever going to succeed. Your first and most important task: finding good clinicians. It's an art, a science, and a heavy lift every step of the way. If you are wise—and most former warriors are pretty wise—this means maneuvering your way into relationships with your own Holy Trinity of Care. You need a competent and capable primary-care physician. You need a competent and capable mental-health therapist. And you need a competent and capable psychiatrist who can pre-scribe whatever meds you may require. Depending on your particu-lar issues, various other specialists will also come into play. But it all starts with the trinity. If it's high-quality health care you're looking for, you will never get anywhere without those three.

The first and most important is the primary-care physician. He or she is the general contractor of your health. Almost everything radiates from there. Finding the right one is challenging enough in the civilian world. At the VA, everything is five times as hard. Long waits for appointments. Heavy caseloads for the doctors, especially the good ones. Endless questions about your need for treatment and reams of forms to fill out. The best VA doctors don't tend to stick around very long. They figure out they can make more money and have easier lives working elsewhere, and they leave. There are a hand-ful of talented, dedicated, committed primary-care physicians in the system, but you might have to try out a dozen before you find one who has the right know-how, temperament, experience, and con-cern. Along the way, you'll find yourself channeling Donald Trump on *The Apprentice:* "You're fired. You're fired. *You're* fired, too." The stakes are high. This is your health, after all. And the search can be mentally exhausting.

But once you find the right VA doctor, it's like you've discov-ered gold. You treasure it. You remind yourself how valuable it is. You can barely get over your good fortune. When I finally found Dr. Jeri Jones at the Brooklyn VA, known officially as the Brooklyn campus of the New York Harbor Healthcare System, I felt like John

Belushi in *The Blues Brothers,* the chubby white guy in dark glasses doing backflips down the aisle of the Triple Rock Baptist Church. I couldn't do anything approaching a backflip. Not yet, anyway. But in my mind, Tuesday and I were right there with Jake Blues. I could hardly contain my enthusiasm.

Dr. Jones was smart, caring, and open-minded. She urged her patients to be actively engaged in their own health-care decisions. She actually listened to me. She was a doctor who didn't gloss over her patients' overall health or focus on only one single element. She spent the time and energy getting to know me in a holistic way, basing her advice and prescription choices on that. It may sound trite to say Dr. Jones cared—but Dr. Jones cared.

As my pain had intensified and my walking had grown more labored, I consulted with numerous specialists inside the VA system, before and during my time as Dr. Jones's primary-care patient. As we spoke about my mobility issues, she encouraged me to do some of my own research. She believed strongly that a patient who understands exactly what he wants to achieve will be far more likely to achieve it. Medicine can't be left entirely to the professionals. I had been seen by neurology specialists already, who put my brain and nervous system through endless testing. I was examined by orthopedists, who focused on bone and muscular issues. Then by physical and occupational therapists, who manipulated my body in many directions and set up exercise regimens. They also sent me to the pain management clinic, where potent drugs were prescribed.

My right leg is what all these physicians were hyper-focused on. The basic issue, most of the specialists agreed, was vascular. The veins in my leg were not delivering blood throughout like they should. Without sufficient blood, the leg was being undernourished. This was causing a lack of feeling, a lack of control—at times an utter lack of usefulness. That's an oversimplified explanation, but once you stripped away all the medical jargon, that's what the various specialists all seemed to agree on.

The doctors had one other thing in common: They all said they couldn't cure it, which was equally maddening and disappointing to me. All those tests, treatments, examinations, medications, and therapies had all led me exactly nowhere. We'd gone round and round for two or three years—appointments, more appointments, more testing, more specialists. All these different well-trained specialists—and not one of them had anything useful to offer me.

However, Dr. Jones was patient and encouraging the entire way. She kept coming up with new avenues to go down, new possibilities, new research. She seemed as dedicated as I was to finding a solution, wherever it may be. But even the most hopeful road comes to an end. Finally, it was time for Dr. Jones and me to have a come-to-Jesus moment, the heavy and inevitable talk we'd been putting off for years. It wasn't quick in coming. By then, she had been my doctor for three or four years.

Dr. Jones sat across from me and Tuesday in her small VA office and reviewed where we stood.

"We have tried neurology," she said.

I nodded.

"You've been to ortho."

I nodded again.

"We have tried PT and OT."

"We have," I said.

"We have tried pain management."

"We have," I said. "So what's next?"

"Well," she said, "as you know, they are working on new braces, robotics, and non-robotics. Those will be available eventually."

"New braces," I said. The tone in my voice said what I am sure the doctor knew I was thinking. *We both know new braces are not going to solve my mobility issues.*

"What I would like to hear," I told her, "is your best estimation of what I am looking at down the line as far as mobility in my day-to-day life, how my condition is likely to develop in the years to come."

Whenever I asked Dr. Jones a direct question, she always answered it. That's one of the reasons I had such high esteem for her. Now, I decided, I was finally ready to hear her answer to the key question about my future.

"You will walk with a cane, though walking will likely become more difficult for you. Some years from now—five years, ten years, it's hard to say—but some years from now, you will likely be in a wheelchair."

I had been carefully charting my own physical decline. Dr. Jones watched me closely for any sign of distress. But the truth was I'd been wondering if this was what the future held. My slow but steady degeneration was happening right in front of my eyes. Still, thinking it and hearing it from a doctor are two different things. It was more shocking than I'd prepared myself for. Her words reverberated in my mind.

I leaned back and took a deep breath. Instinctively, I reached for Tuesday. Just feeling him leaning against my leg kept me steady. Dr. Jones was finally saying out loud what both of us had long ago come to recognize. In a single moment of honest discussion, nothing and yet everything had changed. So much about my life had gotten better. I was happy. I was productive. I loved the people Tuesday and I were meeting and the work we were able to do. Every day, I got emails and social media messages of friendship and encouragement from people we touched and inspired. We were traveling to interesting places. We had each other. We were living a beautiful life. But physically, I was in undeniable decline. My walking was getting more difficult. I was in frequent pain. The tricks that used to help me—shake it off, massage my muscles, take a warm bath—weren't working like they used to.

And now the one doctor I trusted was talking about a wheelchair.

"I haven't run since 2006," I told her. "I want to run again."

"You are not going to run again," she said.

"Running used to be my work," I said. "That was a requirement. That wasn't an extracurricular activity. It wasn't just a hobby." I shook my head, trying to get the words out, trying to explain how much I'd already lost. "Running has ceased to be a part of my life."

"I know," she said. "I know."

Pause. Deep breath. More.

"You will be in a wheelchair."

Those six words just sat there in the air. I could barely make myself draw them in. They exploded in front of me, then seemed to collapse on the floor.

"You will be in a wheelchair." That is what she said.

Even if I sort of knew that already—and somewhere inside me I guess I did—hearing those words spoken so plainly by a medical doctor who had earned my trust—damn, that hurt.

I sat there, digesting the meaning, petting Tuesday, hoping he hadn't heard the same thing I had. Finally, I leaned forward and broke the silence, "That's not me. I don't want to be in a wheelchair. I don't want to evolve from a cane to a wheelchair."

"Well," Dr. Jones said, "you asked, and I feel a responsibility to answer your question realistically. You will most likely walk with a cane for a number of years, and then that won't be enough. I don't know exactly how many. We have already exhausted neurology, ortho, PT, OT, pain management. We've been through the medical gamut. This is reality."

That's what she said. Here's the way a drill sergeant told it to the soldier in me:

"Here's your reality card, Private."

She wasn't being overly dramatic or purposely harsh. For the news she was delivering, she was remarkably matter-of-fact.

She was, I realized later, trying to be as positive as she could be under the very dark circumstances. "Luis," she said, "there are new braces that are coming out, as you know, that may be supportive, robotic, and there are other non-robotic ones that are also available. Or...", she continued, pausing another second, "there is elective amputation, which some people opt for if they feel it will enhance their mobility."

Did she just say amputation?

Amputation?

Amputation?

I had not considered that.

That is not something anyone ever really thinks about.

"There are benefits," she said. "They are making advances with prosthetic technology. People are walking, even running sometimes. It's a serious decision. It's certainly not for everyone. It's not something anyone should do lightly. But it is an option when there is little else that will work."

The words that came out of my mouth were not quite as dismissive as I might have imagined they'd be. I didn't say, "Forget about it." I didn't say, "Are you nuts?" What I said was: "Well, this is obviously something I have to think about."

———◆———

And I did. As I began my due diligence, I discovered three practical realities right away—one procedural, another bureaucratic, and the last one technological.

As a medical procedure, a leg amputation—even an above-the-knee amputation, the kind I would need—isn't considered all that complex. Doctors have been amputating diseased or injured limbs for as long as we've had doctors. Strong guys with sharpened stones were doing something similar before that. Modern medicine has the technique down cold. It involved cutting and stitching with anesthesia to dull the pain. While there is still some artistry involved— mostly involving where exactly to cut and at what angle—this is not a procedure that requires the highest-tech equipment or the most extensive surgical team. I don't want to say, "Any hack can do it." But there are certainly trained professionals who can.

That said, the bureaucratic reality featured some maddening rules and regulations of the U.S. Department of Veterans Affairs. Since the VA was my health-care provider, it would have been natural for me to explore the pros and cons of an amputation with one of its many surgeons. But that was a no-go. The surgery I was considering—a leg amputation to relieve constant pain and promote greater mobility—was considered *elective* surgery. Therefore, the VA would neither perform it nor pay for it, no matter how beneficial the results promised to be. If I decided to have my leg cut off, I was on my own. I would have to find a private surgeon. I would have to arrange and pay for everything, a total somewhere in the neighborhood of $10,000 to $15,000. My decision, my dime. There was one oddity here. While I was on my own in getting the surgery done, if I went ahead and did it, the veterans' health-care system would spring back into action on my recovery. Most importantly, the VA would provide the prosthetic leg for me and whatever other rehabilitation I might need. That was major.

I didn't understood the logic of this half-approval. Then again, it was the VA.

Finally, there was the burgeoning technology of prosthetic legs. Huge advances have been made in recent years. The new designs are sleek and beautifully crafted. They are loaded with shock absorbers and the latest electronics. In their functionality, they are getting closer and closer to healthy human legs. People are running, jumping, swimming, skiing, and doing virtually every other kind of activity on prosthetic legs. Para-athletes are clocking extraordinary times. It wasn't yet true that prosthetic runners are routinely outsprinting the regular kind, but that is beginning to occur. This technology helped me grasp what Dr. Jones was talking about when she said that by cutting my leg off, I might actually improve my mobility. I could walk without one of my legs and maybe even run again.

No matter how encouraging the prosthetic research sounded, this was an excruciating decision to make. I certainly didn't want to lose a part of my body, especially a part as important as my right leg. Even the terms—"cut if off" and "amputate"—sent chills down my already aching spine. I could just imagine the looks on the faces of my family and friends when and if I explained the idea patiently to them. "You might do—*what?*" And Tuesday, too. What would he think? How would he react? The health-care system kept using the word "voluntary." Would *anyone* not facing it understand such a radical choice? Obviously, I could continue down the path I was on, most likely ending up in a wheelchair as Dr. Jones had described. And no one would blame me. But what kind of future was that for me?

Slowly, gradually, with plenty of mulling and more than a few sleepless nights, I wrapped my head around the idea of something that a short time earlier would have seemed totally shocking.

I decided I would have my right leg cut off.

CHAPTER 13

Telling Papá

—◄◉►—

Kintsugi (金継ぎ) *(Japanese: golden joinery)*
*A 500-year-old Japanese art in which broken pieces of metal are restored with
a lacquer that is mixed with gold, silver, or platinum. Thus, something that is
broken is made beautiful and is more beautiful because it was broken.*

WIKIPEDIA

I CALLED PAPÁ IN MIAMI. I HAVE ALWAYS TALKED MORE WITH HIM
than with Mamá. Especially if it's something difficult, I prefer telling
him and then have him clue my mother in.

"How you doin', Papá?" I asked, working hard to sound casual,
not letting on at first that this was anything but a Sunday check-in
call.

"We're good," he answered. "How are you?"

I'm not sure if my father could tell something was coming, but he
probably could. He has a good ear for that sort of thing.

"Listen," I said. "I have something to tell you. It's kind of important."

I took a breath but didn't wait for him to say anything. I just
plowed ahead. "Recently, I met with my doctors. I've decided to
undergo amputation of my right leg."

Gulp!

Even from a thousand miles away, I could feel my father straightening up in his chair. Could my mother see anything on his face yet? Or was he playing it cool?

"Wait a minute," he said. "What's going on?"

I understood this must have been startling, though, honestly, I didn't know how else to break the news. Given the distance, a phone call was the best option. It wasn't the kind of thing I wanted to put in an email.

"Well," I said to my father as directly as I knew how, "I am going to have my right leg amputated above the knee. It's something I have thought about for a long time." Assuring him this was a sound and medically approved decision, I continued, "The doctors think I have a good chance of regaining greater mobility, much greater than I have right now."

My father took a moment before he spoke again, as if he were letting what I'd just told him fully sink in. Or maybe he was just making sure he'd heard me right. Did I really mean what I had just blurted out?

"What's the cause of this?" he finally asked.

I tried to explain. "Papá," I said, "you know I've had a few falls and a couple of blows to the head. Some falls were so hard that I was knocked unconscious. That has affected my balance and my spinal cord. You know quite well how that's impacted me. It's caused me to use a cane. Even with the cane and with Tuesday, I'm having real trouble getting around. The doctors say there's a better than good chance I'll eventually end up in a wheelchair."

"Wait a minute...I don't know," my father said. "I just don't know. There are a lot of alternatives to amputation."

———※———

My father happens to know a lot about medicine. Though his career was in government and diplomacy, he'd been around the medical field his entire life. His father, my grandfather, was a renowned eye surgeon in Cuba and then in Washington, D.C. His mother was a nurse. My dad also knows serious medicine from the patient's point of view, having been through various heart procedures over the years. He has undergone specialized cardiac care for a couple of decades. He has also spent a lot of time in physical therapy. So he is perfectly confident discussing medical issues, very much including his children's.

He's also a very powerful person. Not intimidating exactly, but definitely intense. When he says something, it carries weight. I have never doubted my father loves me, but he has always been hard to ignore. So when he said to me, "Wait a minute," he sounded like he'd just stopped, dropped, and rolled across one of the biggest decisions of my life.

At seventy-four, he still had a great zest for living and a rugged optimism. That's why my heart was almost broken five years earlier when he wrote an email to me, expressing frustration and disgust over my post-Iraq PTSD and decision to turn down employment with the New York City Office of Emergency Management, planning for the city's disaster contingencies. "I'm shocked, saddened, and dismayed," he'd started and it got worse from there. It was deeply deflating to hear one of the most upbeat people I'd ever known sound so negative about me. When his mood sours, look out!

But lately, my Papá and I had been in a much better place. He no longer believed that PTSD was a weakness or an excuse. In fact, he had come to recognize some of the issues I had been struggling with and, I believe, come to admire the efforts I had made and this new service that I've devoted my life to. I gave him huge credit for that. My father had lately been taking joy again in my achievements.

We were close, but in our own unique way. I didn't talk to him or my mom every day, the way my sister did. My parents knew everything that went on with Lucas or Lucia, my niece and nephew. School, friends, who had the sniffles—nothing got past Papá and Mamá. If I called them with daily updates on all of my stuff, they'd spend every day worrying about me. My life is not my sister's. She's a wonderful wife, a terrific mother, and a respected business executive. I am a warrior and a veteran. I don't call or text with an update every time I see my therapist or my physician, not even every tenth time. It really wouldn't be fair to put my parents through that.

The last time I'd seen them was January in Naples, Florida, just before Tuesday's cancer scare. Tuesday and I had booked several events in the area, and we'd stayed around for some extra Florida R&R. They had been up the coast to Sarasota for my aunt's seventieth birthday. On the way back home to Miami, they stopped in Naples to have lunch with Tuesday and me.

We had a really great time during lunch at The Turtle Club at Vanderbilt Beach. It was a picture-postcard day. A gentle breeze blew as we enjoyed delicious sandwiches while sitting beneath a beachfront umbrella.

Ah, Florida!

After some tough times, especially right after I returned from war when I felt distant from my family and even myself, I now recognize how lucky I am to have my parents in my life. I live with a comforting assuredness that if I called my mom or dad and said, "Listen, I really need you to help me," they would come in an instant, wherever I was. They would fly across the country. They would do whatever it took. How long did I need to stay with them? A week? Five weeks? Whatever. There would always be a place for me and Tuesday. Whatever I told them, they would try to support and understand.

But this time, I worried, I might have pushed that parental support a little further than my dad wanted to go.

—◦—

"Listen," he said to me on the phone the day I broke the amputation news. "Let's not be hasty here. You know I go to UHealth Physical

Therapy at the University of Miami Hospital." I knew that. "That's where the University of Miami football players go." I knew that, too. "Those people are doing cutting-edge stuff. Mamá and I would be happy to pay for you to come and get seen by them. You and Tuesday can come to Miami. Spend a few weeks. We'll rent out a little place for you. We can get some other evaluations. You'll get a second opinion. What's wrong with that?"

I realized my father was trying to be helpful. I knew he was genuinely worried about his son. I also appreciated the fact that he was raising his concerns calmly, not erupting in anger or fear. But this was precisely the debate I was hoping to avoid.

"I really appreciate that," I told him, trying to keep my calm, as well. "I know you are getting great care in Miami. And that's a blessing. But I have gotten many opinions on this already from some of the top people around. This isn't some fly-by-night, willy-nilly decision. I didn't wake up one morning and say, 'Hey, cut my leg off.' I have thought about this—a lot. Studied it from every angle. You know me."

I suppose some of this might have been avoided if I'd shared my thinking about amputation going back to when it first became a possibility. I could have let the idea trickle into our conversations. I could have told my parents about my research, the doctors, the reasons I had for moving closer to the decision. But deep down, I must have known that it was never going to be easy for a mom or dad to imagine their son living without one leg. Maybe that's why I'd been putting off this talk until there was no more putting it off.

I tried to bring him into my thinking. He'd been a competitive athlete in college, I reminded him. I asked him to imagine how he'd feel in the same situation. I knew he'd do whatever he thought he had to.

"For nearly ten years, not being able to walk well and be athletic— that's been a big deal to me," I told him.

But he was having none of it. This was fundamentally a medical decision, he seemed to be saying—not an emotional one. Medicine is about saving body parts, not discarding them. I shared the science as well as I understood and could convey it.

The term the doctors used for what I was experiencing was peripheral neuropathy—*neuropathy* meaning disease of the nerves and *peripheral* meaning beyond, as in beyond the brain or the spinal cord. I reminded my dad that peripheral neuropathy is the condition that results when nerves that carry messages between the brain and spinal cord and the rest of the body are damaged or diseased.

For me, I continued, the biggest issue was in my right leg. Either I couldn't feel it or I had shooting pain down there. Both symptoms were making it difficult for me to live a normal and productive life. I was walking with a cane and service dog and still having trouble getting about. I didn't want to live like this for the rest of my life—or even worse, be consigned to a wheelchair. I wanted to do what I wanted to do, and I stressed I wanted to be free from all this pain.

My dad is an intelligent and logical man. He is a good read of human nature and very talented at making arguments. Plus, he had parental passion on his side. But as he continued to dissect my decision, as he tried to talk me out of going ahead with my plan, I could feel my own stubbornness rising to meet his every debating point.

"I'm just not sure you got the right specialist," he said.

"I've seen some of the best doctors anywhere," I answered. "I don't want to spend the rest of my life not walking, much less not being able to do things I want to resume after years away, like sports. I cannot bear the thought of it."

Those were compelling points, I thought. But he wasn't close to giving up. "I just want to make sure—" he said, before I cut him off.

"You are absolutely right," I said. "It's important to get good advice. For the past five or more years…"

"What? You've been thinking about this for over five years?"

I hadn't planned on saying that. I knew it would bother him that I'd kept this secret for so long. But it was just as important to demonstrate this was a thought-out decision.

"I have gotten opinions on all sides—and not just VA opinions." I knew how he felt about the quality of some care from the VA. He'd been hearing my own complaints for years. But before he could throw my own complaints back at me, I made a point of emphasizing, "These are civilian doctors too. Mostly civilian doctors."

"And they are *all* telling you to cut your leg off?" my father said, clearly doubting that.

"Well, it's a little more complicated than that."

"Exactly," he said.

"It's not something a doctor can really tell you," I tried to explain. "The doctor can lay out your options. He can describe the likely outcomes. You have to make the decision in the end."

Any crazy thoughts I'd had that I might simply say, "I'm cutting off my leg" and he'd say, "Good idea, son" were long gone. Of course, I knew that was never going to happen. I knew this was going to be a long conversation. We weren't close to done. But I knew it was important to talk this through with him. I needed him to understand why I was sure that this incredibly difficult path was the right one. He was my father. He cared about me. He did have a great ability to think things through. And as I went through my recovery and my life afterward, somehow or another my parents would surely be involved. They had a right to be included as I was making my plans.

"You have to approach these things gradually," my father said. No rushing. That's what he had learned from his own cardiac treatment. His doctors had settled on a gradual strategy to correct troublesome flaps around the perimeter of his heart. "There are three steps," my father told me, recounting his own medical treatment. The first was to take a strong medication, which he had already started. If that didn't work, the next step would be something more drastic. "And if that doesn't work," my father said, "then they will perform a procedure where they burn off the flaps."

I didn't say the first thing I was thinking, which was, "What do your medical issues have to do with my medical issues? Medicine isn't one-size-fits-all." Without realizing it, he'd just handed me a far more effective rebuttal in our father-son debate.

"Papá," I said, my voice filled with compassion for his own medical struggle, "I understand exactly what you are saying. If the lesser measures don't do the trick, they will burn off the flaps. And that will make you better, right?"

"Yes," he said. "That's about right."

"Well, that's exactly what I'm having done. They've tried lesser measures. Drugs, physical therapy, just about every medical option there is. Those haven't worked for me. Now, they're going to amputate my leg, just like they will burn those flaps off your heart. You do understand what I am talking about."

"It's not the same thing," my father protested.

"It is," I countered. "Very similar...I've already been there. I've tried steps one and two, and it's time for step three." I cut right to the jugular in our argument.

We went back and forth a bit longer.

"No, it's not the same thing," he said.

"It's exactly the same thing," I countered. "You are considering a heart procedure because you hope it will improve the quality of your life and the lesser measures haven't achieved your goals. You hope the operation will give you more years and the ability to travel and do the other things you want to do in your retirement. It's really no different for me, except I am not seventy-four years old. All the more reason why now's the time to grab on to the possibility of improvement."

My father is rarely at a loss for a reasoned argument. This time though, I was the one with logic on my side.

He walked right into an ambush, one he'd inadvertently set up.

I could tell he wasn't prepared for the I'm-just-like-you argument. I had turned his own logic on its head.

"I have done the gradual approach," I explained. "I've been doing that for years. I have been in the pain clinic. I have done the physical therapy. I have taken the pharmaceuticals. The neurologists, the psychologists—I've seen them all. I am now at the point where I really need to move forward. So I'm gonna burn it off—to use your exact language. I am going to have the amputation."

CHAPTER 14

Going In

―――――――⋙«◈»⋘―――――――

May the stars carry your sadness away,
May the flowers fill your heart with beauty,
May hope forever wipe away your tears,
And, above all, may silence make you strong.
CHIEF DAN GEORGE

I TOOK ONE LAST WALK ON MY OWN TWO FEET. TUESDAY AND I WERE both hungry. There was no telling when we'd get another meal not served on a hospital tray!

We had come to San Antonio after I completed my own due diligence and Dr. Patrick O'Shaughnessy completed his. I really did believe what I had argued so passionately to my father, that I had fully explored all other options and that the potential upside of amputation was worth the undeniable risks.

I had chosen San Antonio because that's where Dr. O'Shaughnessy was. I had chosen him because of his national reputation as a talented surgeon who had treated many military amputees. Part of his practice was at San Antonio's Brooke Army Medical Center, one of the top military hospitals in the world. He would, however, be performing my "elective" procedure at a small private hospital

Standing with a commando after conducting a raid on an enemy target as a military advisor to Iraqi Special Operational Forces during my second combat tour in 2005.

Tuesday and I share a moment after receiving the American Kennel Club's Humane Fund Award for Canine Excellence (ACE).

Educated Canines Assisting with Disabilities (ECAD) Co-Founder and Director of Programs Ms. Lu Picard with Blip (Stud Dog) and ECAD Ambassador Tuna. *www.ecad1.org*

Benjamin, a tri-ped and therapy dog in Michigan, reading about Tuesday.

Karin Marinaro and her son Lieutenant
Robert Marinaro, USMC.

USMC Sgt. David Metzler,
Casual Company, Paris
Island, 1955.

Private First Class Cole
Vickery, U.S. Army
Infantryman, and his
mother, Amee.

Tuesday and I love engaging audiences of all kinds, especially children. Our hopes for a better world reside in them.

Delivering a copy of *Tuesday Tucks Me In* to friend and U.S. Senator Al Franken in Washington, D.C. *Photo by Dan Dion.*

Tuesday enjoying and supporting canine and equine therapies at the Special Troopers Adaptive Riding School (STARS) in Sioux City, Iowa.

While delivering a presentation at a Service Dog Summit in Washington state, Tuesday nuzzles me in support. *Photo by Jo Arlow.*

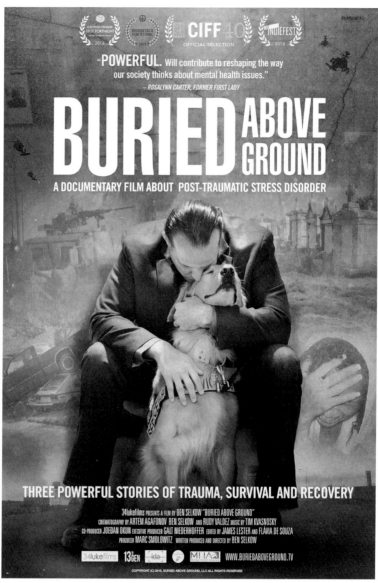

"**POWERFUL.** Will contribute to reshaping the way our society thinks about mental health issues."
— ROSALYNN CARTER, FORMER FIRST LADY

BURIED ABOVE GROUND

A DOCUMENTARY FILM ABOUT POST-TRAUMATIC STRESS DISORDER

THREE POWERFUL STORIES OF TRAUMA, SURVIVAL AND RECOVERY

34lukefilms PRESENTS A FILM BY BEN SELKOW "BURIED ABOVE GROUND"
CINEMATOGRAPHY BY ARTEM AGAFONOV BEN SELKOW AND RUDY VALDEZ MUSIC BY TIM KVASNOSKY
CO-PRODUCER JOEDAN OKUN EXECUTIVE PRODUCER GALT NIEDERHOFFER EDITED BY JAMES LESTER AND FLÁVIA DE SOUZA
PRODUCER MARC SMOLOWITZ WRITTEN PRODUCED AND DIRECTED BY BEN SELKOW

34lukefilms 13GEN ida MHA WWW.BURIEDABOVEGROUND.TV

Award-winning documentary *Buried Above Ground* follows three PTSD survivors—a combat veteran, domestic violence victim, and Hurricane Katrina evacuee—over six years as they each forge their own inspiring paths to recovery.

Day 3 Post-op: Happy to pause with world-renowned surgeon Dr. Munjed Al Muderis and Osseointegration Physiotherapist Lead Sarah Benson after undergoing a life-changing orthopedic procedure in Sydney, Australia.

A golden retriever and ECAD dog, Promise was born on June 27, 2016.

nearby. Before he would agree to proceed, he carefully reviewed my medical records, making sure he concurred with the assessments made by other medical professionals and that I was a strong candidate for amputation. At his insistence, I had also undergone a thorough psychological review—including a lengthy, in-person interview, to make sure I knew what I was agreeing to and that I was prepared for the intense recovery. Only after I met all his stringent requirements had he agreed to operate.

Tuesday and I were due at the hospital at 2 P.M. on February 26, a sunny, 70-degree, Friday afternoon. That gave us just enough time to eat and pack a bag for what the doctors had said would likely be a two-night stay—one night pre-op, one night post-op, then back to my favorite San Antonio hotel. That was far less "bedpan" time than I'd guess most people would have expected for cutting off a limb.

Since Tuesday and I would always rather eat than pack, we left the hotel a little before noon and walked around the corner for an early lunch. Tuesday was frisky. I was stiff and slow. I was really feeling the busy week we'd had—three public appearances, the surgery prep, the nerves I was trying to hide, and the nagging pangs of impending loss.

I'd thought this through from a thousand different angles. I'd gotten the best advice I could find. I had a top-flight hospital, a highly respected surgeon, and an experienced medical team. Though I was confident I was making the right decision, I'd be lying if I didn't admit I was still haunted by introspection. Not that I had doubts. No part of me wanted to back out, even though I knew the rehab would be grueling. I had high hopes for the long-term improvements I expected to get in return. I was excited—euphoric, almost. I could hardly wait for improved mobility and far less pain.

But still. There was no reason to kid myself. This was a very big deal. I was about to have more than half my right leg chopped off, and just being in this position wasn't something most would choose. I was going ahead with this because I was convinced it was the best of some not-so-great options. I didn't wake up one morning thinking, "Gee, it sure would be fun to hop around on one leg!" So yes, there was some sadness too. Just because something seems like the right decision doesn't mean you necessarily arrive at it lightheartedly. And now I was out for my final, two-legged field trip, with a dog and a cane, of course.

I wanted to eat a clean, well-balanced lunch. I wasn't sure when I'd be eating again. I ordered a chicken breast, wild rice, green beans, and an unsweetened iced tea. Tuesday had already eaten in the hotel room, but that didn't mean he wasn't hungry for more. Customarily, I like to have a couple of healthy treats in my pocket for him. This time, it was little quarter-size, organic, made-in-America, chicken-and-oat biscuits. Our restaurant routine has become almost a ritual between us, one I could predict before we even got a table.

Tuesday will look up from beneath the table.

With his snout resting on my right thigh, his soulful eyes will say, "I love you" and "Can I please have a bite? Pleeeeze!"

This was my last meal for a while. As much as I love him, no, we were not sharing. I gave Tuesday both of the biscuits in my pocket. He seemed happy enough.

The walk back to the hotel was equally creaky. I steadied myself with my cane. My right knee was aching badly. The truth was that every step I took reinforced my certainty that this was the right thing to do. This was my final stroll among the bipeds, and Tuesday could see I was having trouble with it. As he was trained to do, he let me set the pace as we went.

It had taken us a little longer to walk back to the hotel than I'd allowed. I glanced at the clock. With the appointment at 2 P.M., we had just enough time to pack and order an Uber car and get over there. As I began putting various items in the overnight bag, I couldn't help but notice it was filling up almost entirely with "Tuesday stuff." His bowl. His squeaky toy. A six-by-six-foot blanket to make a comfy bed for him. A rubber ball. An antler bone. I'll admit it. He might be a bit overindulged when it comes to his collection of toys. We also needed to bring food for him and some more of his organic treats. Couldn't go without those. His brush, of course. And his toothbrush and toothpaste. Pretty soon, there was hardly any room for my stuff in that bag. And hardly a moment to spare. I packed my toothbrush, some meds, and a couple of button-down shirts. Then zipped it shut. It was 1:30. Time to summon the Uber.

I grabbed my cane and the overnight bag and put the leash on Tuesday. Together, we headed down the hall to the elevator and down to the lobby. We weren't moving any more quickly than before. No one said anything, but I'm sure we were a sight. Tuesday and me plus a bag and cane tromping through the lobby and out the front door. By the time we got to the curb, the car was already there. I put the bag in the trunk. Tuesday and I climbed in the back seat, he with far more bounce than I felt—physically or mentally.

We arrived at the hospital, and Tuesday immediately turned on his happy-go-lucky charm. He smiled at the security guard inside the front entrance. He stood politely at my feet as we waited for my name to be called by the admissions-department clerk. I was starting to feel a small case of nerves. As a nurse handed me a clipboard with a large stack of admissions forms, Tuesday cuddled up at my feet. He always knows how to make me feel better.

Tuesday seemed to understand we were here for more than a routine check-up or to refill my meds. We had a bulging overnight bag and now this huge stack of forms. I had an extra knot in my stomach. Being so in tune with my moods, Tuesday could sense my feelings—I wouldn't call it fear exactly, but definitely anxiety or tension. I took a moment to focus on the stress and concluded that it really wasn't the surgery I was worried about. Doctors have been amputating limbs and sewing up the wounds for centuries. But I was undeniably entering a new phase of my life and, therefore, Tuesday was sensing that he too was entering a new phase of his. He stayed, I noticed, extra close to me as I returned the clipboard to the admitting nurse. For a minute or two, she reviewed my information and then nodded that it was time. Together, we all rode the elevator up to my room.

Is it possible the nurse had been charmed by Tuesday? Maybe. She put us in a room that was far nicer than I deserved. It was bright and spacious and, best of all, we wouldn't have a roommate. There was also a small futon that instantly became Tuesday's bed, at least until he found his way into mine. I hung my shirts in the closet, filled Tuesday's water bowl, and laid out his other stuff so it would all be accessible. I took my pants and shoes off, left them in the closet, and put on a hospital gown.

In a short time, a flurry of nurses and administrators started coming by. We were in a private hospital, but I guess it still takes a village to check a new patient in. One gave me a wristband. Another had a waiver for me to sign. Someone else stuck an IV in my forearm. "Anticoagulant," she said when I asked what she was about to start dripping into me. That nurse also checked my vitals and took some blood for pre-op lab tests, making sure everything was in the normal range. If you have too many crazy readings, I assume, they won't go ahead.

Tuesday curled up on the futon and I gave him one of his favorite snack toys, his antler bone. I was fully checked in, but it seemed to me like a small army of nurses and other hospital employees kept finding reasons to come into my room. A lot of them, I noticed, didn't have any obvious business to transact with me. Soon enough, it was becoming clear that I was not the most popular creature in this hospital room.

"What's his name?" a maintenance man with nothing to fix asked me.

"Aw, how cute," said a couple of different nurses who didn't even bother to pretend they were checking my chart or my drip.

No doubt about it. This constant traffic was on account of Tuesday.

"How old is he?" asked a young man in blue scrubs who might have been an intern or a resident. "I also have a golden retriever," he said.

I laughed a little, remembering my father complaining to my mother during one of his hospital stays. "Where the heck are all the medical workers? Did they forget I'm in here?" With Tuesday being here with me and making all those people smile, I was pretty sure there'd always be a nurse or doctor nearby.

While Tuesday was entertaining the staff, I suddenly realized I'd made a huge mistake. Back in the hotel room I'd packed for myself just two shirts. I had completely forgotten to pack even one pair of shorts. Tuesday had enough toys and snacks for an eight-week session of summer camp, but I wasn't prepared for even an overnight stay in the hospital. When it came time to leave the hospital, what was I going to wear? I sure didn't want to exit the hospital in my under-wear. By then, I knew, my right leg would be gone, replaced with a wrapped-up, swollen, and tender stump. I was sure there was no way I'd be able to pull on the jeans I'd worn to the hospital.

Maybe the stress and anxiety I'd been denying had played a role. "That was dumb," I scolded myself.

As nice as everyone was being with Tuesday, I hoped there was a little left for me. Maybe when the time came, someone would lend me a pair of gym shorts. Otherwise, I knew, I'd be wearing that hos-pital gown much longer than I'd planned to and in places no hospital gown should go.

There was nothing much I could do at this point about my post-op wardrobe. So I laid back and tried to relax. I could already tell that Tuesday was eyeing a way to climb up into the bed. It was a twin, not a lot of extra room for visitors. In fact, I remembered, it was about as narrow as the first bed he had ever plopped down on with me.

It was one of the first nights after we'd met at ECAD, before we'd even decided for sure that, yes, we were going to partner up. The fourth night I was there, Tuesday was able to leave his kennel and stay with me. ECAD had narrow, medical beds for visitors. I remembered thinking, "I'm not sure this is going to work." I was 6 foot 2 inches and 220 pounds at the time. He was 75 or 80 pounds, and, I soon realized, he was not used to sleeping in people beds. It turned out that Tuesday never did sleep that night. Neither did I. He kept shifting all 80 pounds of golden furriness throughout the night. No doubt about it, he was excited to share the bed, but he was determined to try any and all positions looking for a comfortable one.

All these years later, he'd gained plenty of bed-sharing experience. Without any fuss, he leaped up on the hospital bed and happily curled up at the foot of the mattress. He might not have been having the same memory, but the narrow bed and the new surroundings took me back to that other, skinny bed on that long-ago, special day when the two of us were just getting to know each other. So much had changed since then, since Tuesday. And here we were about to experience another major change together. I really had to smile.

My surgery was set for 11 A.M. the next day. I wasn't permitted to eat anything past 11 P.M. No food. No water. Nothing in my belly in that twelve-hour window. All I was allowed to do was hang around the room with Tuesday, read, talk on my phone, and—if I wanted to, which I didn't—watch TV. Frankly, TV seemed like too much mental stimulation. I already had plenty bouncing around in my head.

Just as it was getting dark, Dr. O'Shaughnessy swung by. It was a quick, almost perfunctory visit. I think he was making sure I wasn't freaking out. "How you doing?" he asked as he approached my bedside.

"Ready to go."

"Happy to hear it," he answered. "Me, too."

I smiled. That was a good thing.

"How's he doing?" the surgeon asked, nodding down at Tuesday. "Is he ready too?"

"Tuesday's always ready," I said.

Even the doctor's mood seemed to be brightened by the presence of Tuesday, and God knows I wanted a happy surgeon. I didn't relish the thought of some tense doctor working out his aggression on the thigh bone above my knee. That sounded unnecessarily painful. Surgeons aren't always known for their cheerful bedside manner. Then again, most surgeons don't get to see a happy, tail-wagging dog lying with the patient in a hospital bed. Also, Tuesday is undeniably more charming than I am. Better looking too.

"Your blood work looks strong," he said to me. "We are scheduled for tomorrow at eleven."

I figured he knew how to handle the necessary cutting, but I did want to talk a little more about post-op rehab. I told the doctor for what must have been the forty-seventh time how committed I was to doing whatever I could to speed up the recovery process. He said, also for the forty-seventh time, that he understood my sense of commitment. "Some of this," he said, "*is* in your hands." And Tuesday's paws, I thought to myself.

He asked if I had any more questions. I didn't.

Then, he said, "All right. I'll see you in the morning."

I made a careful note of the date in my mind. Saturday, February 27, the day I would have my leg cut off. For the rest of my life, whatever else might happen, I would never, ever forget that date. Who could possibly forget something like that like? With a reassuring pat on my right arm, Dr. O'Shaughnessy turned to leave. "Try to get some sleep," he said on his way out the door. "You, too," he added, looking toward Tuesday.

I didn't think sleeping would be difficult. I was already totally exhausted. It had been a busy day and a busy week. I was dog-tired, and Tuesday was too. We both drifted off to sleep by 8:30 P.M. and we both awoke at 10:30 P.M., just before my eating and drinking cut-off time. I gulped down a glass of orange juice and a bottle of water. I checked the email on my phone and answered a handful of notes, mostly people wishing me well.

I didn't need the sleeping pill the night nurse offered. A little after midnight, I was asleep again.

At around 6:30 A.M., just before the morning nurses entered our room, I awoke well rested. Unlike most people's nightmarish hospital stays, I had slept so soundly, I had only the dimmest recollection of someone coming in during the night to check my IV. The fact that I was out like a light, without any medical help, I took as a sign that I was ready to go.

It occurred to me that most patients check in to a hospital and everything gets taken care of while they rest. But I had a distinct set of tasks to perform. I filled Tuesday's water bowl and fixed him some breakfast. Following protocol, no one offered me anything, and I ate nothing at all. Then we waited. And waited. And waited some more. I'd forgotten how a patient's main job in a hospital is to wait. The etymology of both "patient" and "patience" is from the Latin root *pati-* meaning to suffer or endure. Tuesday doesn't like waiting. He seemed a bit restless. He went back to his futon. Over and over, though, he'd leave the futon to check on me in bed. Then at 10:30 A.M., an orderly appeared to wheel me into pre-op.

Finally, showtime!

From my hospital bed, I shimmied my body onto a gurney, the last time I'd be crawling anywhere on two arms and legs. Yes, these "last times" kept popping up on me. I promise. I wasn't looking for them. But they were hard to avoid. The orderly pulled up the side arms, clicked them into place, and we went for a ride, with Tuesday trotting beside us, his leash in my right hand, heading off to the surgery suite.

When we reached pre-op, though, it was time for us to part ways.

I knew he wasn't going to be allowed to go any further with me—not to pre-op, not to post-op, and definitely not into the operating room. Even though I'd informed the surgical team that Tuesday would look awfully cute in scrubs, even the newest members of the Tuesday Fan Club made it clear that wasn't possible.

Reaching down from the gurney, I gave the back of Tuesday's neck one last vigorous rub. "I'll be back in a little while," I told him. "You can watch me through the window."

A candy striper had won the best job of the day. "There's a nice young lady who is going to hang out with you," I told Tuesday.

He stared up plaintively, but he seemed to understand.

We'd made all the necessary arrangements so that Tuesday wouldn't be totally isolated. Still, I felt a little twinge of sadness watching as he was escorted to the room next to pre-op. A large Plexiglas window separated the two rooms. Tuesday, along with the candy striper, could see me and I could see him.

I was rolled into place, and a different nurse put an oxygen mask around my nose and mouth. They took my vitals again and asked me my name and date of birth. Was that to check if my mind was clear? Were they really curious about who I was? I hoped it was the former. Next, they started a fresh IV line, which I assumed was for the anesthesia.

Mostly, what I did in the pre-op room was to lie there and wait for everyone to ready themselves for the procedure. This is the place, a lot of hospital patients will agree, where the patient suddenly seems invisible. It was strange and, I admit, a little irritating, actually. While I waited there, nurses and doctors and other staff members had a long conversation about what they were going to eat for lunch. "Let's get Subway," one of them said. "We just had Subway yesterday," someone else countered.

It was as if I wasn't lying there or wasn't awake. Even worse, no one seemed to care that I hadn't eaten for more than twelve hours.

I was famished. No one was taking my lunch order, and I knew no one would. Just as I was feeling a little grumpy and considering making a point by announcing what I'd like to eat, the moment of truth arrived. I looked at a big white clock on the opposite wall. It was nearly 1 P.M. when I waved to Tuesday for the last time. Yes, I realized I was thinking it again. It was the last time Tuesday would see me as a biped. My eyes watered a little bit thinking about that. Then, the orderly rolled me into the operating room.

CHAPTER 15

Under the Knife

Imagine yourself as a living house. God comes in to rebuild that house...He is building quite a different house from the one you thought of—throwing out a new wing here, putting on an extra floor there, running up towers, making courtyards. You thought you were being made into a decent little cottage: but He is building a palace.

C. S. Lewis

THE OPERATING ROOM WAS COOL, COLD ALMOST. THERE WERE ALL KINDS of high-tech gadgets and machines in there, things I'd never even seen on TV before. The room looked like something from NASA or a science-fiction movie. One thing I noticed were some bright, pinpoint lights on robotic arms that I think might have been lasers. The whole setup seemed highly advanced.

Surgically speaking, cutting a leg off isn't all that sophisticated or complex. Doctors have been doing successful amputations for a long time. While the techniques have changed a bit over the years, I had the sense that most of the high-tech equipment would remain unused throughout my surgery.

The anesthesiologist came in and said hello. "I'm going to give you a local," he told me. "You may or may not feel anything."

Here I was, on a gurney with fancy saws and equipment surrounding me, and I was beginning to understand that I'd be awake for the entire operation.

"A local?" I asked. "Oh, that's fine."

Actually, that was the first time anyone had even mentioned that I wouldn't be knocked out cold for the operation. No one had explained this before. I'd be awake—or mostly so? But I was okay with it. I am one of those people who hates to miss anything. The team had assembled, and they were ready to start. And now, the anesthesiologist seemed to have my brain and bloodstream where he wanted them.

I was calm but definitely still awake. Mellow is probably the word I would use.

The surgeon stepped up to the operating table. Without saying a word, he rolled me over on my left side. My right leg was now facing the ceiling. I felt the surgeon's hand on the inside of my right leg, the leg he was planning to remove. "There's a pulse where he's touching," I thought to myself. I think he was feeling around my femoral artery. I'm not sure if he was checking for the effects of the anesthesia or poking around for some other reason. I didn't ask. But all of sudden, I could feel my right leg going limp.

That didn't bother me. It seemed like progress. Even if I was going to be awake for the procedure, I knew I didn't want my leg to be. Let's be real. They were going to be cutting there. Unless the nerves were turned off somehow, that had to hurt—hurt something awful.

"Whatever it is you are doing, it is working," I told the anesthesiologist.

Then, Dr. O'Shaughnessy, with the help of a nurse, rolled me on my back and they got to work.

Again, the thing I noticed was the amount of talking in the operating room. It makes sense, I know. They are with their colleagues.

They are in their workplace. They are doing their job. I wouldn't want to sit around with a group of my friends and colleagues and stay silent. But as the patient, it was unnerving. Like . . . *don't they know I'm here? Awake? Listening?*

A lot of it was medical talk. "Pressure here." "Cut there." "And there." "Elevate." At one point, even though I was flat on my back, I saw my leg extended up at a 90-degree angle, like someone was about to snap a wishbone off a piece of chicken—except I couldn't feel anything, which was surely for the best.

That, I think, was the moment things felt a little surreal. It had to be my leg, but it didn't look like the leg was part of me anymore. I was awake. I'd heard conversation. But I hadn't heard any saws or other power tools that I knew would be required to get it off.

I was confused. Had I dozed through the sawing part? Had my mind known to shut it out? Maybe the operation hadn't happened yet? No, that was definitely my leg, and it didn't seem attached. Clearly, even though the drugs hadn't sent me off into unconsciousness, they had definitely inserted a filter between me and what I normally think of as being alert.

The people in the OR seemed to be acting differently. The talking had annoyed me but now there wasn't a lot of banter. However, rock music was playing in the background. That much I was aware of. The surgery took about an hour. At some point, after the 90-degree salute, they took my leg away. But I wasn't looking and I missed it.

The next thing I remember was someone—Dr. O'Shaughnessy, I'm guessing—saying, "Let's suture him up."

I stayed flat on my back, as they had asked me. With the anesthesia inside me and the doctors and nurses standing nearby, I'm not sure I could have moved, even if I tried to. But I didn't. I felt woozy but confident in what they were doing. I tried focusing. I didn't want to lose that confidence by letting my mind wander too far afield. "You don't know what you don't know," as people in the military like to say. And I didn't know what I didn't know. I certainly didn't want to complicate matters by asking too many extraneous questions or trying to micromanage my own surgery.

My lecture to myself: You are here with top people. Don't eff this up, man!

It was my job to lie there and let them do their jobs.

Another thing they say in the army: *Don't be THAT guy.* I didn't want to be that guy.

I was determined to be the best patient doing the absolute right thing for myself.

From beginning to end, I'd stayed awake. But I really didn't feel much, just some light tingling that seemed to come less from the cutting and more from the anesthesia making me numb.

I wondered at one point: Am I going to see my leg in a bag?

I didn't, and frankly I don't think I missed anything.

The doctors may have faked me out on that part of it. They'd distracted me, pulled me into the procedure by announcing what was next. I think they took the leg away as they were suturing. One thing for sure, and I know this because I scanned every part of that room: It was long gone by the time I started wondering, "Where did my leg go?"

It probably took them twenty minutes to suture me up. The team began to scatter, people slowly leaving the operating room. I lay there for another minute, then someone in surgical scrubs wheeled me into the post-op room.

The setup was similar to pre-op. Less equipment. Other beds. A window into an attached room.

I lay in post-op for the next two hours while they evaluated and kept an eye on my vital signs and kept asking me if I felt nauseous. I guess that's a common reaction to anesthesia, and I did have a quick flash of nausea. Also, I told them, I felt hot. My head and then my body started sweating. They were concerned about infection.

Sweating is a sign of infection. But when I mopped my face with a paper towel the hot flash subsided quickly.

Fully awake in post-op, I was grateful they hadn't put me under for the surgery. I really do not like long stays in hospitals. I felt like I would bounce back a whole lot quicker from a local anesthesia if I didn't start out in a coma. The best part of not having to shake off full anesthesia was that I could start experiencing this new me.

The God's honest truth was I actually felt better than I had felt in a long time. My leg—or where my leg had been that morning—felt weird and slightly indescribable. But it didn't hurt any more, and I can't tell you what a relief that absence of pain felt like to me. My leg—what was left of it—was numb, and there was definitely some tenderness where I was cut. But that paled in comparison to the pain that had been my constant companion for years. I felt a real sense of relief, physical relief first of all. That was major. And that physical relief triggered a psychological sense of relief as well. I actually sighed out loud. *Oh, man. A sense of peace. A flash of optimism. One giant exhale.*

But even that wasn't the biggest thing I was feeling as I was lying in the recovery room. It wasn't the pain or the nausea or even the physical relief. The biggest thing I felt was the sense of, *wow, I really did that—and now it's done.* I still felt good about the decision. I didn't have any buyer's remorse or instant regrets. I just felt an enormous sense of complete and mental relief. All the years of wondering, months of thinking, the weeks of planning, and the carefully orchestrated pre-op. *That was all done. I did it. Now, what would come next?* Without a doubt, I was heading into a huge new chapter of my life.

Not that there weren't moments that gave me pause. I will say I could still feel my toes. That was strange. I could feel my toes, even though there were no toes there. I'd read plenty about this and been warned about it by my amputee friends—phantom feeling and phantom pain. But even being prepared, it was kind of weird to feel it.

And it wasn't just my toes. As I was lying there, I also had the distinct sensation that I needed to scratch under my right knee, except, of course, I didn't have a knee, either.

There I was, spending my first moments with just a single left leg. I caught myself reaching toward a part of my anatomy that wasn't there anymore. Somehow, it made me feel better, even if I was just scratching air. What's that expression? If you have an itch, scratch it. Well, I can tell you it applies to phantom itches as well.

These phantom feelings weren't painful, not intensely so, more like little irritants. And I don't care what logic or physics might tell us. I swear to you, they were definitely there.

As I scratched itches in the air, I caught my first glimpse of Tuesday through the window. Tuesday was waiting right where I hoped he'd be, on the other side with the candy striper. His front paws were up on the window and he was peering in at the man on the gurney. One of the nurses tapped my shoulder and pointed.

"I think there's somebody over there who really wants to see you," she said.

He was staring quite intently. His golden tail wagged back and forth high into the air. The clock said I'd been away for nearly two hours. I don't know how much time had passed in his head. But his expression was of happiness to see me and unhappiness about the presence of the Plexiglas. Now, he just wanted to be with me.

Tuesday knew something had happened. He wasn't his usual self. He exuded a combination of concern and curiosity, and he couldn't yet know what had happened in those hours I'd been held captive. I hated that Plexiglas division as much as he did. But it was really cute to see his paws trying to pierce the glass because—I get emotional thinking about this even now—here was someone who loved me unconditionally, showing it without any filter at all. To me, that was beautiful, and I wanted badly, in that moment, for him to know I loved him unconditionally and had missed him too.

I wondered what his reaction would be when he saw the new me. And, now that it was done, as I waited out the post-op time, I was worried about how ugly my stump was going to be. I hadn't seen it yet. I knew I had top doctors. I could only assume that they had done a first-rate professional job. There is a lot of artistry involved in making everything look as good as it possibly can. But from the pictures I'd seen, some stumps were definitely better than others. I hoped it was nice, whatever that meant. I'm not usually too squeamish. I don't gross out too easily. But I have seen some stumps out there that are pretty strange. I was certainly curious, even though I knew I wouldn't get to see the surgical site until the time came to change the bandages. Then, I could stare at it as long as I liked. I was already feeling some swelling and tingling. I had to imagine it wouldn't be a very pretty sight. Not at first.

Even the word plays into this. Stump. It sounds almost menacing, like something out of a horror movie. "Oh, my God, don't let him touch you with his stump!" I almost laughed out loud at the thought. It was definitely too late to worry about any of this.

The two hours of post-op time finally came to an end. The team did one more check of my vitals and then they wheeled me into the room where Tuesday was waiting for our big reunion. He was as excited as a little kid, my boy. As I rolled over onto the gurney, he was already doing his full-body wag. Then, he let out a few sharp happy yelps. The gurney wasn't one he could jump up on. It was too narrow and high. He seemed to understand, even if he wasn't happy about it. Someone turned me toward a door, and we headed down the hallway, retracing the trip we'd taken a couple of hours earlier, again with Tuesday's leash in my hand and him trotting beside the gurney as we rolled.

<hr />

It was 5 P.M. by the time we made it back to the room.

As soon as I had completed my gurney-to-bed scoot and the

orderly rolled the gurney away, Tuesday hopped back up on the bed with me, ready for some cuddling and warmth.

He felt as energized as I felt tired.

My legs, one far shorter than it had been, were spread out on the bed. As Tuesday jumped onto the bed and got his footing on the hospital mattress, he found his way to my midsection and then buried his face flat against my chest and gave me a little kiss.

What struck me was how he curled into a position exactly where my right leg had once been. It was as if he knew that I'd lost a part of me and was there to fill the space. Literally, emotionally, and spiritually.

God, how much I love him, I thought as I allowed myself to shed a few tears at his remarkably perfect display of tenderness.

"Good boy," I told him and kissed him back.

Gently, he snuggled the rest of his body in between my legs. He closed his eyes, and I followed suit, and we nestled into the moment.

A few minutes later, I noticed how hungry I was. So was Tuesday. I hadn't eaten for fifteen or sixteen hours. Other than the treats I'd given to the candy striper to give to him, Tuesday hadn't eaten anything since we left the room. One of the aides brought me dinner, which was extremely tasty for hospital food, though the portion seemed tiny to me. Either I was really hungry or someone told the hospital dieticians that the patients that day were all supermodels with the appetites of birds. There wasn't much to split, but I gave Tuesday some anyway.

I don't know how I was supposed to feel after my first meal with one less leg. Mainly, I wanted to collapse. As soon as I put the dinner tray on the bedside table, I did just that. Both Tuesday and I passed out and didn't wake up until 10:30 P.M.

Unlike the night before, I slept poorly. It wasn't pain from the surgery. Actually, I never felt very much pain. But immediately after the amputation, my muscles and frame started to tighten up. The area near the end of the stump was beginning to bruise. Finding a comfortable position was impossible, and everything seemed to be getting juicy down there.

"Damn."

"God damn it. I gotta get some sleep here."

I was swearing a lot.

Though I was all wrapped up in bandages, I could still see the blood seeping up my leg and toward my butt, which was beginning to chafe against the sheets. I tried shifting my position to air-dry the region. It seemed like every half hour or so I was shifting again. I got no more than a few constantly interrupted bursts of sleep.

And I wasn't alone. Every time I woke up, Tuesday woke up, too. Each time, he looked at me with concern. We went back and forth like that for many hours.

I woke up for good just as it was getting light outside. Not surprisingly, I was ravenous. I asked the hospital staff to bring more food, more than the last visit. "Could I have a man-sized portion this time?" I pleaded.

A nurse came in and, after greeting her new best friend Tuesday, checked my IV and said she had some pain meds for me. I hadn't asked for any, and I wasn't really feeling much pain.

What I was curious about were the dos and don'ts of proper wound care. How to wrap the site. How to protect it from danger. How to keep in clean.

"How often should I change the dressing?" I asked. "How tightly should the bandages be? Where should I place the gauze?"

"Once a day for the first two weeks," the nurse said. "After two weeks, once every other day."

On the Internet, I had read different theories on compression in the post-op period. Different doctors have different perspectives about this. The goal for all of them is to make the swelling subside as quickly as possible. I had some questions about that as well, though this time the answers seemed squishy and vague.

"Tight but not too tight. . . . Just wrap it normally. . . . You'll know."

Maybe I would, but I didn't know yet. As eager as I'd been to get out of the hospital quickly, the reality was setting in. I did not know what I was doing.

They gave me some antibiotics and some pain meds that I wasn't sure I needed. And some gauze. They told me the doctor would come after lunch to talk to me and then I'd be able to leave. That's it. That was all the instructions anyone would be giving me for now. Oddly, I was hungry again.

I had a good lunch. Around 1 P.M., the doctor came in. I hadn't seen the stump yet, and I was curious. It was wrapped up tightly and I hadn't touched it. I wasn't about to mess with this on my own.

"You want to have a look?" Dr. O'Shaughnessy asked.

"Definitely," I said.

He started with the Ace bandage, unwinding like he was working on a mummy. Around and around and around, the stump got smaller and smaller as he went. Then, carefully he pulled away the gauze.

I could hardly see any bare skin there. The whole thing was an oozy, bloody, multicolored mess. "The bruising is beginning to set in," the doctor said.

Then, a nurse cleaned the area around the stiches, and I got my first clear look.

I won't lie. It was jarring, looking at where my leg used to be and not seeing a leg there anymore. But I could see where the surgeon had cut and the skin from the top and the skin from the bottom were neatly sutured together. So, yes, I was definitely now an amputee.

CHAPTER 16

Moving Out

We will march with a broken leg
So we can get that Golden Egg
Sound off (one, two!)
Sound off (three, four!)
Cadence count (one, two, three, four, one, two—three four!)
PVT. WILLIE LEE DUCKWORTH, 1944

I WOULDN'T EXACTLY CALL IT REVOLVING-DOOR MEDICINE, BUT THEY certainly didn't urge us to hang around the hospital for long. That was fine by me. I took it as a sign of a successful procedure without complications and their faith in me.

"No reason you have to stay here any longer," Dr. O'Shaughnessy announced bright and early the next day. And so less than twenty-four hours after he'd cut off my right leg, I was rolling out of the hospital in a standard-issue folding wheelchair, wearing a pair of borrowed shorts. The overnight bag was in my lap. A huge supply of gauze was in the overnight bag. With Tuesday's leash in my left hand, we hopped into a waiting taxi.

Hopped. Literally.

Of course, I'd have been happier if the driver had taken us straight to the San Antonio Prosthetic Limb Superstore, if there were such a place. But there wasn't, and I'd been warned repeatedly: Because of inevitable swelling in my residual limb—medical professionals, I noticed, never called it a "stump"—I'd have to wait for a couple of months, at least, before being fitted for one of the high-tech prosthetic legs I'd been hearing about. Until then, I'd be making do with a wheelchair—or the brand-new pair of aluminum crutches waiting for me back at the hotel. I was pretty sure both the chair and the crutches would suck.

For me, these first hours out of the hospital, and so many of the days to follow, were like my earliest school days. Make that school *daze.* I was a kid all over again, wide-eyed, awkward, nervous, pretending I wasn't, but still understanding that I had so much I needed to learn. At least this time, I could bring my dog to class. Basic mobility was going to be lesson number one.

Woozy as I was leaving the hospital, I'm really not sure how I got out of the car, across the lobby, into an elevator, back to our hotel room, and into bed. But there I was. Despite the dramatic surgery, I really wasn't in all that much pain. Maybe the anesthesia was still doing its thing. I couldn't say. I was propped up, relatively comfortable, with my laptop balanced on my one remaining knee, staring at a mountain of emails, knowing that if I didn't start clearing out the inbox, I would have a whole lot of relatives, friends, readers, and well-wishers wondering what was going on with Tuesday and me. Just as there had been a lot of last-one-before-surgery events, I was quickly noting the many firsts I hadn't even considered. Balancing a laptop on one raised knee is not as easy as it looks. Tuesday was curled up at the foot of the bed, looking relieved that we had gotten through this first stretch pretty much—I was going to say *intact.* But that wasn't right. Unscathed? No. On my own two feet? Definitely no. From the very start of being a one-legged man, I discovered that half of my favorite expressions, I couldn't use anymore. Just getting settled into my room, I was as busy as a one-legged man in an ass-kicking contest—wait, that one would be truer than it had ever been! Then, my cell phone rang. The ring reminded me that I still was far from an expert at being an amputee. I'd forgotten to bring the phone to the bed with me or leave it within easy reach on the bedside table.

Damn!

How stupid was that? It was way over on the desk. By *way over,* I mean a good ten or twelve feet, which would not have been an issue a week earlier but now was a challenging fact of life. It kept ringing, ringing, ringing. I told myself, *I will need strategies for all the things I've spent a lifetime doing without forethought.*

Slowly, I set the laptop down on the bed. I pivoted to the left so my leg-and-one-third were dangling off the side of the bed. I knew I couldn't rush this. I didn't want to put too much pressure on the good leg. I knew balance would be an issue, and I didn't know how much strength I had—something like half of what I had before, I presumed. And I had some expert advice swirling around in my head. One point almost everyone made: A leg amputee should be careful not to over-use the good leg. That was a sure route to strain or injury—and then where would you be? One leg gone and the other with a sprained ankle or a busted-out knee! However hard this was going to be just got ten times worse! There was going to be a whole new rhythm to things I used to take for granted, things like carrying the coffee across the hotel room, setting the TV remote control within reach, and, of course, fetching the cell phone off the desk. Just forty-eight hours earlier, I could have gotten up and gone anywhere without a second thought. My body had basic balance, even with one bad leg and a crunched-up spine. Clearly, I was going to have to learn almost everything all over again. Everyone had agreed I had to be careful, especially at the start, when my balance sucked and I didn't know what my limits were. Welcome to the amputee's minute-by-minute learning curve.

The phone kept ringing. And rang some more. By the time the call went to voice mail, I was only halfway across the floor.

———◆———

There were many other lessons to come. None was more important than my first-of-the-day cup of morning coffee. Even if I could hop to get it, I was certain to drop the cup and burn my hand if I tried hopping back. No matter how difficult any of this learning would be, I knew a cup of coffee was essential to getting started. This would be my first field trip in the wheelchair.

In preparation for day two, I'd made a plan. As Tuesday watched intently, I shimmied my butt off the bed and into the canvas seat of the wheelchair. That was a workout all by itself. We got out of the hotel room without much trouble. The door was wide enough. The chair rolled smoothly. We took it slow. We rode the elevator to the lobby, where the breakfast room was. I had Tuesday's leash in my right hand. I used my free hand and the leash hand to keep the chair rolling with a little assist from my remaining, good leg.

Tuesday understood immediately how to walk alongside the chair without getting rolled on, always keeping an inch or two between himself and the spinning, rubber wheels. I didn't have to instruct him on any of this or even practice. He proved once again how intuitive he is. The same way he knew how to keep a proper distance from moving buses and cars, he just got it.

As we rolled into the hotel breakfast room, I felt a little wave of self-confidence. Maybe this wasn't going to be so bad. From the chair, I was able to reach the coffee-service counter. I filled a large paper cup, added milk, slapped on a plastic lid and stopped in my tracks. I hit a mental roadblock. How was I going to get the coffee, Tuesday, and me back upstairs? The added element of the coffee cup brought a whole new level of difficulty to this first of many routine exercises.

I didn't have a cup holder on the wheelchair. Who knew I needed one? Holding the coffee between my legs seemed like asking for trouble. It was a manual chair. I had to wheel myself. And hold the coffee. And hold Tuesday's leash. I couldn't just sit there. So I got started as well as I could. I propelled with my good leg instead of my arms. It was a decent start, and we were moving along toward the elevator door. But we also had to get onboard.

Do you have any idea how high that threshold can be for a one-legged man in a wheelchair with a cup of coffee and a service dog? *Smooth sailing* is not exactly the way to describe it.

This new way of living was going to take some ingenuity and planning. I tried what I would call a Reverse Fred Flintstone. Just like the Stone Age car he propelled with his feet. Pedal-pushing forward with only my one leg, I couldn't get the chair to move ahead. But by turning around, I figured out, my pushing was stronger and we could clear the threshold into the elevator. One hand on the leash, one hand holding the coffee, one leg powering us backward. I just had to be careful I didn't run over one of Tuesday's paws.

I knew what Tuesday was thinking. He was thinking: *This is certainly awkward. You'll never steer yourself that way!* And he was right. Though we fully cleared the elevator door, we also smashed into the back wall at a weird angle. And when the door closed, I realized immediately I couldn't reach the panel or the "two" button for our floor. Tuesday was in the corner, throwing me an eyebrow. "First of all," he was saying, "can I help? Second of all, what do you think you're doing here?"

Eventually, I spun the chair around, reached the button, and, when the door slid open, I rolled backward over the threshold and onto our floor. I Fred Flintstone-ed the chair down the hallway and to the door to our room. Somehow, I fished the key out of my pocket and managed to unlock the door. Tuesday went in first, then I wheeled the chair in behind him. I put the coffee on the desk. I parked the stupid wheelchair and picked up the crutches so I could stand. I balanced myself between the crutches, leaned on the desk, and removed the lid on the coffee cup.

All I can say is that was the finest cup of coffee I'd tasted in years. After all we went through to get it, it had better be.

Those early days were all about relearning the basic tasks of life. Getting in and out of the shower on one leg. Brushing my teeth and drying my hair while maintaining equilibrium. Pulling items down from the top shelf at the supermarket. Strapping groceries onto the back of my chair. Learning to love un-cracked sidewalks and gently sloped curb cuts. Wondering what idiot would design a door in the twenty-first century that a standard-size wheelchair couldn't roll through. I don't know that I was any better or worse than anyone else would be facing these challenges for the first time. It did make me think our country would be a much better place if every junior high school in America had Wheelchair Week, where all the kids would have to get around entirely by manual wheelchair. Talk about a valuable learning experience!

Tuesday was his typically patient self as he learned to make adjustments too. I asked him to help more than I ever used to. I swear I even wondered if he could learn to make coffee. He recognized that now it might take an extra nudge to get me outside. And some of these things I just stunk at. I got frustrated. I wasn't improving as quickly as I thought I should. Tuesday could see the wheels turning, figuratively and literally, in my head and on the chair.

Everyone had tried to warn me about the steep learning curve.

But still, I had underestimated how much physical exertion this would take. I had to compensate for the lack of one function by intensifying the effort of other functions. Adjusting to that was clearly something every amputee has to deal with—and I would too for the rest of my life. I was out of balance now, and I would need—from my good body parts, from equipment and devices, from wherever I could find it—to bring the balance back in. That would take more oxygen, more muscular strength, more drive, more stamina, and, most of all, more good cheer. Frustrated as I was, I knew I had to find some ways to preserve that last one especially.

Call me stubborn, but I steadfastly refused to let this amputation change our plans. The one thing I didn't want to do was miss anything we had agreed to do. That would sound like surrender. Just because I'd had my leg chopped off, that didn't mean I would use that as an excuse to shortchange the important mission that Tuesday and I were on. We had places to go, people to meet, and causes to throw ourselves into. I refused to skip any of it, even if I had to roll, crutch, or hop my way there. By whatever means of transport, I knew Tuesday would be at my side.

Perhaps that explains what I was doing just ten days after surgery, 550 miles from San Antonio, appearing with Tuesday in front of 225 children of service members at Fort Bliss, outside El Paso. Or then again, maybe I was just nuts, taking field trips like this so soon after surgery, as I had barely begun to recuperate.

The Fort Bliss kids were terrific. They didn't appear to care that I had arrived in a wheelchair. They didn't seem to notice my awkward appearance or my clumsiness getting around. They laughed and clapped at my stories about traveling with Tuesday, and they had a thousand questions about what it means to be a service dog.

Just seven days after the Fort Bliss kids' event, seventeen days after my surgery, Tuesday and I were due in St. Petersburg, Florida, where we'd been invited to speak to 300 academics. And two weeks after that, we had back-to-back events in the Los Angeles area. At every stop, we'd be giving talks, signing books, posing for pictures (with this stump!), shaking hands, and talking about veterans and service dogs and PTSD.

I wasn't neglecting my recovery. In between all of those engagements, we would keep returning to El Paso. That city would be our home away from home while we waited for the swelling in my residual limb to subside sufficiently so that I could be fitted for an interim prosthetic leg. The weather in El Paso is cool and dry in the spring, and I had heard about a talented physical therapist who practiced at the VA hospital on Fort Bliss. I was eager to work with him.

We still packed and traveled, only now with the folding wheelchair and what felt like a boxcar load of Ace bandages, medical tape, and gauze. And I really did still feel like me, the same person I was before the operation, just with one fewer leg. My mind was in the Olympics. It was my body that was in the shop. But in those first weeks after the amputation, when adults looked in our direction, they saw someone startlingly different than the person in my mind. I was wheeling myself around in public with a stump where one of my legs had once been. Then, add Tuesday to the equation, and you had a guy in a wheelchair without a leg—who had a service dog trotting along by his side. That was a lot to take in.

I wasn't used to being quite this much of a spectacle. The only thing I didn't have was a helmet with a siren and a spinning light on my head!

Wherever we went, I started noticing that people were staring at us. I was certain I could tell what they were thinking even if they didn't say a word. They were thinking: "Oh, my God, what happened to that guy? Poor bastard!" As someone still fighting the awkwardness of PTSD, I hated every second of that. But what were we supposed to do? Stay home? Hide from the world? Wait around until my prosthesis was ready, then begin our lives again? That didn't sound like Luis and Tuesday to me.

I did what I could to make myself more presentable. I kept my stump wrapped and neat. I made sure I was nicely dressed. But then at some point it occurred to me: It really didn't matter how well covered my stump was or if my shirt was pressed. In this condition, I wasn't blending in anywhere. So we swallowed hard and just pushed on.

CHAPTER 17

El Paso

Everyone has oceans to fly, if they have the heart to do it.
AMELIA EARHART

EL PASO AND THE VARIOUS SIDE-TRIPS WERE ALL ABOUT DOING GOOD
and killing time. How long would it take for the damn swelling to go
down? That's what I wanted to know. How long until I could be fitted for my new prosthetic leg? Two months, the doctors were saying.
Maybe more. For the next few weeks at least, Tuesday and I would be
unhappy hostages of the fluid in my stump, a prisoner of my crutches
and my wheelchair.

My brain hadn't officially recognized that I was minus a limb,
physiologically or psychologically. I knew I was sitting in a wheelchair. I wrapped my leg every morning in Ace bandages and gauze
and changed them constantly throughout the day. I was getting off
the couch. We were keeping a breakneck travel schedule. But in these
weeks after surgery, I also waited anxiously for someone to say I was
ready for my interim prosthesis.

I hated to admit it, but I was also feeling some pain. My absent
leg twitched. Sometimes, it would cramp. It wasn't just the surgeon's
sutures, though I could certainly feel them. The healing was messy

with all the blood and puss and other gook. But the wound wasn't the awful part. I was far more tormented by the nerves. With the surgery, the nerves in my leg had obviously absorbed a major assault, and now they were yelling back at me. Going off like fireworks was more like it—sharp, intense, and random explosions of pain. Flying in all directions. Following few predictable patterns.

Many times a day, these firecrackers erupted, and I'd say to myself, "Damn, that hurts. When is it going to stop?"

The strangest thing was that these nerve explosions ran up and down what had been my right leg, including all the places where the leg wasn't anymore. Here's a lesson I learned quite vividly: Just because pain is labeled "phantom" doesn't mean it doesn't hurt. In fact, in some ways the phantom pain was the worst of all. It's hard to get your head around that phantom pain. You start to wonder sometime around the tenth excruciating jab: Am I imagining this? If I am, what the hell do I do to turn it off? The pain wasn't constant. I could go hours without feeling anything. But I swear to God it was real. Every time the nerves held one of their late-night pain parties, they roared with abandon until dawn.

Thank God for Mario.

Based outside Fort Bliss, Mario was one of the best physical therapists I ever worked with. He was also a below-the-knee leg amputee. That fact didn't define him. In fact, I'm not sure I ever would have noticed it. He wore long khakis and got around quite comfortably. Mario got me focused, helped me deal with my pain, and—this might sound exaggerated but it's accurate—taught me how to be an amputee. He had faith in my commitment to get stronger as quickly as I possibly could. The exercises he suggested all seemed to help. I wondered if he saw some of himself in me, but I never asked him. And I never asked him how he had lost his leg. If he wanted to tell me, I figured he would. All I knew was that he was in his mid-fifties and still quite strong. And as we worked together in the physical therapy clinic, I developed faith in his instincts and abilities—and more faith in my own. That was all the good part, but I was still feeling those awful bursts of pain.

I'd started with the pain meds as soon as we'd arrived in El Paso. I knew the dangers of that. Yes, the pills turned the pain off—or dulled it down. But those pills also dulled my senses and fogged my brain. And I knew that once you got in the habit of taking those pills, it could be very hard to stop. I'd had plenty of friends over the years who'd gotten into trouble with pain pills. I was never certain who was addicted and who just liked the blessed relief. But I knew more than a few people who had tried and failed to stop using, often time and time again. That was a club I didn't want to join. Still, three weeks after surgery, I found myself downing up to fourteen pills every eight hours.

The Sunday before Easter, I asked Mario directly: "So how do I get rid of this pain?" I didn't share with him the amount of pills I was taking but he knew that pain meds were part of my recovery. "I don't want to become the next disabled-vet prescription junkie," I said. "Tuesday and I have too many things to accomplish."

I expected Mario to say, "Yeah, I hear you. You should definitely talk to your doctor about that." Physical therapists aren't prescribers. They are usually reluctant to weigh in on matters of pharmaceutical pain management. So I was surprised when Mario brought out a small, black device and handed it to me. It was slightly larger than one of those pagers people used to carry in the pre-cell-phone days. It had a couple of buttons on the front and four wires poking out of the top.

"This is a TENS unit," he told me, explaining that TENS stands for transcutaneous electrical nerve stimulation. "Basically, it zaps a small amount of electric current into your body as a means of controlling pain. It doesn't work for everyone, but you might give it a try."

I was skeptical. I had faith in Mario, but I wasn't sure that shocking my stump was going to ease anything, let alone phantom pain. Truthfully, the TENS sounded painful on its own. "Use it eighteen hours a day," Mario said. "Just carry it around with you. Not when you are sleeping or bathing, but all the rest of the time. And change the frequency and the intensity every thirty minutes. It'll be more effective that way."

I did everything exactly the way Mario told me to. I inserted the four electrodes beneath the Ace bandages at different parts of my stump, which was a bit of a hassle. But I did it. I could feel an electric current pulsating through my leg. But the current wasn't painful. It was steady and dull. Every half hour or so, I turned it up or down in frequency and intensity. And Mario was right. That made all the difference in my little world. Within twenty-four hours, damned if my pain didn't really begin to subside. Instead of a 9.5 pain level, I would call it a 1-point-something, which is probably the level of pain two-thirds of Americans wake up with every day. Not bad for a couple of weeks after an amputation. Within a few days, I was almost totally off the pills. Why keep taking them? The pain had abated almost to zero.

I never expected my physical therapist to do anything more than stretch my body and teach me some new exercises. But as far as I was concerned, Mario and TENS were miracle workers. I don't know how to divide the credit between the two of them. I just knew I wasn't howling anymore.

***

I hated my wheelchair. I hated it because it was a wheelchair, and I hated it even more because it was such a crappy one. Heavy. Clunky. Slow. Hard to fold and harder to steer. Forty-four pounds of metal, rubber, and canvas, all constitutionally unwilling to cooperate with me. I hadn't chosen the chair. The hospital had given it to me. Believe me, even as a novice, I would not have picked this one. And I couldn't help but notice, as I was cursing its inadequacies for about the 127th time, the three tiny words embossed on the undercarriage.

"Made in China."

I didn't need to be a disabled U.S. Army veteran to see a small irony there. But it wasn't just where or how the wheelchair had been manufactured. Those were the easy things to focus my anger on. What I really hated most of all was the fact that I was so dependent on the chair.

Time and prosthetics were the only long-term cure for that. But in the meantime, couldn't I find a better chair? I had many disabled friends. I'd heard them describing wheelchairs that were lighter, faster, and more maneuverable. I never heard anyone say, "I love my wheelchair." But I did have the strong sense that some chairs were far superior to others. If I had to wait for my prosthesis, I wanted a better chair. I *needed* a better chair, which first and foremost meant a lighter one. I asked around and got directions to a large medical-supply store near Fort Bliss.

"I'd like to see your top-of-the-line, folding, lightweight chair," I told the salesman, whose name was Fernando. Fernando skipped right over the half dozen chairs on the display floor and disappeared into a back room, while Tuesday and I killed time in the bandage aisle, checking out the different styles of wound wrapping. Damn, I was learning all kinds of new things!

Fernando finally returned with what looked to me like an Olympic wheelchair. It was made of seamless, aerospace-grade titanium, all fancy and aerodynamic. It weighed barely one-third of my old clunker, which suddenly felt like something out of World War I. The new chair, an Aero-X by TiLite, didn't have wings or a rocket-propulsion system, but it looked like it might as well have. It had 1.6-ounce Performance 5-Spoke Soft Roll Wheels and a

TiShaft Back Release Bar, a Curved Axle Plate, and a Tru-Fit System that was just this side of a custom-made chair. And it had a snap-in, air-cushioned seat saddle and a back panel made of camouflage material. This was clearly a chair designed for a warrior or a veteran. How, I wondered, had I even allowed myself to sit in my ancient, clunky, steel model?

"Can I try it out?" I asked Fernando.

"Sure," the salesman said.

He set the air cushion in the right position and made a couple of other adjustments so the chair would fit someone of my height. Then, he said: "Have a seat."

I hoisted myself from my chair into the sleek aluminum one, which immediately tumbled backward, dumping me onto the floor. Tuesday darted in my direction. Fernando did too, as did two or three other store employees. I had used exactly the same maneuver and the same amount of force I'd been using to sit in my own chair. I had no idea I was launching myself, cartoonlike, into an exaggerated, military-style somersault.

Thankfully, my long-ago paratrooper training protected my back. I had the presence of mind and the ingrained muscle memory to execute a fairly impressive parachute-landing fall or PLF. Harness the momentum. Keep the body supple. Roll with the fall. That's how they taught it at the U.S. Army's Airborne School in Fort Benning, Georgia. The lesson was still planted somewhere in my brain. With my two good arms, one good leg, and a stiff shot of adrenaline, I managed to pull myself back up, hardly missing a beat. Even more important, I also managed to protect the stump. Anything to protect the stump! Everything else was fair game to be hit or wounded or injured—just not my head and not my stump. The last thing I needed was a fall that resulted in my stump exploding like a watermelon. I didn't want anything slowing my recovery.

"I'm okay, I'm okay," I announced immediately to the crowd around me, even before I had any idea whether I was okay or not. I wasn't going to lie there. That would have been totally lame. I think Fernando was happy I wasn't race-rolling to a nearby lawyer's office to file a multimillion-dollar injury suit.

At that point, two things seemed obvious to me. I had to learn to control this chair, and I also had to buy it. The list price was $5,400, though Fernando said a steep disabled-vet discount was a distinct possibility. I would have to figure out later if I could get the VA to cover the cost. For now, that chair was coming home with me.

I drove that Aero-X like I stole it. Learning to pick up speed. Turning on a dime. Slamming to a sharp stop. With this chair, there was no limit—none that I'd been able to reach, anyway. The only governor was how hard and fast my arms could spin those skinny racing wheels. And despite my various ailments, I was happily discovering that I still had my upper-body strength.

I wiped out a couple of times. I flipped to the right over a stupid crack in the sidewalk. Once, I misjudged a curb height and landed, knee first, half in the gutter, half on the grass. But these were indignities and learning experiences more than anything to stop me. And for someone who hated being in a wheelchair, I could see that this one did have its attributes.

We had to go back and forth a bit—what else was new?—but in the end the VA agreed to pay for it. Once I got my prosthetic, I knew the wheelchair wouldn't be my everyday mode of transportation. But I'd still require one from time to time—for emergencies or even unplanned little rolls around the house. Until someone invents a personal rocket ship or a practical hovercraft, I will probably always need a wheelchair or a pair of crutches within reach. So while I waited for my swelling to abate, I figured I might as well use the thing—and maybe even have a little fun.

Tuesday and I went out to a spot behind the hotel in El Paso. I was on the pavement. He was on the grass next me.

"Go!" I yelled.

With all the strength in my arms, I hurled the wheels forward. Again and then again and again. I was off and picking up speed. I glanced over at Tuesday, who was running hard to my right. Pretty soon, I was really flying and so was he. Faster and faster and faster. This machine was responding to anything I put into it. It really was up to me. And I was loving it.

Tuesday and I were conducting our own man-dog version of the Tour de France, though being in West Texas I guess it was more like *La Vuelta del Paso*. We'd found our own Fast and Furious, and I could feel the competitive rush coursing through me. My racing partner was breathing hard, but he wasn't slowing down.

I could feel the beads of sweat gathering on my forehead. Future callouses began developing on my hands. I'd already passed the blister stage with the old chair. I was breathing at least as hard as Tuesday was. I glanced ahead of us at the fence that would be our finish line. I wasn't sure I could beat Tuesday there, but I was giving that dog the run of his life. As we both pressed on, I could feel the breeze against my face. It was cool for West Texas—no, more than that. It was enlivening and invigorating and exhilarating, too. God, I'd missed that feeling. I was moving under my own power. I was going fast. I was maintaining my balance and keeping control of the chair. Tuesday was pumping hard to keep up with me. We were two friends, running side by side, yet still giving the race everything we had. There were no limits.

In the end, Tuesday still kicked my ass. He made it to the corner three or four seconds before I did and waited there patiently for me.

He could still outrun me, even when I was driving a $5,000 titanium chair. But I gave him a run for his money. I know I did. He was really panting when we both got to the fence at the hotel property line.

I loved every minute of it, and so did he.

For a minute there, we were a cohesive military unit answering the call to move out quickly. *Double time!* That's how it's referred to across the Armed Forces.

Carpe diem, Tuesday! We were definitely seizing the day!

CHAPTER 18

Getting Fitted

—«◄●►»—

The future is the shape of things to come.
H. G. WELLS

THE JEWELL CLINIC REALLY WAS A CROWN JEWEL.

Over the years, Tuesday and I have visited scores of veterans' medical facilities across the country, probably more than a hundred by now. Some are old. Some are new. Some are staffed by wonderful, caring people. Some are not. But we haven't seen too many that are like the state-of-the-art Jewell Clinic of the Eastern Colorado Health Care System. Opened in 2010, the Jewell Clinic definitely does not live up to the downbeat VA stereotypes. It is small for a VA facility. Clean. Modern. Friendly. Not teeming with my fellow walking-dead zombies. All the employees seemed to know each other, and were unfailingly friendly to us each time we arrived.

Tuesday and I had come to Denver because of the clinic's reputation for helping patients with mobility and rehabilitation issues. I'd asked around and done quite a bit of online research and concluded that this would be the right place for me to get my new leg. The Jewell staff had deep experience. They had access to all the latest prosthetic technologies. And they had Bill-the-prosthetist, who everyone seemed to agree was uniquely talented in the art and science of properly fitting artificial limbs.

Here was something else: We had a 9 A.M. appointment. Tuesday and I arrived a little early, prepared for the usual VA wait. Instead, we were greeted by Bill and led into the examining room at precisely 9 A.M. Wow! Just wow! On time? No way!

On our way in, I noticed quite a few people with canes, crutches, walkers, and wheelchairs. There was actually something comforting about that, as I rolled along in my own chair with Tuesday trotting by my side. I'd been feeling self-conscious and different. Here, I wasn't a freak. For the first time since my surgery, the world didn't seem populated entirely by perfect bipeds. The world looks very different from 6 feet 2 inches than it does from 3 feet 1 inch.

I would describe Bill as a slightly more muscular version of TV's Gilligan—tall, lanky, sinewy, and sandy-haired. He gave off what I would describe as an artsy, mechanical vibe. I could tell he was a guy who worked with his hands. The room had a typical examining table and a stool and also a set of parallel bars, about twelve feet long.

Tuesday had to say hi before we got started. He nudged up against Bill, who petted him nicely. "Do you have a dog?" I asked.

"Yeah, I do," Bill answered politely. But he was clearly focused on getting started—quite businesslike, actually—so I didn't try to make any more conversation with him. Some people, I know, just aren't the talkative type.

Bill asked me to climb out of the wheelchair and stand inside the parallel bars, holding on with both my hands. He looked. He poked. He prodded. Then, he handed me a long, rubbery item he called a sleeve. The sleeve was maybe a foot and a half in length and a foot in circumference. The rubber felt slightly sticky. It was roughly three millimeters thick. He asked me to sit back in my chair and slide the sleeve onto my stump. "This should be just large enough to slide up the full length of your residual leg and fit snugly," Bill told me "Roll it up your thigh to the point where your thigh meets your hip."

I pulled it carefully over the stump. That created a strange sensation, but I didn't care. This was the first step.

It seemed snug to me. "Fits like a glove," I marveled.

"We need it to fit better than a glove," Bill said. "Much better. Now stand up again."

With both his hands, Bill pulled and pinched at the rubbery material, maneuvering the excess to the top of the sleeve. With a pen, he marked where the excess began. He felt around my right glute and my inseam, making sure he squeezed all the extra rubber to the top. Finally satisfied, he slid the sleeve off my stump and, with a pair of industrial scissors, he cut off the excess along the pen marks.

"Slide this back on," he told me.

The man was good. There was no excess rubber anywhere. "Definitely better than a glove," I said.

With the trimmed sleeve in place, Bill handed me what looked like a cutoff set of long underwear, made of a slightly gauzier material. "Pull these on," he said. I slid one side onto my good leg and the other side onto my stump.

The long johns were extra high-waisted, reaching almost to the middle of my chest. Bill told me to pull them up as far as I could, stretching the wrinkles out. All of a sudden I felt like uber-nerd Steve Urkel from *Family Matters*.

"Did I do that?" I muttered to myself in Steve's nasally voice.

One thing you learn real quick in the military. You've gotta maintain a good sense of humor.

Bill wanted everything to be as smooth as possible against my skin.

Then, he stopped for a moment and began to prepare a mixture that looked exactly like plaster of paris, the stuff we used to make models with as kids. Then, he returned his attention to my leg.

At the end of my residual limb, he pulled the excess long john material into a point, keeping the material as taut as possible. He cinched it together with strong, thin string—could it really be dental floss?—carefully, almost surgically winding up the excess into a perfect little ponytail, wagging from the bottom of my stump.

"Will you stand now?" Bill asked.

With me upright and between the parallel bars, he leaned back and inspected the rubbery sleeve and the long johns one last time, making sure everything was smooth and taut and no wrinkles had slipped in.

"Sit back down," he said.

As kids, when we played with plaster of paris, we poured the plaster powder into a bowl or a bucket of water and stirred it up. He had a bucket of water and something in there acting as an accelerant, but he also added rolls of white gauze to the mix. The mixture mustn't have been anything too toxic. I noticed he wasn't wearing gloves.

"Stand," he said.

With every abbreviated instruction, I was struck by how little narration Bill was offering on this amazing day. But I did as he asked me to. I stood.

I stepped back between the parallel bars, which gave me some added stability and helped me remain still while I balanced on one leg and he went to work. He squatted in front of me like a sculptor assessing his raw stone or clay. He lifted some gauze from the plastery liquid and began wrapping the soggy strips around my residual leg. This went on for several minutes. Wrapping. Laying on plaster. Wrapping some more. Laying some more. Around and around he went, up and down and middle, the entire length of my residual leg. From the tip of the stump all the way to the top of the inseam, all of it was being wrapped in this plaster-soaked gauze.

Now I could see why Bill insisted that the rubbery sleeve come all the way to the top. He couldn't allow any imperfections in there at all.

"The higher we go," Bill finally said, "the more leverage you will have. That'll give you that much more control." Bill was the expert, and I had no doubt he was right.

He spent maybe ten minutes rolling on the wet, gauzy layers and making sure there were no bumps or wrinkles or looseness or excess material anywhere. The more he wrapped, the more I realized this was definitely tighter than a glove.

As Bill slapped on more and more water, I could feel the plaster hardening and tightening around my residual leg. It wasn't painful, just noticeably constricting, gripping around the entire circumference of what was left of my leg. You know what it felt like? It felt like a more extreme version of one of those blood pressure cuffs. The pressure kept increasing, and all that plaster was hardening into a cast. Unlike a blood pressure cuff, it didn't deflate. It just kept feeling tighter.

So how would this pressure be relieved? The long johns, Bill told me, weren't just to protect my skin. They would make it easier for him to slide the hardened plaster away.

When he decided the plaster was hard enough, Bill got his fingers around the cast and delicately began to shimmy his new creation off my stump. He tugged smoothly but firmly so the plaster wouldn't crack. After a few more shimmies and one small pop, he was holding a three-dimensional mold of my residual leg. Not a picture. Not an estimate. An actual impression of what was and wasn't there.

Now, I really did feel like a model for one of the greatest sculptors of our time. And the mold Bill had created would help him forge a new body part for me.

Then, he handed it me. "Pretty cool, huh?" he said, nodding his head appreciatively at his latest work.

"Yep" was I all I could manage. But it definitely was.

He peeled back what was left of the long johns. He helped slide off the rubber sleeve and clean up the mess. He told me something, proudly, that he hadn't before. Some other prosthetists, he said, have started using 3-D printers and computer-assisted design to help establish the dimensions they will try to achieve. "The new technology has its benefits," Bill said. "But I still get better results with an old-school cast."

It's ancient technology, he said. But it's human scale, and if done correctly it produces an eerily accurate representation of the residual limb. "That's the craftsmanship, right there," he said.

I liked the sound of that.

One person, working with another, bringing talent and experience and a caring human touch. If plaster casting was Bill's preferred method, count me as a plaster-cast guy.

"I'll make a vacuum socket for the interim prosthetic based on the cast we have made," he told me as Tuesday and I prepared to go. That socket is what would fit around my limb and hold the actual new leg in place. Bill wouldn't be subcontracting any of this to an orthopedic workshop somewhere, he assured me. He would create the all-important leg socket himself. He had taken the measurements. He had interacted with the patient. He had the mold. And I was completely certain he had the talent and skill to get it done.

"So go make me a leg," I said with a smile.

"I will," Bill said in that same deadpan tone. But then I noticed a slight change. The more Bill talked the more he sounded almost excited. "I'm going to fit you with a leg with a microprocessor," he said. "A C-leg, it's called. C for computerized. It's made by a German company named Ottobock. Top of the line. It's popular with para-athletes. It's an amazing piece of equipment that blends the latest technological achievements with some old-school prosthetic craftsmanship."

Between Bill's version of enthusiasm and the idea of coming at the challenge from two directions, I was smiling even more than before. I was thankful that we had chosen Jewell and Bill. His approach and knowledge was exactly the kind of thinking that appealed to the army officer in me. I'd spent much of my life studying old and new battle strategies. Now, I was working with someone who'd obviously been studying the strategies and science of prosthetic legs.

Bill mentioned the C-leg's electronic innards, how the leg's sensors could absorb fresh data from my real-life experiences and feed them into the operating software. He mentioned Bluetooth remote connectivity. He said something about "constant refinements." I couldn't take all of it in so quickly. But I knew that I'd soon be spending hours on the Ottobock website, soaking up every last detail about this magic-sounding device that was going to help me walk *and move well* again.

My mind was flying with possibilities that seemed finally within reach. Bill made sure I didn't get ahead of myself. "This will be your *interim* leg," he cautioned. "The size of your limb is still changing, even though most of the swelling has gone down. Your leg will keep changing in the months ahead. You probably won't get your permanent leg for two or three months—maybe even a year from now."

I should be prepared for a steep learning curve, Bill warned. "It's a good piece of equipment, but it won't walk for you. You still have to do that yourself. Be prepared. You are facing many grueling hours ahead. You'll be working with a physical therapist who will help you build your strength and show you some techniques. Balance, leverage, stopping, starting, climbing stairs, leg swing—you'll have to learn all of that. It can take a while."

"I know and understand," I answered. And I did.

However long it took, I knew I was going to be impatient. I was mentally ready to start right away. Slap on a leg and get going. But I'd been warned by doctors and psychologists, by surgeons and nearly every firsthand report on the Internet that this was a slow, painful process. However hard it was going to be, I told Bill, I was ready for it. I was ready to start right away.

From beginning to end, it was a great visit with Bill. We were in and out in an hour. I could almost see my future ahead of me, standing once again 6 foot 2 inches tall.

"Is next Friday okay for you?" Bill asked. "Same time?"

"Absolutely," I answered.

This was all moving very quickly, something I wasn't used to at the VA. I didn't come this far to spend an extra weekend in a wheelchair. I was grinning as Tuesday and I rolled out of there.

———

For most of the next seven days, I stared at my laptop in the hotel room, digesting every morsel I could about the Ottobock Genium C-Leg, "proven to support your active life through amazing microprocessor technology." It wasn't just a leg. It was one of "the world's leading microprocessor prosthetic leg systems." Tuesday and I went out for food and to let him do his business. But other than that, I was committed to becoming a Rain Man–caliber expert on this sleek piece of hardware that I was convinced would enable the return of my mobility.

Nothing else seemed half as interesting as that.

This thing was loaded. The easy swing initiator. The preflex knee. The enhanced-response shock absorption. The equalized stride control. The Adaptive Yielding Control. Dynamic Stability Control. Adaptive Swing Phase Control. I wasn't sure what all those features were, but I liked the way they sounded. The careful accommodations for sloping and uneven surfaces. My time on crutches and in a wheelchair had certainly highlighted plenty of those.

"The Genium microprocessor prosthetic leg is quite simply the closest technology has come to natural walking," the website said. "Imagine work, family, or leisure time activities without having to think about your next step. If your active life demands more function, this is the system you need."

Yes, I could imagine all of that. Yes, my active life demanded more function. Yes, I was ready for my C-Leg. Now all I'd have to do was trust Bill's fitting technique and learn to walk again. And I didn't have to imagine when. That date was not only in my calendar. It was a constantly ticking countdown in my mind.

Friday, April 29, was going to be L-Day, Leg Day, the day I would finally walk out of this place and into the world on my new bionic leg. I would remember that date, as surely I would remember February 27, seven weeks and a lifetime earlier, the day my right leg was severed and carried out of the room. Tuesday and I might even start celebrating those dates every year. They would be my other birthdays.

I could hardly wait.

CHAPTER 19

Dog Fight

───《○》───

Sometimes following your heart means losing your mind.
UNKNOWN

SNOW WAS FALLING IN DENVER ON APRIL 29.

Tuesday and I took a cab through the slush from the hotel to the Jewell Clinic, arriving out front ten minutes early for our 9 A.M. appointment. Just how I always like it. As I pulled myself out of the taxi and maneuvered my wheelchair onto the sidewalk, I let Tuesday off his leash. That way, he could trot onto the wet, snow-dusted front lawn and do his business before we went inside. Nothing unusual there.

"Get busy, Tuesday," I said.

The flakes were still falling, a light, late spring snow in the mountain West. I was still fumbling with the chair when I vaguely noticed a woman walking a German shepherd up the sidewalk toward us. I had no reason to focus on dog-walking pedestrians. I was almost giddy with anticipation about trying on my new leg.

Then, *bang!*

All of a sudden, without a word of warning or any provocation that I could see, the German shepherd lunged forward, yanking the leash out of the woman's hand. She was a small woman, elderly and frail. She went tumbling immediately to the sidewalk. The dog took off running across the lawn—straight at Tuesday.

Barking. Snarling. Racing at full speed. Dragging an empty leash behind. With all that speed and ferocity, the German shepherd pounced on gentle Tuesday, who was only trying to get his business done.

Standing where I was, outside the taxi, balancing on one leg with the metal wheelchair in my hand, I didn't have a close-up view of everything. But I could see enough to know this was trouble. Big trouble.

The other dog was young and strong, a classic female German shepherd—black and brown with small touches of white, ninety or one hundred muscular pounds. The dog was wearing a T-shirt with writing I couldn't read.

As I hurriedly opened and dropped my lightweight chair to the sidewalk, I started shouting as loudly as I could.

"Stop that!"

"Get off!"

"Leave him alone!"

I can yell loudly. Usually, my voice is strong and urgent enough to scare any animal—or at least freeze a violent situation in place. But this time, my shouts had no effect at all.

The German shepherd was now right on top of Tuesday and the two of them were in the slushy grass, a mixed-up tumble of fur and limbs and snarl.

With a quick glance to my side, I saw that the elderly woman had managed to get up off the ground. As quickly as I could, I was in my lightning-fast Aero-X titanium chair and rolling hard—a few turns down the sidewalk and a turn onto the lawn. Which is exactly where the chair got stuck. The ground was too soft, the racing tires too skinny, my weight too much, for me to roll myself and that chair across the lawn. But I had to get there, however I could.

Things were getting uglier fast. I could see now that the German shepherd had its mouth around Tuesday's right ear. *Oh, my God!* The shepherd's teeth clamped down and locked there. Tuesday's entire ear was in the female dog's mouth.

I'll never forget the look in Tuesday's eyes. He desperately tried to pull away. He was shaking his head and wiggling his body—all to no avail. His strength was simply no match for the power of this young, hyped-up German shepherd.

The shepherd barked and growled. I was still yelling. All I could hear from Tuesday, even at this distance, was his hard breathing and his whimpers and cries. In a full-out dogfight, a retriever is no match for a shepherd. My heart was breaking for Tuesday.

To say I was upset would be a huge understatement. I could hardly imagine anything worse. Tuesday had come with me to the VA clinic, and there he was—my partner, my companion, my round-the-clock best friend—being viciously assaulted before we even got in the door. All I wanted was to rush to him, rescue him, comfort him, save him from this brutal attack. But I was stuck in the mud.

By now, people were stopping and staring. The fight was causing a giant ruckus, impossible for anyone to ignore. Patients coming out of the building, employees going into work—everyone seemed to halt on the sidewalk and stare at the frightening scene.

I did the only thing I could think of. With the strength of my two arms and one good leg, I launched myself out of the wheelchair and into the air. As I hurled toward the angry tangle of canines, the shepherd was still in full attack mode. Her iron jaw and razor teeth were clamped on Tuesday's soft and tender ear.

No one in his right mind would approach a seething German shepherd with sharp teeth bared. Who said I was in my right mind? The dog I loved was under fierce attack.

Fortunately, I landed just a few inches from them. Executing some bizarre three-legged crab crawl, I dragged myself forward, using my hands and good leg. I had to get there and save Tuesday. I was yelling as I crashed into them.

Now, I was just mad. Madder than an angry dog. Certainly madder than the German shepherd. I must've looked some sort of hellhound because that's exactly how furious I was.

"Stop!...Stop!...Let go!"

I know it wasn't the smartest thing, what I did next, but I had to do something. I curled my fingers around the snout of that snarling German shepherd, trying to pry her mouth and teeth apart. But as hard as I tried, the dog wouldn't open her jaws. Tuesday's ear was still inside her mouth.

I didn't care what it took. I couldn't give up there. I was not going to let this crazy brute bite Tuesday's ear off. That was exactly where this seemed to be heading. I was sure.

So I cocked my right arm back. I balled my right fist. I punched that German shepherd directly in the head with everything I had.

The shepherd looked stunned, but not stunned enough to loosen its grip. My punch seemed to have affected her focus, but not enough to loosen her bite.

So I punched a second time, harder still.

Again, the dog looked slightly shaken, and again did not let go.

At this point, the lady who was walking the shepherd caught up to us and grabbed her dog's leash. Small as she was, she started pulling. Almost simultaneously, my taxi driver, who'd been out of the cab and standing behind me, ran up and grabbed Tuesday's leash. Now, the two of them were in a dog leash tug-of-war, trying with all their might to separate the animals. That might have been a good thing except for the obvious fact that the German shepherd still had its jaws clamped around Tuesday's right ear. So the harder the lady and the cab driver pulled, the more likely the shepherd was to yank his ear right off.

How many amputations can one family bear?

"Don't do that!" I yelled at the lady.

"Drop the leash!" I shouted at the driver. "NOW!"

I don't think either of them understood why I was shouting so urgently, but they did what I said.

That's when I punched the shepherd a third time, even harder than before. This canine combat had caused serious adrenaline to flow. I was hoping this blow would be effective. It was everything I had. This time, my fist caught the animal at the socket of its right eye.

Incredibly, the dog still refused to let go.

It was a battle of wills—mine and the shepherd's with Tuesday's safety on the line.

I could still hear Tuesday's high-pitched whimper, as he glanced toward me in desperation as if asking: "Can you please help me, Luis?"

With whatever strength I had left, I cocked my arm back for yet another blow. But thankfully, I didn't have to throw this one. It was at this moment that the dog loosened its grip on Tuesday's ear, then fell backward and over. Tuesday collapsed onto the lawn, shaken, dazed, and confused.

Both dogs were blessedly still.

Thank God for that. I'm not sure what else I could have done.

I just wanted to comfort Tuesday. I leaned over, too grateful to notice the cold, wet ground, and pulled him into my arms. I held him there, letting both of us calm down. He had an almost vacant look in his eyes.

"What just happened?" he wanted to know, as I held him tightly and quietly let him know it was over and he was safe. But his expressive eyes were filled with questions. "What made the shepherd do that? I was just over here to take a poop."

I couldn't do a thorough medical exam on the grass outside the clinic. But I was relieved to see Tuesday still had his ear. I wasn't sure that would be true as the attack unfolded. Amazingly, he wasn't even bleeding, and as I ran my hands through his wet coat, I didn't see any obvious puncture marks, which relieved me and certainly relieved him. Given the viciousness of the encounter, frankly, I was expecting much worse. I'd have to give him a fuller inspection when we got safely inside the clinic and then later at home. Both Tuesday and I were still breathing heavily. But after such a frightening attack, I was happy blood wasn't gushing and his chewed-up right ear wasn't on the snowy lawn. As I collected myself, I realized how much worse this might have been.

At this point, the fear and anger gave way to a mixture of adrenaline and emotion. I started yelling at the lady who had lost control of her dog, as if there were anything she could do now.

"You idiot!" I screamed. "You have to control your dog! That's the law!"

"I'm sorry, I'm sorry," she was saying. "This has never happened before."

I had no idea if this was true or not, and at that moment I really didn't care. I could see she was an old woman with only a couple of her teeth left, and super-skinny. She did not look well. In hindsight, I suppose she didn't have the physical strength to control such a powerful dog. And maybe that was the point. If you can't control the dog you are walking, you need a different dog. Try a Pomeranian or shih tzu.

All I really knew was that her dog had attacked my service dog as I was going into the VA clinic to get a new leg. Given how out of control that shepherd was, I certainly could have been bitten or worse and Tuesday was lucky to be alive.

My eyes darted back and forth from the lady to Tuesday. His coat was wet and dirty from rolling on the ground. I was an even bigger mess.

My shorts and shirt were sopping wet. My butt was caked in mud. The Ace bandage around my stump was soaked and black.

I calmed down a little, but I was still irate.

"You are lucky, so lucky, I didn't kill your dog," I barked at the lady. "That is totally unacceptable."

I could tell she wanted to say something but didn't know what to say. A couple of people from the clinic told her she should probably take her dog and leave. "Just get out of here," one of the employees said.

Several people came over to me and Tuesday, asking what they could do to help us and if we were okay. I am sure they were worried about both of us, the golden retriever who'd just been attacked by a German shepherd and the one-legged guy with the Ace-bandaged stump launching out of his wheelchair and hopping into the middle of a vicious dogfight. I didn't see it unfold from anyone else's perspective, but it must have been one hell of a sight.

CHAPTER 20

Try On

――❰◆❱――

Slow and steady wins the race.
The Tortoise and the Hare, Aesop

AS EXCITED AS I WAS TO BE GETTING A NEW LEG, THAT'S HOW matter-of-fact Bill seemed when Tuesday and I rolled up to him in the Jewell Clinic hallway.

"Hey, Luis," he mumbled. "Hi, Tuesday."

"Hi, Bill," I answered, trying to regain my composure for the important business ahead. "Sorry to be such a mess. But a German shepherd just attacked Tuesday on the lawn outside. I can't believe that just happened."

"That was Tuesday?" Bill said softly. "Yeah, I heard a commotion outside."

"It was really something," I told him, still a little breathless and edgy. "But we're ready to go. We're here."

"Okay," Bill said, leading us into the examining room and leaving the door open. "Why don't you wait here, and I'll go get the leg."

No, Bill wasn't much of a talker. But if this was Christmas morning, he was Santa Claus. He had the only present I wanted this year.

Regardless of what had just happened outside, I wasn't going to let anything interfere with our long-awaited appointment inside. The only exception, of course, would have been if Tuesday had needed medical attention, which he didn't. Maybe if I'd gotten my hand bitten off, in which case I would need a hand *and* a leg. But short of that, Tuesday and I had a 9 A.M. slot with Bill the prosthetist, and damned if we weren't right on time. I took a small piece of pride in that. Nothing, not even a mad dog attack, could stop us now. Who cared if we didn't look our usual, crisp selves?

"Sit and relax," I told Tuesday, who I could tell still needed another minute or two.

Certainly Tuesday still looked disheveled. He wasn't his shiny coat, impeccably groomed self. He'd need a thorough brush out and probably a whole lot more. I saw a dog bath and shampoo in his near future. And still I looked far worse than he did. My Ace bandage was soaked and blackened. My shirt and shorts were stained and wet. I was scuffed up in ways I was just realizing, and that was just what I could see while sitting there. And it hit me, my finger was pulsing with pain. The ring finger on my right hand. I didn't know if it was broken or sprained or what. But somehow it had gotten jammed in the tussle. And now I couldn't make it go straight.

While we waited for Bill to return, Lina, a nice VA desk manager, came in to check on us and noticing my discomfort, offered to tape up the finger for me. "I can wrap the two middle fingers together to keep the injured one more secure," she suggested. That sounded good to me.

Several people who'd been outside—VA workers, I believe—wandered in to say hello.

"Are you okay?" they kept asking.

I should have just thanked everyone for their concern. But I probably just mumbled back. I was even more upset than I realized. The attack outside had been so unexpected and completely unprovoked. I was having trouble believing I'd just jumped into the middle of a dog attack to save Tuesday. The VA is supposed to be a safe environment. That's a given for humans, but it should also be true for service dogs. Tuesday had been assaulted by another dog like this only one other time. That was in Brooklyn. We certainly weren't looking to make a habit of it. Now, I was just trying to shake off my grumpiness and focus on what was coming next. I'd climbed into the cab happy and I wasn't going to let that shepherd rob me of this much-needed reason to smile.

Finally, quiet Bill returned with his hands full. "This is your leg," he said.

It was the Ottobock Genium C-Leg and the socket he had made from the plaster mold. I couldn't believe my new leg and I were finally in the same room.

<hr>

It looked just like the picture and the videos I'd seen on the Ottobock website. What was I expecting? I don't know. But I was still thrilled to see it in person. I'd never had someone present me with a body part before—not too many people have—and this one was about to become mine.

I'm not quite sure what to compare it to. Like a life preserver floating by in the ocean? Like meeting a new friend? The feeling was unlike anything I'd ever had or imagined. I stared at it for a good, long moment, just taking it in. It was incredible. I thought the leg looked sleek, modern, and cool. I sure hoped it worked as well as it looked. I couldn't wait to slide it on.

"This is my new leg," I called over to Tuesday. "It's called a C-Leg. Pretty cool, huh?" He cocked his head to the side. A disembodied leg was not something he'd seen before.

At Bill's instruction, I had brought a new pair of tennis shoes along—a pair of Nike running shoes. Perhaps it was a little presumptuous at this stage in recovery, but fitting nonetheless. I put the left shoe on my own foot and I handed him the right. He slipped it onto the foot of the C-Leg, tying the laces and adjusting the shoe.

Each move made the leg seemed closer to real, closer to what I'd so eagerly anticipated. Tuesday was staring intently at me, picking up on my nervous excitement. This is really happening, I thought to myself. I was trying to take everything in.

The next thing that struck me was how big the socket was. We don't usually think about how wide the top of our legs are where the edge of the hip meets the top of the thigh. It's the widest part of your leg and usually the least noticed part. You are at least vaguely aware of the size of your ankle, your knee, and your calf. But not this part. The circumference of your leg up there is probably larger than you realized. I know mine is. The socket of my new leg had to match that precisely. Otherwise, the leg wouldn't fit as snugly as it should.

It is not just the thigh the socket wraps around. It is the hip too. Before the operation, I'd never given any of this much thought. In the movies, didn't a prosthetic just snap into place? But I'd since learned from the websites and literature and online videos that the flushness from the thigh to the hip is what provides the leverage and support. That maximizes the stability. That's what allows someone to move and walk. Still, none of my research had completely prepared me for this moment. Now that I was staring at the actual leg, I was seeing all of this from a whole new angle. It was fascinating, intimidating, and thrilling all at once.

"This is amazing, Tuesday," I said.

Bill might not feel like talking, but I knew Tuesday was always happy to converse.

With a nod and furry shake, I got a firm "you bet" back. He was at least as excited as I was.

Now, Bill was ready for action.

He had me move between the parallel bars that took up a large part of the room.

"Put this on," he said, handing me the liner, a poly-fiber sleeve that would sit between the socket and my stump.

He pointed at my upper leg. "Make sure there are no air pockets," he said. "There can't be any room."

I did as Bill told me, just the way I'd seen in videos, and pulled the liner up as tightly as I could.

"Now, stand," he said.

I did, holding onto the rails for stability.

"I have to feel the very top of your leg," he warned me. I'm glad he warned me first because that was a little uncomfortable, the way he had to grab up there, in the tight and narrow fold where my butt meets the top of my leg.

"Do what you have to," I told him. These are not places I was used to having a lot of company.

But this was important, I knew. He needed to check up there to see that the seal of the socket was airtight. I'd have to deal with any discomfort and cooperate.

I stood there, between the parallels, not sure what came next. Then Bill placed my prosthetic leg right in front of me.

"Now," he said, "I want you to take your residual leg with the sleeve and slide that into the socket and the prosthetic leg."

Shhhuck! The leg slipped right in.

He pointed my attention to a white, quarter-size button near the upper part of the leg. "Once the leg is in, you press this button to create a vacuum."

The goal, he explained, was to deliver my residual leg into the socket as far down as possible while using the button to release the air and create a vacuum that will hold it in place. I felt like I was back in high school physics class.

I wiggled the stump slightly in and out and from side to side until Bill was convinced it was all the way in.

It felt like it was to me.

In. Snug. Secure. No wiggle.

I had a right leg.

It wasn't my flesh-and-blood leg. It was a leg some genius engineer had manufactured for me. But it was still one hell of a leg. And I was standing on it. Seeing it coming out of my hip and my thigh, I have to say, it felt pretty damn awesome.

For the first time in nearly two months, I really felt as though I was standing. I felt balanced. Not confident. Not secure. Not proficient yet. Not close to any of that. But I didn't feel off-kilter the way I had been feeling, living with only half the usual number of legs.

Now, I felt like I had retrieved an important counterbalance that I hadn't even known I needed until it was gone. This was the exact 180-degree opposite of phantom limb pain. Now, I had a limb. I was feeling limb sensation instead of phantom-limb sensation which is a whole lot more pleasing, I can promise you that. I felt comfortable. Balanced. I'd felt somewhat balanced with crutches, but this was better. Better than having the best crutches on earth. I don't want to say the leg made me feel whole. It made me feel whole in a way I hadn't felt since before the amputation.

"Put a little weight on it," Bill directed.

I did. And then I put a little more. And a little more.

In the research I had done, I had learned that many amputees are initially reticent and don't trust the leg. Naturally, I wanted to do the opposite. I wanted to push the envelope.

I shifted, trying to place half my weight on the new leg and then stood as normally as I could. It wasn't surprising but definitely a relief to discover the new leg could hold me. It really was a leg.

Of course, I hadn't gone anywhere with it yet. I hadn't moved at all from the exact spot where I'd first stood. Both sneakers were planted in place. The new leg hadn't shown its stuff, and neither had

I. The parallel bars were there if I needed them. But I didn't. I was holding myself up without the bars.

I think Bill was impressed I could hold myself up at all and shift my body weight around. I was determined to be the best prosthetic patient he'd ever had.

"Most people aren't able to do that initially," Bill told me. "It's not just about the strength. You have to trust the leg. It can take time to be able to stand and balance. Walking and then running will come after that."

I knew the answer, but I asked the question anyway, "Do we really have to wait?"

———※———

Our session had been scheduled for ninety minutes, and I didn't want to waste any of it. As I stood on the leg, I concentrated hard on not holding onto the rails.

Occasionally, I had to reset my balance. But one day soon, while walking on the sidewalk with Tuesday at my side, I knew there wasn't going to be any bar to hold onto. I didn't want to allow myself even a moment of feeling dependent on these.

I understood the whole concept of training wheels. I'd used them as a boy when I learned to ride a bicycle. Even then, I remember balancing myself on the two skinny tires, challenging myself not to let the tiny side wheels touch the ground. And as I recall, the best thing about a good pair of training wheels was the glorious day you could rid yourself of them.

"I'm ready to take some steps here," I told Bill.

Bill nodded and invited me to take some short ones.

"Hold onto the bars and take a couple," he said.

Immediately, I could tell, this walking thing was something I would really have to learn. Or relearn. Or forget what I had learned before and learn all over again. Whatever it took, there was no looking back anymore. It was time to get started—one baby step at a time.

Walking, it turned out, was far more complicated than I realized.

Bill assessed how I was standing, then he coached me on how to move my hip back and then swing the leg forward. He watched me try it a couple of times, then he stopped me to adjust the leg. He fiddled with the ankle. He studied my gait and my stance again. Then, he turned something in the knee. Those changes were very subtle. I couldn't really tell what he did. But he was treating my leg like a car that needed a tune-up even before it went out on the highway and then some more precise adjustments once it finally hit the open road.

I'd seen babies, their faces contorted in concentration, take their first tentative steps. I was the baby now. They usually got it, and so would I.

I told Bill I felt a little pain where the top of the new leg hit the bottom of the old one, a little pinching where the round end of the socket tightened around my leg. Could he do something with the socket or add a layer of protection to the sleeve?

Low-key Bill, the man of few words, replied as I knew he would—with a single word. "Okay," he answered without quite offering a specific plan.

Then, he increased the height of the leg a centimeter or two, and I could feel the difference immediately. He watched my gait again and pronounced an improvement. "Better," he nodded. Turn by turn, adjustment by adjustment, Bill was making the leg mine.

It was one thing to read the Ottobock website or to watch the videos. It was another thing entirely having the C-Leg connected to me. I was putting pressure on it. It was sending pressure back. Flexing the knee and turning the ankle, I used the leg to hold me.

I practiced, and Bill followed me inside the parallel bars. I couldn't wait to cast aside these training wheels. He kept fine-tuning, and all the while, I knew, the electronics inside the leg were doing their special thing. Measuring. Monitoring. Adjusting. Getting used to me while I was getting used to the leg.

That's how it was—that's how it would be—with this new C-Leg. A symbiotic relationship: While I was adjusting to it, it was adjusting to me. It had a brain, but the leg wasn't fully bionic. It didn't move without me. I still had to swing it. I couldn't expect the leg to drive me. I had to drive the leg.

That first day, I didn't walk outside the parallel bars. I didn't run any marathons or tango on *Dancing with the Stars*. That didn't mean I would never run or tango—just not the first day. But I grew more confident balancing myself, and I even turned around a couple of times. Like pivoting in ceremonial drills while in the military. *About face!* And I took I don't know how many little steps forward. *Forward. March!*

Looking over at Tuesday, I asked, "How do you like this footwork?"

I really felt like I was getting somewhere.

"I don't know how many people say this to you," I told Bill as we were getting finished. "But it is an interesting feeling—psychologically, mentally—finally getting here. There are the mechanics of this whole thing, the process of learning how to operate the leg. The excitement of the first steps. But there is also the psychology of it that is entirely different from crutches or a wheelchair. This thing is literally going to be a part of me, a new part, even though it isn't made of flesh and blood. I have to make it as much a part of me as my other leg. This leg and I, we are in this together for sure."

It was a heartfelt mini-soliloquy.

Bill nodded as usual.

"Can I take it home?" I asked him.

"No," he said. "You can't take it home. You have to see Tom to start your gait training. I'll give the leg to him. When he says you're okay to take the leg home, you'll take the leg home."

Really?

Tom was a physical therapist at the VA hospital in downtown Denver who specialized in working with patients who had new prosthetics. If Mario in El Paso had taught me how to be an amputee, perhaps Tom in Denver would show me how to walk like I wasn't one. I was just as eager to work with Tom as I had been with Mario. I'd heard nothing but good things about him. But did I really have to leave my leg at the clinic until Tom gave me the green light? Wouldn't it be far more useful to start practicing on my own?

Bill refused to budge.

"No," he said.

"Come on," I pleaded.

"No."

"I'm serious. Let me take it home. I need to practice."

"Talk to Tom."

CHAPTER 21

Test Drive

—— ««◉»» ——

*We cannot walk alone. And as we walk, we must make the
pledge that we shall always march ahead.
We cannot turn back.*
MARTIN LUTHER KING JR.

THERE WAS SOME CONFUSION ABOUT OUR WEDNESDAY APPOINTMENT
time. Tuesday and I showed up forty-five minutes early at the VA
hospital in downtown Denver to see Triathlon Tom.

The hospital's physical therapy clinic had none of the quiet effi-
ciency of the Jewell Clinic, which I was starting to think of as the
Department of Veterans Affairs's exclusive boutique. The downtown
facility was tiny and crowded with old equipment. I half expected
to see the Universal weight machine we'd used in high school gym
class or one of those madcap 1950s vibrator belts. But the downtown
clinic did have Triathlon Tom, and that's the reason we were there.

As we waited for the appointment, a short, stocky man was struggling inside of the clinic's parallel bars, taking painfully labored steps
with his new leg prosthesis. He wasn't moving very much. "You
mind if we watch?" I asked him as Tuesday and I plopped down on a
padded table, me on crutches. "I'm trying to learn."

"Please," he said. "Then, I'll watch you. We'll both learn something."

I liked his attitude.

His name was Quiñones. He was around sixty-five years old, and balance was not coming naturally to him. I didn't know how long he'd been practicing—but longer than I had, since this was my first day.

His posture was tilted. He gripped the bars like he was scared he might fall off a cliff. His baby steps weren't even baby steps, more like a stand-in-place shuffle. He seemed terrified he might fall. I didn't know what to tell him, so I went with vague encouragement.

"Keep going," I said, the sort of thing you say when you aren't sure what to say. "One step at a time." But you know what? It turned out that such words are near to the truth. Learning to walk with a prosthetic leg takes persistence, and it really does come one step at a time.

Tuesday and I are such fortunate creatures. When you are on a mission that millions of people believe in, a lot of them are willing to help. Or maybe that's just what happens when half your pack is an irresistibly cute canine. Whatever. Talented people keep stepping forward in the most generous ways. They share their ideas and their expertise. Some host us in new cities and help organize events. Sometimes, they act as if it's their job to help, extending boundless kindness, decency, or professionalism. That was Triathlon Tom.

A 6-foot-tall, athletic, happily married father of young fraternal twins, Tom was a staff physical therapist with the Denver VA, one of thousands of caring men and women toiling admirably in America's often-maddening veterans' care bureaucracy. He was also a top-notch team member of the Eastern Colorado VA system's Amputee Clinic. So it didn't surprise me when Tom told me offhandedly that he would be competing in a triathlon the next morning. He approached everything, including me, like an all-in, multi-event, leave-nothing-behind competition that he couldn't wait for. This man was on a mission of his own—showing me and other disabled veterans, amputees especially, how to walk again. He was so much more than a "federal bureaucrat." As far as I could tell, there was nothing he couldn't do, up to and including dealing with my impatience to walk again and getting me to swing my new bionic leg as if it were my own.

Tom had many ways of achieving this. Encouragement. Criticism. Precise readjustment. Endless repetition. Channeling my impatience and frustration in productive ways. He used all of it. "Point your toe a little to the left," he'd say. "It's heel-to-toe, heel-to-toe. You walk the leg. The leg doesn't walk you." Walking, it turns out, is far more complicated than putting one foot in front of the other, to use another expression I think I might have tried on Quiñones. It's a far more complex activity than most lifelong walkers realize, a fact that I only fully appreciated when I was the one expected to master it all over again.

In my first session with Tom, he had me climb into my new leg, which Bill-the-prosthetist had delivered to him. Then, Tom strapped me into a harness with a hook attached to the ceiling and told me to take a step. Then another. And another. The only other time I'd seen a contraption like this was in a community theater production of *Peter Pan*. With so much of my weight being supported by the harness, cable, and pulley, those steps were easy. Too easy, I thought. "This isn't walking," I told Tom. "This is hanging on a hook. I want to walk." I asked him politely if he would remove the harness. "Can we get rid of the freakin' harness?" I asked with a devilish grin. He agreed to let me try without it. I think he liked the fact that I was already pushing boundaries, his and my own, though he might have doubted how well I would do. We moved to the parallel bars.

Without the harness, the full weight of my body was now divided between two legs, one that God had given me, one that was manufactured by Ottobock. But let's be frank, I wasn't exactly trim. During my time in the wheelchair, I'd put on a few extra pounds. I was tipping the scales at 220 without my right leg, which had been my previous weight with the leg.

The leg definitely felt awkward. It felt exactly like what it was, a foreign object smack against my body. It didn't feel like part of me. But using the parallel bars to help my balance, I was able to sort of walk. I have to add the "sort of" because it was not a smooth walk. I wasn't gliding along. I was stiff. My motion was labored. It wasn't a confident gait. But I was, indeed, putting one foot in front of another, and that was hugely encouraging to me.

"Very nice," Tom said.

He had some suggestions about how I was plopping my new foot down. "There is a rhythm we are trying to achieve," he said. "We're not just dropping something on the floor." But he seemed pleased I was taking steps, one after another, and I was pleased not to be suspended in a stupid harness like some oafish Peter Pan.

Tom made me leave the leg with him after that session. "The next time I see you, you can take it home," he said. I would much rather have taken it back to the hotel with us right then. I spent the next two days frustrated I wasn't practicing with my leg.

When we returned to the VA hospital on Friday to see Tom, I got right to walking in between the parallel bars.

I really wanted to progress as quickly as possible. In fact, I needed to progress rapidly because Tuesday and I had an ambitious travel schedule planned in the months ahead. I told him I really wasn't sure if I needed the bars anymore to stabilize myself.

"You want to skip the bars?" Tom asked.

"*Yes,* I want to skip the bars," I said.

"Sounds good."

Again, I didn't go very fast or very far, just around the cramped physical therapy clinic. I would call my steps labored and tentative. But I was making them and stringing them together, far more of them than I had the last time we were there. Now, it was starting to feel like walking. But apparently, I wasn't done with Tom's stability aids. He seemed concerned I might fall. So he cinched a belt around my waist and held it behind my back, following me as I stepped across the room. I felt like a dog on a leash. Sorry, Tuesday. I didn't like that at all.

Tom seemed overly concerned about me falling. Partially because I'm a big guy, which meant he'd have a difficult time catching me. Partially, I think, because other hospital patients had fallen and then needed urgent attention from the clinic staff. Nevertheless, I was perturbed by the onslaught of Tom's be-carefuls and take-it-easys and watch-your-steps.

"Listen," I snapped after a few steps with the belt. "I'm gonna fall. People fall. Kids fall. Bike riders fall. We all stumble and fall. Then we pick ourselves back up."

Impassioned by the situation, I went on.

"With or without amputation, I'm going to fall."

And I did.

A couple of times.

At my first U-turn and then later on.

It hurt.

But nothing terrible happened.

I got up and kept walking some more.

Thank you, Airborne School in Fort Benning, Georgia. With the number of falls you have to endure learning to become a paratrooper, I'd better know how to fall.

As much as I was pushing to do more and do it more quickly, Tom seemed to like my drive and my positivity. "A lot of people are scared of the leg," he said. "You can't be scared of the leg."

As I kept practicing, he called over two other therapists—and a couple of physical therapy interns—to watch. "This is his second session," Tom said. "He thinks he's ready for stairs."

He seemed proud of me.

That's why I was so pissed when, after that second session, Tom still wouldn't let me take my leg with me. He had promised, hadn't he? "I get that you're impressed by my progress and how much I'm walking," I said. "But I need to practice on my own."

"You'll take the leg on Monday," he said. "Not today. You shouldn't push yourself too quickly. You won't be happy if you injure yourself. Monday, you'll get the leg."

"That better happen," I warned him, just making sure. "If not, I swear I'll take it hostage—or I'm going to Home Depot and making a peg leg. I need to practice a lot. Tuesday and I have places to go and things to do."

Was I joking? I'm not sure.

It was a long weekend. I wouldn't call it a waste, as there are always things to do, but someone in my shoes needs a lot more "homework" than the average soul. So, that weekend I remained a prisoner of the crutches and the wheelchair.

On Monday, Tom offered some intense gait critiques. The swing was still the tricky part. Mastering the swing, making the leg go back and forth in a natural manner, is the real skill of walking with an above-the-knee prosthesis. I'm not saying I got it instantly. That wouldn't be true. But I was feeling the knee and it was bending and I was starting to get a rhythm down. I felt incredibly good about what I was mastering and had no doubt that, in another week or two, Tuesday and I might well be climbing Pike's Peak.

Then, Tom made a suggestion that brought me right down to earth. "You want to try the stairs?" I think he'd been at least partially joking when he made that stair comment to his physical therapy colleagues. But now this was serious, and we were going to give it a try.

What a humbling experience that was!

"Okay, Luis," Tom said after we rode an elevator together up to the second floor, and he led me to the top of a stairway. "When you go down a step, you need to make sure your foot is halfway off the step before you take the next motion. Otherwise, if it is not halfway, the knee won't bend when it's supposed to, and you won't step down naturally."

That seemed like an awful lot of instruction to walk down one step. But looking down, I realized I had never thought about exactly how that stair-descending rhythm works. Climbing requires an entirely different motion, Tom warned me.

I tried what Tom suggested and let me just say: It's amazing how high six inches can be. I felt like I might need mountain-climbing pylons to lower myself one small step.

This seemed crazy, like it couldn't possibly be the way a normal person goes down the stairs. It couldn't be how I'd been walking down stairs my entire life. Tom assured me that it was. It seemed like too much planning, too much positioning, and too big a drop. And I didn't quite get it that first time.

"Gives me something to work on," I half mumbled as Tom and I retreated to level ground.

We did end that third session on a happy note. If we hadn't, I really might have done something reckless.

"You ready to take the leg home today?" Tom asked.

"Yes," I answered firmly.

"Are you sure?"

"I am very sure," I said.

Tom gave me a big smile. I knew he was playing with me. But as soon as I had the leg in my hands, Tuesday and I exfiltrated the area as quickly as possible before there was any chance for the plan to change. I took the leg back to the hotel and finally started practicing on my own.

Now, my process was divided in two—with Tom and without Tom. Both were vital to my progress.

Over many physical therapy sessions spanning a few weeks' time, Tom looked on as Tuesday and I walked the hallways of the hospital. He wasn't merely following us around though. He spotted and coached me as I walked, turned, and negotiated around people and obstacles. He kept giving me pointers, and I kept trying to walk as naturally as I could.

Swing, balance, land, don't fall, walk.

You have to learn to sense when and how to swing the prosthetic leg so you take even, smooth, rhythmic steps forward. Besides balancing, that's the hardest part. You've got to train your brain to understand how the leg swings itself and also how the leg moves. And you've got to practice where the foot and the leg land in relation to your gate. I never thought about any of this complicated coordination before my operation. We take all that for granted, those of us who have spent our lifetimes walking on our own two legs. Too bad I didn't pay more attention when I was two.

The mechanics, the balance, and the locomotion of sitting, standing, and walking are all different with a prosthesis. The new leg, no matter how advanced it is, isn't you exactly. It's an $80,000 contraption that's jammed up against your thigh and groin. Mastering that takes real mind control—and time.

As I walked around the VA hospital, I wanted Tuesday walking with me. But the first time we tried that, I had trouble keeping him under control. He hadn't seen me walk much in the past couple of months. He seemed thrilled for me—and for himself as well. We were walking together again. But as we did, people kept coming over, wanting to pet Tuesday or just say "hi." Patients, staff, techs, trainers, everyone. Often at the VA, I let Tuesday interact with people. They almost always want to meet him. Military veterans love dogs. And Tuesday loves them. It's a win-win situation. Except for times when I need Tuesday to perform tasks for me, which happens more often than people think.

Initially, he wouldn't sit and stay. He wanted to walk beside me. He wanted to help me. He knew I was struggling.

A few times, I got impatient with him.

"Tuesday, STAAAAY," I said sharply.

I rarely have to admonish Tuesday in public. But he wouldn't sit and stay as I practiced my walking. I really needed to focus on the leg and on myself—not on Tuesday's many fans and tripping over him.

I didn't want to yell, but I couldn't whisper. With so many people around, he wouldn't have heard.

Back at the hotel, we took walks through the building's many hallways. Smooth. Level. Carpeted. Mostly empty. We circled the lobby and went to the restaurant. Then, ever so slowly, we ventured outside, a vast expanse of crooked sidewalks, uneven entrances, and daredevil curbs. Tuesday accompanied me everywhere. As I got better at this, he'd be at my side wherever I went. I liked having him and he liked being there. This was our longstanding reality. We might as well both learn the new mechanics.

I tried to take things slowly. I couldn't leave the leg on all day. My body wasn't ready. Even I could see that. The leg was attached to the socket, which in turn was vacuum-squeezed onto my stump—it took a lot of energy to maintain all that. Honestly, it was exhausting. It wasn't easy on my muscles, my nerves, my bones, or my skin. This was all just part of the deal, I told myself. All I could do was get stronger, get more comfortable, and improve my technique, which meant continuing to work and learn with Tom.

In all our sessions, Tom watched me keenly. He kept making

adjustments, some large, some small, analyzing my gait. Straight steps. Turn around. Up and down. We hadn't done backwards, but I had to think that was coming. He was really honing in on all the little things. And with each new maneuver that I got right, he gave me loads of positive feedback.

"I want the critical feedback too," I reminded him. "This is how I'll get better."

Tom, I was happy to learn, was willing to offer plenty of that.

With his guidance, positive and negative, and my obsessiveness plus Tuesday's love, I continued to make progress. I was determined to be the fastest-learning walker in the history of above-the-knee amputees. Every second I wasn't on the leg, I felt like I should be. Some days, I pushed myself till my stump was tender, my thigh was raw, and my back ached. Eventually, I learned to pace myself a little. But I was right to believe that learning to walk was worth the effort and not a job for slackers. Fearlessness—or was it stubbornness?—was a huge advantage.

There was something else I noticed as I continued working with Tom at the clinic and taking short walks around the hotel lobby. I was starting to feel some limb sensation. Not phantom limb sensation. The real thing. As if that Ottobock leg was actually becoming more a part of me.

This was something I wasn't sure I would ever feel again, and now I knew I would never get tired of it. It felt like I was getting back a piece of myself down there, and that was even better than just getting back on my feet.

Tom's valuable instruction kept coming. "Allow your right hip to extend outward. Make sure your arms swing naturally as you walk so your entire movement flows." I appreciated the advice and critiquing, and I was walking pretty well, I thought. Upright. With confidence in the leg. Without too many missteps. Together, we worked hard. And the progress was right there to see.

Things you take for granted with a natural leg are a lot less intuitive with a manufactured one. Oxygen use is one. It's harder to walk on a prosthesis. It takes more effort. It requires more energy—researchers say an above-the-knee amputee uses a full 80 percent more than a normal two-legged person walking.

Another thing I never noticed so clearly before: Sidewalks are all uneven. Curb cuts aren't where they are supposed to be. Ramps aren't there when you need them. The leg gave me far more mobility than the wheelchair had. But it still wasn't a walk in the park, though, come to think of it, the ground in most parks isn't so level, either.

Suddenly, that hospital hallway seemed like a breeze, even with Tuesday occasionally two-stepping around my feet.

PART III

Paws Forward

CHAPTER 22

Older and Wiser

—————————=»«◉»«=—————————

I don't know where I am going, but I am on my way.
VOLTAIRE

"HOW OLD IS TUESDAY?"

People have been asking us that question for years. But as Tuesday got older and so did I, I noticed that the question seemed to come up more frequently. I was pretty sure it wasn't just idle curiosity.

"He's ten," I'd say, quickly adding, "going on three."

That was my way of joking about Tuesday's exuberant energy and the boyish, goofy side of his personality. Sometimes that ended the questioning, but often it did not.

"So what happens when Tuesday is too old to work?"

Oh. Yes. That.

Even though I tried to laugh it off, this is a big deal. A very big deal. That question, and whatever the answer, is important to me. It is important to Tuesday. It's important to all the people who meet Tuesday and read about him and learn from him.

Dogs don't live forever, just like people don't. Most of the time, dogs don't live as long as humans do. Most likely, I will outlive Tuesday, if you want to get real about it. That's never something I care to dwell on. But, yes, okay, those are the very real facts of human and canine life.

This whole complex subject of dogs' longevity has long been reduced to simplistic formulas. Ever since I was a boy, I've been hearing people talk about "dog years" and "human years." One dog year, as it's commonly known, is the equivalent of seven human years. You've likely heard this, too. So if your dog is five years old, he or she is supposed to be akin to a thirty-five-year-old human. Since many dogs live to be nine or ten or eleven or twelve years old and most humans live into their seventies or even their eighties, that rough formula makes a certain amount of sense.

But wait. The details, it turns out, are more complicated than the old seven-to-one equation. For one thing, different breeds have different longevities. Also, counting years isn't always the best way to judge a dog's comparative age. The fact is that canine aging doesn't happen at the same pace that human aging does. Think about it. Don't newborn puppies seem to age more quickly than the old formula would suggest? A one-year-old canine is probably more like a fourteen- or a fifteen-year-old human, not a seven-year-old. And then doggie aging tends to level off.

Then, we get to golden retrievers, Tuesday's breed. They can live to be fifteen or sixteen years old, though experts have been trying lately to figure out why the breed's average life span has declined in recent decades. Colorado's nonprofit, the Morris Animal Foundation, has undertaken a $25 million study to get to the bottom of this sad trend that may be a result of certain cancers. But it didn't take cancer scares or mathematical equations for me to focus on what I have always known. Chances are, I'll live a lot longer than Tuesday will.

I hate even thinking about this. *Damn mortality!*

I find it very difficult to imagine living without him. Partly, that's because of all he's done for me. Partly, it's because I just love him so much. I never know how to separate those two, so I don't really try. I just hate the thought of living without Tuesday. I have felt that way ever since I first met him. It's even stronger now. So I've blocked it from my mind, as much as possible, the fact that he wouldn't always be at my side. I've refused to dwell on it.

I'm not alone in feeling this way. It's about relationships. As I have long understood, it isn't enough to say that other owners *think* of their dog as a member of the family. That dog *is* a member of the family, and a vitally important one. You wouldn't say your son or your mother feels like a member of the family. Those people *are* your family, in every sense of what *family member* means. Tuesday is family and so much more. His role is enormous. He has been my guide, my confidence builder, my prosthetic, my assistant, my colleague, my brother, my friend—the roles of importance are never ending.

Saying all that does not make it any easier to address the questions people ask that begin with "what happens when..." But, of course, ignoring something doesn't make it go away. The fact is that Tuesday keeps getting older, and, at some point, he will be tired and need a break.

At some point, Tuesday will die.

There. I said it. I feel like I need a hug. Or even better, I need to give Tuesday a hug.

I came to see that this indulgence really wasn't fair to Tuesday or fair to me. I wasn't doing either of us any favors pretending he could live forever and be strong enough to work as my service dog. I had to quit ignoring this or repressing it or believing that Tuesday would be the first dog in the history of the world to be stuck eternally in time. The dog that lived forever.

He is amazing, but I don't think even he can achieve that.

I've counted, and the numbers move in only one direction. Up.

Tuesday probably had another four or five or six years of life ahead of him. None of this was for certain, of course. But a fourteen-year-old golden retriever is a senior golden retriever. Even a twelve-year-old is up there. And no one could say how Tuesday's service dog abilities might decline with age. Most service dogs begin to lose a little something by the time they are ten or twelve, sometimes earlier than that. When Tuesday turned ten, I could happily see he was still energetic, dexterous, focused, and spry. But he wasn't five anymore, and he wasn't SuperDog—well, okay, maybe he was SuperDog, but you get my point. He's not like the family dog who, after he's too old and tired to fetch the Frisbee, can just hang out on the porch and watch butterflies. Tuesday's responsibilities have always been demanding. We work long hours. We travel extensively. He needs quick reactions and sharp senses. He's done it all with a ridiculously cheery disposition and boundless energy. At some point, wasn't all of that bound to fade?

More recently, I'd been noticing the questions have gotten even more direct.

"How many more years does Tuesday have in him?"

"What will you do when Tuesday gets too old to work?"

"Will you get another dog?"

Some of this got me angry. Oh, I know, the questions were probably well intentioned. But, would you ask a middle-aged woman, "What will you do when your husband dies? Will you get another husband? Will he be similar to your first one? Have you started looking around?" On some level, the questions about Tuesday are legitimate. But I'm sorry, there's something a little awful about these questions. Disturbing. Disquieting. What was I supposed to say?

———◦———

The terrible truth was that these people did have a point.

Tuesday was getting older. Indeed, he wouldn't live forever.

Eventually, painful as it was to contemplate, he was going to get too old to keep working as he had. At some point, he was going to leave us. We had to figure how we would bring another service dog into our tight two-man pack. But before I did anything remotely like that, I had to discuss all of it with Tuesday. I don't believe in big secrets, especially from him. I knew I could only proceed in a way that made Tuesday comfortable. I needed Tuesday's blessing.

We had to talk about this.

There was no getting around it. But when? Where? How? It wasn't a subject I wanted to address casually, just letting it pop up as we were walking to the supermarket or sitting by the hotel pool. I had to find the right moment. I didn't know how I'd handle the moment. Honestly, I had no idea how he was going to respond.

So I found a quiet moment, while the two of us were sitting on the bed. We didn't have to be anywhere. No one was showing up. We had all the time we needed. I tried to feel him out.

"Are you getting tired, Toopy?" I asked him.

He looked up at me, knowing from my tone that this was more than idle chatter. But what was I getting at?

"We work so hard together," I began. I knew he could hear the sincerity in my voice. "We start early and we go all day. Sometimes, we barely stop to eat. Often, we work until way after dark."

He gave me one of his there-must-be-a-point-in-there-somewhere looks.

"I ask so much of you," I continued. "You're not a puppy anymore. I know I'm not young either. But you're ten years old now...."

Yes, I was stalling, and Tuesday knew it.

Finally, I just blurted it out.

"I think it's time for us to transition with another service dog."

That might have been the hardest sentence I have ever said to Tuesday.

"They call this a successor dog," I explained. "Your successor. I'm not exactly sure when this will happen. The new dog isn't even born yet. You're gonna still be my service dog for another year or two."

It was all so emotional. Very.

Tuesday didn't look angry or hurt or even sad, which relieved me. I certainly didn't want him to feel like I was laying him off or downsizing or excessing him or any of the other terrible phrases that are used in business today when a person is told a job is being snatched away. I wanted this to be different. I wanted it to be a natural progression, a mutual process and timed right. And right at the top of my many considerations, I wanted to make the transition when Tuesday was ready to make it, too.

"We'll have to find a new puppy," I said to him, "and that's a very exciting thing. I'll need your help with a lot of this. Together, you and I will welcome the new puppy with love into our family. You'll help to teach the puppy everything and show him how to be my service dog. Do you think you can do that? I know you can. We'll have to show him what he needs to know—or show her. I think maybe we should get a girl."

Tuesday perked up when I said "a girl." "What do you think about that, Tuesday?" I asked. "Maybe we should get a girl this time. You and I could probably use a little female presence around here. What do you say? Bring a girl into our all-male pack?"

Tuesday's smile said, "I like that."

Since Tuesday was fixed, my successor dog could not be his direct offspring. Tuesday will never have the experience of being a father. But this talk of a new pup in our lives seemed to bring out something paternal in Tuesday. He'd been babying me for years, but he'd never had the experience of raising a little Tuesday. He has such strong leadership instincts. I knew this could be special and exciting for him.

"This is sounding better all the time, isn't it, Toops? And you'll still have lots to do around here."

I think Tuesday was getting excited. He looked ready to run right off to the trainer and bring home his brand-new housemate. But I explained to him that none of this could possibly happen for a while.

"First, the new puppy has to be born," I told him. "Service dog training could easily take a year or two. Then, there will be that period of transition, where the puppy will still have to learn what to do. We will get to know this new puppy. For a long time, you will still be my service dog. Our pack is just going to grow by one."

Even though Tuesday couldn't be the biological dad, my thought was that the new puppy should still come from Tuesday's bloodline. Maybe, I hoped, she could be a niece or a grand-niece or a blood relation of some other kind. I loved the idea of having a dog that was related to Tuesday, trained in part by Tuesday, and welcomed by Tuesday into our lives. The perfect successor dog, just like Tuesday, but younger.

"We will work together," I told Tuesday. "You'll teach her things. The new puppy will get to know me and get to know you, and we will get to know her. You're a very good teacher, Tuesday. You have those strong pack instincts and we're adding a new member. I've learned so much from you. I know you will take to this new role beautifully."

That was certainly true.

But still, I needed to explain the meaning of *successor dog*. It didn't mean Tuesday had failed. Or stopped giving his all. Or that I loved him any less. Or that I'd ever want to live without him.

"Over time, the new puppy will gradually take over as my service dog," I told him. "And as you get older, you'll do as much as you feel like doing. There are all kinds of things you can do. We'll keep traveling, helping veterans and other people. You'll keep educating adults and children about the wonders of service dogs. I know how much you like meeting new people. There are thousands of new people we will meet. You could do more therapy dog–type work, helping people with their big life challenges and showing them how much you love them and how important animals are. You're gonna love this. I promise you."

Maybe I was worried too much about this. As much as I had dreaded addressing the subject, he seemed to take it perfectly well. I'm not sure he understood exactly how everything would happen. Truth be told, neither did I. But he knows I love him, and he loves me. Together, I had no doubt, we would figure out how to make all of this happen.

The baton was going to be passed forward, from Tuesday to one of his kin. Transitions like this one have been occurring since the very beginning of time. I guess dogs don't need humans to explain nature to them.

———◆———

With that issue finally out in the open, I was able to concentrate again on Tuesday, the best service dog anyone has ever had. All of this transitioning could easily take another year and a half. Tuesday and I will continue to work until he lets me know that he needs to rest. Then, I'm thinking we might get an RV, and we'll drive around, meeting veterans, pursuing our advocacy and education campaigns, and doing our live events—Tuesday, the puppy, and me.

Tuesday will work less. That's not to say he will be retired. Just as with working people, working dogs don't usually want to stop their work abruptly. Their work is part of who they are and what they live for. We've all seen it. People who retire, those who go from working a full-time job to doing nothing at all, they quickly get miserable. They get depressed. They feel useless or worthless and worry they have nothing to live for, so they die. That's no good for humans, and it's no good for dogs. Gradual transition is better for everyone.

Tuesday will segue from being my service dog to being more of a therapy dog. He'll continue bringing joy to adults and children, smiles to people's faces until one day, hopefully far off into the future, he reaches the place that animal lovers call the Rainbow Bridge.

Do you know about the Rainbow Bridge?

According to a story that has brought great comfort to many when they need it most, that's where our animals go after their time on earth ends.

No one knows for sure who wrote the story. But it's been translated into many languages and circulated by animal lovers for three or four decades now. The way it's told, there is a multicolored bridge "this side of Heaven" and a green meadow beside it. When a beloved animal dies, he or she goes to this place.

According to the story, the dog or cat or other animal has a heavenly place to run and play and hang out all day with other animals, enjoying abundant food and water and the warmth of spring sunshine. "All the animals who had been ill and old are restored to health and vigor. Those who were hurt or maimed are made whole and strong again, just as we remember them in our dreams of days and times gone by. The animals are happy and content."

The only thing missing? A certain, loving "special person," who is still alive on earth.

Then one fine day, the animal "stops and looks into the distance. His bright eyes are intent. His eager body quivers. Suddenly, he begins to run from the group, flying over the green grass, his legs carrying him faster and faster."

His special human has arrived.

The two of them do not waste a second. They jump into each other's arms and embrace. They kiss each other's faces. They gaze with deep affection into each other's misty eyes. Then, side by side, they cross the Rainbow Bridge into heaven, "clinging together in joyous reunion, never to be parted again."

That—or something like it—will happen for Tuesday and me. I have always believed in some kind of afterlife that includes all the creatures we love. I couldn't be happy without him, and I am very sure he couldn't be happy without me. And now I know that the new puppy will someday be with us, too. Whatever else happens to me in the years to come, I couldn't imagine spending eternity without the both of them.

CHAPTER 23

Successor Dog

The only thing I know that truly heals people is unconditional love.
ELISABETH KÜBLER-ROSS

"YOUR SUCCESSOR DOG WILL BE BORN THIS SUMMER," LU PICARD SAID
to me. "That dog will take two years to train. In your case, you'll be
involved in everything, as much as you want to. And, you need to
start thinking about a name."

Lu has a thick New York accent and a gruff exterior. She oozes
moxie. And yet she has a gentle spirit and a truly noble heart. She is a
tough trainer—and not only of dogs. Her technique always involves
training humans too.

She lives on a farm in Connecticut, and training service dogs is
far more than a job for her. Lu was working in the business world
when her father suffered a stroke. She could see how much he hated
being dependent on her. At first, she wasn't exactly sure what to do
about that. But she looked at the family dog and thought to herself, "He's smart. He loves us. Maybe he can pitch in." She got busy
working on his skills. She started with little things that turned out to
be not-so-little. She taught the dog to help her dad get up from his
chair and also to retrieve little items like his glasses, the TV remote,

or his favorite magazine. Pretty soon, Lu noticed her dad seemed more active and less depressed. For some reason, her proud father was more comfortable accepting assistance from a dog than from any of his other family members. Lu was astonished at the difference the dog could make. She knew already she had to get more involved in the service dog–training world.

She quit her full-time job to start ECAD, which originally stood for East Coast Assistance Dogs. She and her husband, Dale, bought land in Connecticut to develop a training site. Dale gave up his own business to work full time for ECAD. They built kennels and an office suite, and redesigned the house where Lu, Dale, and their two daughters live. It became a full life mission for the family, breeding and training these amazing animals. Over the next two decades, ECAD's growing staff and dedicated volunteers trained hundreds of service dogs and placed them in the homes of disabled clients all across the United States and beyond.

Training each dog takes a tremendous amount of time and patience. It also takes a lot of help. Lu has perfected her methods over the years, though she is always looking for new ways to do an even better job. Her dogs are some of the most highly educated animals anywhere. They have to be. Their owners depend on them.

ECAD dogs are carefully bred and all go through an intensive two-year education program. Each dog has to master a full curriculum of communication and assistance skills. Nurturing skills are just as high a priority. The wet-nose nuzzle. The extended paw. The wagging tail. Lu's dogs must learn all of that. These are dogs with extraordinary talents and proven temperaments.

Over the years, the ECAD mission keeps expanding. Lu gets new ideas, and clients demand more. A program called Canine Magic provides service dogs to children with autism. Project HEAL focuses on the needs of military veterans living with physical disabilities, PTSD, and traumatic brain injuries. An annual summer camp teaches children the responsibilities of being dog owners by working with assistance dogs in training. To reflect this broader mission and constant activity, Lu gave a new meaning to the ECAD acronym, Educated Canines Assisting with Disabilities. Today, it stands for Educating Canines Assisting with Disabilities. But those are just words. From Lu's father's living room to the dogs being trained today, ECAD's central mission remains exactly the same: educating and delivering highly trained service dogs into the hands of people with disabilities, helping them to lead more independent and fulfilling lives.

Tuesday, a proud ECAD graduate, has certainly done that for me.

———◦◉◦———

As Tuesday and I travel across all of God's beautiful creation, we have been able to meet—this is no exaggeration—thousands of dog trainers along the way, many of whom have made a specialty of working with service dogs. Some have fancy long strings of letters after their names, meaning they've been certified as trainers, animal behaviorists, or veterinary consultants. But those letters don't begin to describe the love and dedication they bring to the field. With few exceptions, they are the best sorts of people, making the world a better place one paw at a time. Our new friends include some of the best dog trainers in the world. But even after meeting so many committed and hardworking trainers, there's one thing I know: Lu is a real gem, among the very best of them. I know that sounds partial, but it is the truth.

So as soon as I started thinking about my next-generation service dog, it wasn't a hard decision to go back to Lu. That's not to say I didn't consider alternatives or reach out to old friends for advice. One person I spoke with was Dr. Bonita "Bonnie" Bergin, a legendary trainer who invented the modern concept of the service dog. A former special education teacher, Bonnie has made a huge impact professionalizing the dog-training world—lifting standards, creating international associations, and building a vibrant network of canine researchers around the globe. Her accredited Bergin University of Canine Studies in Rohnert Park, California, awards associate's, bachelor's, and master's degrees in dog studies, and she is always on the cutting-edge of the latest developments in the field. Bonnie really is the trainers' trainer. Among her students was Lu.

Bonnie had some good advice for me.

"You'll need a uniquely trained dog, even by service-dog standards, with all of the travel and work you do," she said.

It's not that I needed confirmation of what I already knew, but after we spoke I was even more positive. She made me fully comfortable with the idea of returning to Lu.

———⋙⟐⋘———

Lu explained the basics to me.

One of her golden retriever breeder dogs, Daisy, would be having a litter fathered by Patriot, one of Lu's stud dogs. "That will be in late June or early July," she said. "Of course, we don't know how many puppies she will have or whether all of them will make suitable service dogs. But I have a very good feeling about Daisy."

Daisy is in Tuesday's bloodline. The relationships are a little complicated, but the best way to think of it, Lu said, is that she is one of Tuesday's cousins. I would learn a lot about all this in the weeks and months to come. But the family ties gave me confidence. It made me feel like I knew these puppies already. I knew where they came from. "If all goes well," Lu said, "one of the puppies in that litter will become your next service dog."

But Lu was already thinking about picking the right dog for me.

"From zero to eight weeks, they'll all be with me and the nursery team," Lu said. "I will be looking for one that is temperamentally right for you. I'll be sure to send that one into New York City to be with a family there." Lu has developed a 1-to-10 scale to measure how intensely the animal is affected by his or her surroundings. "I will be looking for one that is medium line," she said. "Hopefully, I've got a girl who's, like, a five on that scale so she's not too environmentally aware but she's not environmentally afraid." Then, as was the case with Tuesday, the young trainee pup will go through Lu's extensive ECAD training program to become a world-class service dog. Over the course of two years, the future service dog will complete several distinct phases of beginning, intermediate, and advanced training, each designed to hone specific abilities and instincts. Much of the basic training will be conducted by volunteer inmates at a state prison in Connecticut. Other exercises will be handled by loving families who will take the trainees into real-world environments—crowded stores, busy street corners, popular restaurants, sporting events, local parks, and anywhere else a working service dog might need to go. Every day will include complex task training and human socialization. Only then will Lu know, with my input, which of Daisy's puppies—if any—will be the right one for me. But I was already trying to think of a name.

I had nothing to do with naming Tuesday. When he was born on September 10, 2006, he was one of four in a litter of precious purebred golden retriever pups. If you look up the date, you'll see it wasn't even a Tuesday. It was a Sunday.

It's an unusual name. In fact, the only famous person I've heard of with the name was actress Tuesday Weld. As far as I know, she never starred in any movies about dogs, and she was often referred to by reviewers as a film sex kitten, so I don't think that was where the name came from. But it seems everyone wants to know:

Why Tuesday?

Over the years, when the question has come up, people have offered a bunch of different possible explanations: You met on a Tuesday. The name was inspired by the Rolling Stones' song, "Ruby Tuesday." The

9/11 terror attacks happened on a Tuesday. The truth is that I don't know why Tuesday was named Tuesday or even exactly who picked the name.

I do know that the name came from one of Lu's donors, who also named two of Tuesday's littermates Linus and Blue. I don't know why he or she picked it. Perhaps, the donor really was a hardcore Rolling Stones fan. Or not. Tuesday was two years old when I met him. He'd been living with the name quite happily since he was born. By that point, the name and the animal seemed inseparable to me and him. Why change it? I wouldn't want someone changing *my* name!

Sometimes, as we have traveled around, people think the name is goofy. Who ever heard of a dog being named for a day of the week? And, a Tuesday no less! There are definitely a lot more dogs named Bailey, Max, Charlie, Sophie, Buddy, and pretty much anything else. Tuesday and I can hardly do a public event where someone doesn't come up to us and say, "Where's Wednesday?"

They always think that's hilarious. Tuesday and I just groan.

So, as Lu and I first began talking about a successor dog, I already knew the new dog wasn't going to be named Wednesday. Or Thursday. Or any day of the week.

This wasn't a decision to be made lightly. I knew that from the start. A lot of different elements can go into naming a dog. The dog's appearance. The dog's personality. The story of how you met the dog. The dog's pedigree and background. Some of these things you may not know when it comes time to pick a name, especially if he or she is a rescue. And, as we already knew, sometimes a dog comes already named by someone else.

To complicate matters a little more this time, Tuesday is a famous dog. People all around the world know who Tuesday is. Hundreds of thousands of people have met him and many have told me they've even named their own new pups Tuesday. While our new pup won't be Tuesday's biological son or daughter, he or she will be Tuesday's successor—and therefore forever intertwined with Tuesday in people's minds. Compared and contrasted. Associated always. Truly connected for life.

I guess that's why the successors to famous animals sometimes just inherit the first dog's name.

The German shepherd Rin Tin Tin was an international film star after being rescued from the battlefield in World War I. The dog was so popular, Hollywood chieftains couldn't afford to stop making *Rin Tin Tin* films, and neither could the military. If Hollywood had tried, the U.S. Army might well have sent tanks up Sunset Boulevard. That's how valuable a recruiting tool Rin Tin Tin was. After the original dog died in 1932, the name was given to several related German shepherds featured in movies, on the radio, and then on TV. Rin Tin Tin Jr. had his moment, though he was not nearly as renowned as his father. Rin Tin Tin III, said to be Rin Tin Tin's grandson, but probably only distantly related, appeared in a film with child actor Robert Blake in 1947 and helped promote the military use of dogs during World War II. There was a IV and V and the Rin Tin Tins never really stopped.

Something similar happened with Lassie.

Several collies named Lassie appeared on radio, in the movies, and on TV. That's what often happens, I guess, when a canine's celebrity outlives the actual dog. *Lassie Come Home,* the first movie, hit theaters in 1943, starring a dog whose real name was Pal. All the Lassies back then were male descendants of Pal, who played a female dog. On-screen, it was Lassie and Timmy, but offscreen they answered to names like Spook, The Old Man, and Howard. Since then, there seems to be no end to dogs named Lassie. *Pet Vet* hit TV in 2007. The animated *New Adventures of Lassie*, featuring Lassie Parker, started in 2014. Who knows? There could be twenty more Lassies to come.

But I was not going to do that with Tuesday.

I was adamant from the minute I started thinking about this. I didn't care how famous Tuesday was, there would be only one.

Somehow, to me, repeating the name seemed disrespectful and confusing and just not right. I knew I didn't like senior, junior, and the third. It was obvious that there could only be one Tuesday. He's one of a kind. My love for him is one of a kind. Our friendship is one of a kind. Whatever the charms and talents of the new dog, each unique animal deserves its own identity.

I had to think of something different. Special. Perfect. In my mind, I did sometimes think of the new dog as Puppy. But he or she would grow up some day, and that didn't seem like a lifelong name or very dignified. An intelligent adult service dog shouldn't answer to "here, Puppy…heel, Puppy…let's go for ice cream, Puppy." I wouldn't want to be called Baby, even though I was a baby once— and a cute one, my mother always told me. I'd have to think of something right.

Initially, even contemplating a name for Tuesday's successor was painful. I've loved Tuesday more than anything in my life. What name—or being—could possible succeed Tuesday? So I told myself I would take my time. I wouldn't rush it. The new puppy wasn't showing up tomorrow.

Then, it hit me.

Promise.

We would call the new puppy Promise.

That name was perfect. It's forward-looking. It's optimistic. It's easy to say. It makes you smile. It's something everyone can understand and remember. It could work with either a girl or a boy.

Promise really was the essence of this new service dog, a perfect jumping-off point for what I knew would be a whole lot of love and a million adventures ahead.

The promise of love.

The promise of service.

The promise to be a canine ambassador everywhere.

The promise to learn from Tuesday and to teach us as well—and to carry on this amazing mission he has been on.

The promise to spread the word about service dogs, veterans, mental health, and living with disabilities, the visible and invisible kind.

And all the promises that go the other way—from Tuesday and me to Promise: That we will love, support, protect, and entertain this new member of our family with hugs and furry kisses like you wouldn't believe.

Yes, we would call the new puppy Promise.

I started saying the name, just to hear how it sounded.

"Good girl, Promise. Good girl."

"Look at you, my little *Promesa*." In Spanish, promise is *promesa*, ascribed to the female gender and is lovely to the ear. Promise and *promesa* originate from the Latin language dating back thousands of years.

I thought it sounded very Promise-ing.

It just seemed so far away. But I knew the day would come so quickly and would soon feel like tomorrow: Tuesday, Promise, and me.

But even as I try to write this, my eyes well up at the notion that Tuesday's time will eventually come and he will leave us. I hope that's not for a very, very long time. When it happens, it will feel like a piece of my heart has been ripped out and handed to me. You're never supposed to see your heart. It's in your chest. Being handed your own heart is a thoroughly unnatural experience, so vulnerable. But it will be real, and nothing in the world can change it.

Have you ever loved someone so much that you cannot fathom life without him or her? If you are reading my words, I suspect you are that kind of person, one who has loved and been loved unconditionally. Unabashedly. Unwaveringly. We all want that, and we all want to pass it on.

Though I consider myself to be a spiritual person and someone who prays and believes, I think I can only truly say that I've spoken with God a few times.

That's not because I haven't wanted or tried. Rather, it's because I could not see or listen beyond myself. Without question, it is a flaw. One that perhaps many of us possess. Still, it is powerful. And I am working on it.

Perhaps I will get there, to a new understanding and acceptance, before Tuesday and Promise and I start our own unique journey together.

What I knew for certain was I could hardly wait to meet this new little bundle of love.

CHAPTER 24

Special Delivery

If you are what you should be, you will set the whole world ablaze!
ST. CATHERINE OF SIENA

THE TEXT MESSAGE FROM LU CAME RIGHT ON TIME, EXACTLY SIXTY-TWO days after Daisy and Patriot got to spend some quality time together at Gracie-the-dog-breeder's house in Connecticut.

"Daisy's delivering," Lu's message said.

Lu had told me to expect Daisy's litter sixty to sixty-three days into her pregnancy. And yes, Tuesday and I had been ticking off the days. In that litter, I hoped, would be Tuesday's protégé and successor, my next service dog. To call this *major* would be a major understatement, given how much Tuesday has meant to me.

Hopes were super-high all around. Lu was excited. So was Dale, her husband, and PJ, their grandson. So was Gracie, who had been the first to suggest the Daisy–Patriot match and promised to check in frequently when the blessed day finally arrived. But no one was more excited than Tuesday and me. We both appreciated how much one puppy from this new litter could change our lives.

As these puppies were born, so too would our future be.

This was to be Daisy's first litter. She'd been medically checked and declared fully ready to mate. Lu needs a steady stream of potential service dogs, and the Daisy–Patriot pairing had all the earmarks of potential success. "Both of them have excellent bloodlines," Lu told me back in April as she and Gracie were making plans for the breeding rendezvous. "They're both strong and smart and healthy." Though this would be Daisy's first go-round as parent; Patriot had been bred three and a half months earlier with Gucci, another of Lu's golden retrievers. Six weeks in, the results of that coupling looked quite promising, everyone agreed. And besides all that, Lu reminded me of something else I already knew: "Daisy's related to Tuesday."

That last point, not surprisingly, was the one I found most persuasive, other than the fact that I fully trusted Lu. She's a phenomenal trainer who understands the importance of starting with exceptional dogs then getting the best out of them with the most rigorous training she can dream up. If Lu said, "Daisy and Patriot," then Daisy and Patriot it would be.

As many times as Lu had been through this, she had the birthing routine down cold. A big part of this, I would learn, involved not flipping out even when crises occur along the way. When the big day arrived, Dale shoved aside some of the furniture in the breakfast room, which was right off the kitchen of their two-story colonial house. He and PJ dragged in a large, square "whelping box," four-feet-by-four-feet, designed to protect the puppies during the delivery, which could take hours or days, and in the period immediately afterward. No one knew yet how many puppies there could be, but it might be six or eight or ten or more, and all of them would need to stay comfortable and safe. The litter could also be smaller. But looking at Daisy's belly, Lu felt confident the puppy total was more than two or three.

The box had three-inch rails around three of the sides, creating a little hideaway where the first puppies out could huddle when their mom decided to press her back against the box wall while giving birth. "We don't want anyone getting crushed or smothered," Lu explained. A smaller rail across the front would keep mom and babies from wandering around the rest of Dale and Lu's house.

There was a thin pad on the box floor. "If I put a thick comforter down," Lu explained, "the mom might not feel the puppies underneath her. The thin pad will absorb what it has to and be a whole lot safer for everyone." I knew enough about human births to imagine that delivering this many puppies could not possibly be a tidy affair. "Of course, we'll have to change that pad three or four times a day."

Of course.

Despite her no-nonsense attitude about dog training, Lu, I discovered, also has an artistic side. She had decorated the walls of the whelping box with brightly striped nursery cloth with drawings of little animals. "I do that for my own pleasure," she told me. "I'm sure it doesn't matter one way or the other to the dogs."

With the box in place and fully prepared, Lu was ready to go just as soon as Daisy was.

I wasn't there for the birth, which started just before dinnertime on June 27 and went past dawn the next morning. But I pressed Lu for every last detail, so I kind of felt like I was there.

The first puppy popped out at 5 P.M., a precious, gurgling male with squinty eyes, the tiniest wisps of light-brown hair, and a body no bigger than Lu's right hand. He greeted the world in what looked like a wobbly water balloon, really a thin membrane of placenta. The sack burst immediately, and the fluid leaked all over the pad in the whelping box.

First-time mom Daisy looked utterly stunned, as if she had no idea on earth what she had just done. Did she think she was pooping? Was she just feeling sick? Lu leaned toward the first theory, but who knows? Never having given birth before, Daisy certainly seemed to be having trouble grasping the basic concept of what was going on. She had a troubled look on her face that seemed to say, "Oh, my God, I'm in trouble now. I just messed up the house."

Lu and Dale immediately launched their happy voices, hoping to reassure the startled new mother.

"Oh, look what you made!" Lu declared. "So beautiful!"

"You are such a good girl!" Dale said. "Yes, yes, yes."

Even PJ joined in. "Look at the beautiful puppy!" he said.

It's pretty much impossible not to be joyful when witnessing a birth.

All that delight and encouragement worked. The affirmations seemed to ease Daisy's concerns. She didn't yelp at all—just a little whimper and then a small coo as she glanced at her firstborn and then quickly turned her head away. Normally, dogs don't make much noise while they are giving birth, something they've learned from their ancient ancestors. It's biological. It's for self-protection. A delivering animal who makes a racket in the wild is only calling attention to herself at a highly vulnerable time. She'd be easy prey and so would her offspring.

Lu watched and waited for Daisy to lick the newborn clean. But Daisy didn't seem to know about that important step in the canine birth process. The little puppy was lying there right on the whelping pad, dripping with fluid and birth. Daisy just stared. After a couple of minutes of encouragement and waiting, Lu took a soft rag and wiped off the remaining birthing fluid. She watched as the puppy stretched his tiny legs and blinked hard, getting used to the unfamiliar light.

Usually, Lu tries not to touch the puppies too much in the first three or four days. Their nerve endings are just settling down, and it's good for them to get used to connecting with their mother. That's part of the bonding process. But Lu couldn't leave the puppy dripping, and there were important things to do.

The first puppy looked healthy. His breathing was strong and steady. As Daisy instinctively concentrated on the birth of her next puppies, Lu got to work. The puppy's weight was good, one pound, one ounce on Lu's kitchen scale. His color was right, about halfway between medium gold and light brown. Lu wrapped a thin, red collar around the puppy's tiny neck so she and everyone else would be able to tell this one apart from all the others that would be coming next. She had a bagful of collars in other bright colors—yellow, green, blue, orange, pink, and so on—enough for however many puppies the litter might comprise. As she placed the baby back in the box, Daisy looked like she was about to deliver puppy number two.

The fun had only begun. Daisy's next two offspring, a male and female, arrived at fifteen-minute intervals. Lu gave the boy a blue collar. The girl got pink. Then, after a short break another boy eased out. He got a black collar. One by one, the mother and her babies huddled together in the whelping box—finding warmth, getting comfort, honoring their ancestral traditions as pack animals, not sure where else to go. There are few sights more precious than that, and the heap would soon get larger.

There was a two-hour break between numbers four and five and a three-hour break between five and six, though number seven came twenty minutes after that. The puppies all looked healthy. They all weighed within an ounce or so of one pound. Everything seemed right on target—except for Daisy's initial clumsiness as a mom. As the puppies piled together in the whelping box, Lu was growing concerned about Daisy—what was it? Inexperience? Confusion? Standoffishness? "She's not licking her babies," Lu said to Dale.

Licking is important. It's instinctive for most delivering animals. Besides cleaning the offspring, that close physical contact also stimulates the newborns to pee and poop. For the first few days, their muscles aren't sufficiently developed to get things moving inside on their own. The muscles need that extra stimulation. Otherwise, things start backing up. Even in these earliest hours, Lu was noticing that the whelping pad didn't need changing as often as she expected, and that was not a good sign.

Lu tried to show Daisy how to lick, demonstrating the action with her own tongue on her finger. Daisy seemed to catch on, but only a little and only temporarily. Daisy licked one of the puppies, then she stopped. She wasn't much of a nurser, either. She would nurse a puppy for a few minutes, then she would stop. Lu was happy when Gracie arrived at 2 A.M. to have a look.

The women agreed that this was not a crisis yet, but that they should pay close attention. Even in the midst of birthing a litter, this was not usual. Maybe a little more human intervention would help.

By then, two more puppies had arrived, the final two, for a total of nine: six boys and three girls. And despite Daisy's early adjustment issues, everyone really was looking good. The heap was now a full-fledged pile, and there was constant noise and movement inside the whelping box. Squeaking. Tumbling over each other. Purring and moaning and just incredible-looking cuteness. With Daisy lying down beside them, the ten of them really did look like a family. Or was it more of a football team all diving after a fumble? The ball had to be in there somewhere!

It had been a very long night. Everyone was excited but tired. Every two hours, Lu and Dale—with additional help from PJ and Gracie—gave each of the puppies a thorough ten-minute massage. It wasn't exactly the equivalent of being licked by mama, but it did the trick of stimulating the little ones' nerve endings to get things moving inside. With nine puppies at ten minutes each, this took a while. It didn't leave much rest between the cycles. The humans took turns on massage duty and relieving each other for short naps. And slowly, even Daisy seemed to catch on. Her nursing picked up, and so did her licking. She seemed to finally be grasping that something very big had just occurred and she had a major role to play. Young, inexperienced Daisy, it seemed, was finally grasping the idea that she was a mom.

Things were looking up for almost everyone, human and canine, as the first twenty-four-hour cycle was completed and the second began. Then came the really tough news.

Lu had been keeping a special eye on one of the puppies, a female who had an orange collar. She *looked* fine—good weight, decent color, nice-enough coat. But the inside of her mouth, Lu noticed, felt a little chilly. In the whelping box scrum, she didn't seem quite as active as some of the others. Lu made a point of taking some extra time with Orange Girl, cuddling her little body, checking her more frequently and giving her some extra belly rubs.

By 6 P.M., Orange Girl seemed more, not less, lethargic. She still didn't feel warm enough. At 7:00, Lu was happy to see her lying on her mother's belly. That would be good for both of them. But the puppy wasn't nursing—just lying there. Lu checked on the litter at 9 P.M. and again at 10. Orange Girl was struggling. Everyone else was fine. That's where things stood when Lu, who had hardly slept in thirty-six hours, finally went in for a post-midnight nap. Gracie said she'd keep a special eye on Orange Girl.

Gracie woke Lu at 3 A.M.

"She isn't doing well," Gracie said.

Lu got up immediately.

By that point, the puppy was hardly breathing. She seemed to be fading in and out of consciousness. She definitely wasn't thriving like a second-day puppy should.

At 4:30 A.M., Orange Girl died in Lu's loving hands, leaving her mother Daisy, her father Patriot, and eight brothers and sisters behind. She just didn't have the strength to keep going.

This wasn't the first time such a thing had happened. Lu had been through it before. But it never gets easier seeing a beautiful creature not make it. "Poor Orange Girl," she told Dale. "She was just a little baby. She was born and lived for less than two days."

Lu couldn't help asking herself if there was something else she or anyone could have done, even though she knew the answer was no. Not all newborn puppies are meant to live. Darwin, Mother Nature, God—explain it however you want to. Lu didn't have the answers. She just understood it's the way things are.

"I don't like it," she reminded herself. "But we can't always prevent it, no matter what we do. This is nature's way—or God's way—of protecting the species and helping to keep the breed strong."

If a puppy is going to fade like that, it usually happens in the first ten days. But not always. One time, about four years earlier, one of Lu's newborns lived for four weeks and then succumbed. That puppy had been the smallest of the litter. She never made the transition to eating from a bowl. For four long weeks, Lu had been worried while also learning to love the small dog. That was much harder than this time. It threw Lu into a genuine funk.

"What are you doing?" Dale asked her. "You know better than that."

She did. Lu realized that she had to be strong. She'd done all she could, and there were so many other pups that needed her attention. She pulled herself together and learned a lesson from the experience.

With Orange Girl, she allowed herself a few minutes of genuine sadness. How could she not? Then she mostly let it go. She couldn't afford any more than that, she told herself. The others puppies needed her. Daisy did too. She had to move on.

In those early hours before the sun rose, Lu went to the whelping box and gently lifted each puppy. One by one, this strong, experienced dog trainer held each baby retriever to her heart and whispered her love. She pulled each one to her cheek and pressed soft kisses the way only a mother can. Finally, she leaned down and, being careful not to wake Daisy, kissed the mother to them all. Lu then went back to her bedroom and exchanged tired and tender smiles with Dale.

There were eight darling pups in the room just off the kitchen. One day, she knew, she'd be sharing their love with eight wonderful people whose lives these beauties would almost certainly change for good.

CHAPTER 25

Mad Dash

—— ⟨⟨◆⟩⟩ ——

*There are no limits. There are only plateaus, and you must
not stay there, you must go beyond them.*
BRUCE LEE

WHAT A MAD DASH THIS WAS GOING TO BE! FROM NEW YORK CITY TO
Rockville, Maryland, to Denver, Colorado, to Miami, Florida—all
in three days. But this was the life we'd chosen, I reminded myself.
And I couldn't see skipping any of it.

Daisy was recovering. Lu still felt sad about Orange Girl, but had
reached a place where she could accept what had happened as the
natural order of things. I still had no idea which of the other puppies would end up being my next service dog. One of the two girls,
I assumed, but maybe not. Maybe I'd been too quick in thinking it
should be a girl next time. Was gender really the best way to find
the right match for me? Tuesday had worked out beautifully, and he
was a boy. I didn't resolve any of that. I didn't have time to. Lu didn't
even know the personalities of the various puppies. Those personalities were only being formed. Plus, Tuesday and I had places to go and
people to meet, actually a whole lot of them.

We had been asked to join a panel hosted by the Substance Abuse and Mental Health Services Administration of the U.S. Department of Health and Human Services, the SAMHSA/HHS. Yes, the federal government is justifiably renowned for its alphabet soup of departments and agencies. But this was an important gathering. The topic was recent developments in the field of PTSD. I believe they considered Tuesday and me a recent development and the expertise we possessed on the subject to be of value.

The logistics were, admittedly, a little tight. We'd have to check out of our hotel in Brooklyn and take an Uber car across the East River to New York's Penn Station and then an Amtrak train to Washington, D.C., and then a taxi from Union Station to suburban Rockville. And that was just the first leg of our frantic cross-country jaunt. When we got done with the federal panel, we would grab a late-night flight to Denver, where we would see Bill-the-prosthetist at the Jewell Clinic, who was going to fit my final-final leg socket and a brand-new, high-tech, spring-loaded Ottobock foot. Then, as soon as we got the new gear fitted and attached, it was back East on an overnight flight to Miami, where we would finally catch our breath for a couple of weeks of hanging out with my parents. We hadn't seen them since before the operation. They sounded excited to see us. I know I was looking forward to spending time with them. Tuesday was too. Oh, I forgot one thing. As soon as we landed in Florida, we had agreed to read *Tuesday Takes Me There* to a group of children at Books & Books, a beloved local book store in Coral Gables.

To make all this work, we would have to leave New York in the middle of the night. Our train to Washington was scheduled to depart at 3:25 A.M. At that hour, navigating the usually snarled New York traffic would be a breeze. So around 2 A.M., I climbed into my prosthetic leg. Tuesday and I ordered the Uber from Brooklyn, which delivered us and all our stuff to the sidewalk outside Penn Station a little before 3:00.

I should probably describe what I mean by "all our stuff." My clothes and toiletries and Tuesday's toys and snacks were jammed into one suitcase and a medium-size duffel bag. I hoisted the suitcase into my wheelchair, which I used as a makeshift luggage cart. Then, I plopped the duffel bag on top of the suitcase. I had my folding crutches in one hand and Tuesday's leash in the other. Even though neither of my hands was empty, I still had to steer the wheelchair.

By my count, that was four assistive devises in all. The wheelchair. The crutches. The prosthetic leg. And Tuesday. Plus, all the normal stuff. No one could accuse us of traveling light.

The station was eerily empty at that time of the night. So when our train was called, we didn't bother hunting for an elevator to the platform. I figured we could ride the handy escalator down.

Holding Tuesday's leash, I collected all our stuff and gently pushed the wheelchair onto the moving escalator. That part was easy enough. Here is where the learning curve got really steep, as steep as a train station escalator, you might say: We were aboard the escalator. It was rolling down. Clearly, I should have given more thought to the physics of the situation. Even *some* thought. I didn't think about physics at all. But in an instant, the weight of the load shifted downward on the wheelchair. I felt a sharp tug on my hands and arms. I held on as hard as I could and tried to pull the wheelchair back toward me. The pressure got intense quickly. I lost my grip and then lost my balance. The wheelchair toppled forward, down the escalator. Almost simultaneously, I fell headfirst, Tuesday's leash still firmly in my right hand. He tried to hold both of us steady, but the weight of my tumble pulled him along with me.

The whole thing lasted maybe three seconds...but bouncing down those rolling metal steps felt like a thirty-minute ride. With my first gasp of panic, my mind slowed immediately. I was absorbing every sight and sound.

I credit all my years of military training and experience for this. A lot of people who get forged in the fire of combat, dealing with crazy situations day after day, become adept at slowing their minds in moments of crisis. It is a skill, as learnable as shooting a rifle or marching in single file. It's not a simple reflex. It isn't fight-or-flight. It's a matter of weighing relative options in real time, taking the time to strategize, making judgments as you go. Suddenly, it's not a car crash you're in the middle of. It's a ballet.

I could have been Mikhail Baryshnikov, riding an escalator with a dog.

The wheelchair seemed to flip in exaggerated slow motion. The suitcase toppled over. The duffel bag rolled forward, and the crutches went flying, both momentarily suspended in midair above the rolling escalator. I tumbled behind the chair, trying to protect my good leg, trying to protect my prosthesis, trying to protect Tuesday, and trying to protect myself—all at once.

I was also eager to avoid getting jammed at the bottom of the escalator, where the steps were folding down and sliding into the metal teeth of the landing. To me, that seemed like a special danger zone. In my mind's eye, I could see all our equipment landing there, then Tuesday and me colliding on top of all that, as the metal steps collapsed into the metal teeth of the landing.

Protect the prosthesis. Protect the good limb. You mess that up, and you'll spend months not getting around. Minimize the blows on the way to the plat-form. Avoid those metal teeth if at all possible. All those thoughts were rushing through my head. In the swirl of the fall, my mind screamed. I didn't hear Tuesday wail or whimper. I swear it was like watching a scene from a movie with highly detailed visuals—with the sound turned off.

Was it luck? Was it slow-mo strategy? Was it angels watching over us? I don't know. The bad news was that we fell with such momentum that there was no stopping in midair. The good news? That the escalator stopped before we hit the bottom and two guys came to our rescue just as Tuesday and I came tumbling down.

I'm not sure whether one of them pushed an emergency button or the escalator stopped on its own. But one man caught the duffel bag and then the runaway wheelchair. I let go of Tuesday's leash so he could jump clear of any obstructions. Meanwhile, the other man grabbed the suitcase and scrambled to get the crutches. Tuesday and I both got banged around a bit, but my new leg didn't fall off. Both men helped me to my feet.

I know how badly I could have injured myself. People break their necks—even die that way. I know how Tuesday could have been hurt. A fall like that with so much equipment on a moving escalator—it truly could have been disastrous.

In fact, from what I could tell as I began to take stock of the situation, I didn't break anything. As I hit the bottom, I guess I did get bitten on the ankle and calf of my good leg by those escalator teeth. My skin was nice and bloodied up. But I was on my two feet. Tuesday was on his four and wagged his tail in surprised excitement. Remarkably, considering the many moving parts here and all the unforgiving surfaces, I had a bleeding right shin, a scraped-up left elbow, and that was about it. Tuesday, thankfully, seemed entirely unscathed. I profusely thanked the two men who sprung up to help us. They acted like it was no big deal. They both petted Tuesday, and I told them again how grateful both of us were.

As quickly as the escalator incident had started, it was over. All of us boarded the train. We found our seats and got settled for a gentle predawn ride down the Eastern Seaboard, arriving in our nation's capital a little after dawn.

═══◦▩◦═══

We had to nix going to the PTSD conference. Despite our best intentions, the physical and emotional start to our trip took its toll. By the time Tuesday and I got to our hotel in Rockville, both of us were so exhausted we could barely stand, much less speak intelligently. So, we spent the rest of the day calming our nerves, resting our bodies, and getting the night of sleep we'd so dramatically been robbed of. After a quick hotel dinner, we headed to Dulles Airport for our late-night flight to Denver, where we were due at 9 A.M.

On the ride to Dulles, I felt angry with myself for missing the panel. We had promised to attend. I knew we had some useful insights to share. We had just wasted all that time and money and effort, rushing down from New York—for what? To sit in a hotel room and then fly out immediately to Denver? But the more I thought about it, the more I came to see that there was a life lesson in here that Tuesday and I needed to learn.

"Take it easy!"

It's true. Too many people have far too sedentary lives, adversely affecting their health and welfare. I never wanted to fall into that trap. I would rather stay on the offensive, moving around, getting things done, taking on bigger and bigger challenges. But even for creatures like Tuesday and me, there are limits. And maybe we'd just come face-to-face with one of ours.

I also understand that the only way you know your limits is to push them and find your breaking point. We had certainly done that. As a new amputee, I am not saying what we did was smart. Clearly, we should have found the elevator instead of taking our escalator-wheelchair joyride. But that said, I would rather have an accident like this one happen three months in instead of two years post-op.

But yes, we do need to be a bit more cautious. Both the escalator tumble and the dog attack helped to remind me of that. *Don't be stupid, Luis! You need to protect your body! You especially don't want to injure your good limbs! You need them, now more than ever! Be a little gentler on yourself, okay?*

Before I get off this, let me give myself some credit for the level of mobility we had achieved in the first twenty-four hours of our continental dash. Talk about planes, trains, and automobiles! We pushed our limit. We found it. And we responded accordingly. Given what we were up against, that was its own kind of success. If we'd gone to the conference, who knows whether we'd have made the flight to Denver or our appointment at the clinic. That in turn might have affected our red-eye to Miami and the children's event and seeing my parents—and, wow, who could say where and when those dominoes would stop falling!

———•◦•———

We didn't just show up in Denver. The appointment was carefully planned well in advance. A week before Tuesday and I left New York, Bill-the-prosthetist and I spoke on the phone. That way, he'd be ready when we got to the VA Eastern Colorado Health Care System's Jewell Clinic.

"How many socks?" he asked me.

"Two," I'd told him.

"Good to know," Bill said. "That's in the range of the shrinkage we would expect."

These weren't socks like the kind you buy in Walmart or the Gap. These were socks that could tell a story as well as a doctor's medical chart. A newly amputated limb is something of a moving target. Everyone expected my stump to shrink. The swelling goes down. The muscles atrophy. A prosthetic leg has to accommodate for that. Making those adjustments is a big part of what a good prosthetist does.

When Bill first fitted me back in April, my residual limb fit snugly inside the poly-fiber socket that Bill had made for me. But over time, the socket had gotten looser and he suggested I wear a special sock around the residual limb. The sock would tighten the fit, he promised. And it did. For a while. But the stump kept shrinking, and pretty soon I needed two socks to fill the growing gap. That two-count gave Bill a rough estimate of how much my limb had shrunk—two socks' worth.

"How else does it feel?" he had asked me on the phone.

It wasn't easy to put into words, but I did the best I could. "It's like the limb doesn't quite reach to the top front of the socket," I said. "I feel room up there. It's definitely looser now than it was before."

Bill assured me all this was normal, a predictable part of the fitting process. And he knew what do to about it. "You'll leave Denver with a far better fit," he promised. I liked his confidence.

Our late-night flight from Dulles landed in Denver just in time for us to flop into bed. The next morning brought one of those perfect Colorado summer days. Sunny. Crisp. Hardly any humidity in the air. The kind of weather that has drawn people to the Rockies since pioneer times. It was an air of optimism. Tuesday and I arrived at the Jewell Clinic a little before 9 A.M. and found Bill in an unusually talkative mood. Maybe the weather had affected him too. During our past visits, Bill had kept his thoughts mostly to himself. This time, with a little prodding, he was almost expansive—for Bill.

"How long have you been doing this?" I asked him, not at all sure he was eager for conversation.

"I've been a prosthetist for seventeen years," he said.

I asked how many prostheses he figured he'd created. "It must be up in the thousands," I offered.

"Yeah," he answered. "For a number of years after 9/11, when the wars in Iraq and Afghanistan were heating up, I used to do a few hundred a year. Now, it is less than that. There aren't as many wounded combat veterans coming home now, and there are also more prosthetists out there. But we still stay pretty busy."

I was happy to hear him talk about himself at all. There's a level of trust to be achieved in simple conversation. I like knowing about the mechanic who works on my car, and my leg is a whole lot more important to me than my car. I don't want my leg to be the project of some anonymous toiler. I want to know there's a real human putting his heart and his soul and all his talent into something as important as that.

"It is very rewarding," Bill said of the responsibility. That was the mind-set of someone who cared, and I was reassured to hear him say it.

For a less experienced prosthetist, this visit could have been a lot more trial and error. But Bill had a clear idea what I needed. He brought out a test socket that he had fashioned for me. The Ottobock bionic leg would fit into that. This wasn't my final socket. It was just to test the fit. But I could see immediately that the test socket was smaller and sleeker than the one I had been wearing for the past three months—and, I bet, far easier to slide over a pants leg.

I thought to myself: "So these are the advantages of limb shrinkage?"

He asked me to take off my leg. Then, like Geppetto in *Pinocchio,* headed back to his workshop, where he got busy with his Allen wrenches swapping out the old socket.

"Try this on," he said when he returned. "We may still need to make a few adjustments. But let's try the fit."

I slipped on the test socket and immediately I could feel the difference. It was snug, even without the socks. Bill watched me walk to assess my gait. Then, he copped a feel. I don't know how else to describe it. He slid his fingers into my buttocks so he could check how well the socket was resting against my ischial seat, that delicate area between the butt and groin. He came around the other side and did more pushing and poking. He was trying to gauge if the socket was too tight, too loose, or just right.

The new fit felt pretty good to me, though Bill noticed a few things he still wasn't happy with. "I'll keep this overnight," he said. "I'll use it as a guide to make your final socket."

I removed the leg. He kept the tester and reconnected my old socket. I got ready to wobble out of there on my loose, two-sock fit.

"That's all we need for now," Bill said, seeming eager to return to Geppetto's workshop. "See you tomorrow afternoon."

I was equally eager. "Come on, Tuesday," I said. "Let the man get to work."

———◆———

Ever since the Penn Station escalator fiasco, I'd been asking myself, "Do we really need to travel with all this stuff?" While we were in Denver, I vowed to cast off some of the things we really didn't need any more and do a better job of organizing the rest. I bought a canvas bag to carry the crutches. I swapped the duffel bag for a laptop-friendly backpack. And here was the big one: We went to a self-storage facility, where we stowed the wheelchair and some smaller excess items. I know I said I would have the wheelchair with me forever. But with my soon-to-be refitted prosthesis, I didn't think I'd be needing the chair on a regular basis anymore. Yes, it was one sleek chair. Yes, I'd had fun racing with Tuesday. And yes, I'd be happy if I never saw it again for as long as I live. This was a huge leap for me. I'd had a wheelchair, this one and the clunker that preceded it, since my operation, first as my primary means of mobility then as a ready fallback. Clearly, the escalator gods had other ideas. All I could think was *good riddance!*

With less stuff to carry and no wheelchair to push, I knew I would have a lot more balance. As we walked, my hands were free. That would help me stand straighter. When you are more than 6 feet tall and pushing a luggage-cart wheelchair, you can't help but lean forward.

From now on, I told myself, I would be a "light fighter." That was the term we used in the army for a foot soldier who carried everything on his back. No armored personnel carriers. No marching from the battlefield to the barracks every night. It was all in the rucksack, period. "Pack light, freeze at night," we used to say in the infantry. Light fighters all the way! Now, I was returning to that light life.

We got all that done and still made our 1 P.M. appointment at the

Jewell Clinic. I could hardly wait to check out the final-final socket
Bill had created for me. I was literally grinning as we walked into the
clinic. Tuesday could feel my excitement. He bounced through the
door beside me. When Bill led us into the examining room, I know
he could also feel the anticipation. He took my old leg and loose
socket into Geppetto's workshop, spending a full thirty minutes with
his Allen wrenches and screwdrivers. I didn't know exactly what he
was doing, but when he returned, the top of the leg was attached
to my brand-new socket. It was just as sleek and tapered as the test
socket, but the real one was made from a different kind of plastic and
it was a cool-looking black. It also had a thin layer of padding where
the earlier model was just the hard plastic.

But that wasn't all. At the other end of the leg, I also noticed, was
a brand-new Ottobock 1C61 Triton VS foot. *VS* stands for vertical
shock. It didn't look too different from the old one, but I'd checked
it out online and knew this one was far more advanced. This lightweight carbon foot boasted "enhanced shock absorption and torsion
resistance." It is suitable, the manufacturer says, for "a particularly
broad range of applications from everyday use to recreational sports."
Unlike earlier models, the IC61 had a spring in the back toward the
heel. That little spring was designed to change the whole kinesiology
of walking—imitating the way the muscles, tendons, and ligaments
in a real foot all work together in a smooth and efficient way. All this
promised greater flexibility and much more functionality. It was, as
the company advertised, more like a foot. I was certainly excited to
take it for a test walk.

I gently shoved my limb into the socket. I know that sounds like
an oxymoron, but a gentle shoving is what it takes. Then I depressed
the valve to release the air inside the socket. Finally, I stood and
slowly walked around.

Damn, that felt nice!

No more wiggle. No more wobble. No more socks.

I remembered back in April, when Bill explained to me the ins and outs of prostheses, I had said to him, "It should fit like a glove," and he had said to me: "It needs to fit better than a glove."

I started to understand what he meant. Forget gloves. A prosthesis has to fit like a transplanted heart. Maximum fit and maximum comfort. Everything in the spot it's designed for, connected in the way it's supposed to be. No wiggle room at all.

It was, at that moment, almost perfect. We were getting close. I could tell. This was like being in a shoe store and having the clerk hand you a perfect pair of Johnston & Murphy dress shoes. Whatever shoes you came in wearing, the Johnston & Murphy fit was so much better.

Oh, this is nice, I thought. *Sleek and comfy!*

I hadn't even left the clinic, and already I could tell the new fit gave me an extra shot of confidence and support.

But as I paced around Bill's examining room, I began to notice that something was amiss. The new foot seemed to have more bounce in it—which was good, right?—but the bionic leg didn't have enough resistance anymore. The knee movement was off. I took a step, and the leg started to buckle. The swing was too quick. It was unnerving.

"The socket feels fine, much better," I told Bill. "But we need to adjust the resistance."

Like a NASCAR racer coming into a pit stop, these bionic legs need continual adjustment and tune-ups. That was becoming clear.

With his Allen wrench, Bill gave the screws connected to the pylons a couple of extra turns. I didn't understand all the mechanical details. But those pylons tightened or loosened certain hinges, which altered various settings. He did this four or five times and made other adjustments. No doubt about it: You get a real appreciation for the amazing human body when you try to replicate the way it works. He shifted the height of the leg, making sure it matched the height of my good leg. He altered the resistance. He adjusted the ankle. He focused especially on the new foot. Was the toe at the correct angle? How was the connection with the foot? Each time, the leg got a little better. All these small adjustments were huge.

After the fifth or sixth modification, Bill went into the leg's computer using a Bluetooth connection. He changed the settings on the microprocessors in there. I could see the little blue light blinking.

Then, there was the new foot.

That spring and whatever else was in there really made a difference. Neither the leg nor the foot had a propulsion system. It wasn't robotic. It depended on me to move. But that spring supported and amplified my body's natural effort. It made everything more efficient and put a little bounce in my step, easing the physical impact like a shock absorber. Now, when I took a step, my foot didn't simply plop on the ground like a dead weight. Now, it landed gently and then sprung back up. The difference was truly noticeable. I didn't feel flatfooted anymore.

This new version of the leg was an undeniable improvement. And with the thrill of that came an adrenaline rush. Clearly, I knew, I needed time to take the setup on some longer test walks to make sure I wasn't missing anything. But for now, it was feeling pretty darn great. I had only one small, lingering complaint.

Up near the top, where the socket fit snug against my groin, I felt rubbing against my skin. Pinching, really. It wasn't pressure on the bone or the tissue. It wasn't internal. It was external.

I mentioned it to Bill.

He took the leg back and returned to his workshop, where he applied a layer of foam adhesive. "This should help," he said. I tried it on. Once again Bill had done his magic.

CHAPTER 26

The Homecoming

If light is in your heart,
you will find your way home.
RUMI

PAPÁ WAS WAITING FOR TUESDAY AND ME AT THE MIAMI AIRPORT
when our overnight flight from Denver arrived at 6:30 A.M.

We hadn't seen my parents since Naples in January, two months
before my surgery. I have to say I was a little nervous about how they
were going to react. Neither of them had been too keen on my decision to amputate. Really, what parent would be? My dad especially
had pressed hard for me not to go forward with the operation. Once
I made my decision though, he did stop nudging me. I give him
credit for that. I don't know if he ever fully agreed with my decision,
even after I explained it to him, but he did quit bugging me about
it, and I was grateful for that. Knowing my father, I'm sure it took
some self-control on his part. Now, for the very first time, he and my
mother were going to see the results.

I knew this would be a potent moment—for them and for me.
They were the people who had created me and brought me into
the world, the ones who'd counted my ten fingers and ten toes one

ancient, blessed day decades earlier. And here I was, presenting myself to them with five fewer toes, not to mention one fewer leg.

Yikes!

All of that was on my mind as Tuesday and I made our way off the plane, down the concourse, and toward baggage claim.

I was glad I had waited to visit them until I was off the crutches and out of the wheelchair. My parents didn't need to see their son like that. This way, their first vision of me would be on my new leg, even if I wasn't exactly running any marathons yet. I wanted to present a cheerful image. I wanted them to know that everything was fine. I'm not sure I could have pulled that off a month or two earlier.

Especially with a major life decision like this one, I wanted my parents to see that I was okay. That I wasn't dependent. That I was moving ahead. That I could exercise sound judgment in the toughest decisions of my life. Isn't that the whole point of growing up? The whole point of being a parent? To raise children who become strong, thoughtful, independent adults? It ought to be, anyway.

I am a dog parent. I can only imagine what it is like parenting a human being. But I'd always believed this was a key part of how we measure a parent's success. When children grow up, do they establish lives of their own? Do they move out, start their own families, establish careers, and so on?

Most people probably wouldn't have handled the big unveiling the way that I chose to. It's natural to want your family and other loved ones around you in your times of greatest need, providing the unique comfort and support that strangers, acquaintances, and professionals cannot. But there's a flip side to that approach, and it weighed on me. I didn't want to shock them or drain them and disappoint them or burden them unnecessarily. Protecting Mamá and Papá's feelings did mean missing out on some parental love and attention. I understand that. I wouldn't necessarily recommend my approach to anyone else, not for something as life-altering as this. But it felt right to me.

I gathered up our luggage, and the moment finally arrived.

As Tuesday and I stepped into the south Florida humidity, Papá was parked in the arrivals lane just outside the terminal. When he saw us coming toward him, he climbed out of the car and called out, "Luis! Tuesday!"

I noticed that he used both names.

He rushed over and gave me a warm, long hug.

"And how's Tuesday?" he asked, bending down and running his fingers through the fur on the back of Tuesday's neck. "How are you, boy?"

I didn't get a sense of any negative judgment or deeper issues. He didn't say a word about the leg. Not yet, anyway. My father just seemed happy to see us.

"Do you want to get breakfast or should I drop you at the hotel?" he asked. "Your book event is at ten, right?"

I nodded. "I think we could probably use a nap," I told my father. "A couple of hours to recharge."

"Good idea," he said. "You want to be ready for the presentation. I'm sure you didn't get much sleep on the plane." He dropped us at the hotel, which was just a block from my parents' new condo, and said he'd return for us at 9:30.

Even the ninety minutes we slept made a big difference. I felt downright energetic as I dressed, adjusted my leg, and gathered Tuesday's leash and his rubber fold-up bowl. But as I walked around the hotel room and led Tuesday to the elevator, the pinching I'd noticed in Denver was back. I wouldn't describe the pain as excruciating, but it was definitely irritating, and it wasn't going away. If anything, it was getting worse. It was small, but it was there. Have you ever stepped on a splinter so tiny you can barely see it? That's how this was. Sometimes, even the tiniest splinter can make you wince—or even hobble. It's impossible to ignore. That's how this pinching was. I knew, as I walked to the elevator, I didn't have time to do anything about it before the children's book event. I'd just suck it up until later. But as soon as I had a chance, I'd have to figure something out.

Mamá was standing in the lobby, waiting for us. She was dressed nicely. She always is, even on a summer Saturday morning. And she met us just as warmly as my father had. She also didn't so much as mention my leg. But she gave me a big hug and, though she didn't quite do the same for Tuesday, she did say hi. Mamá's not a big dog person. She never has been, despite the years she spent with Max in the house. But she didn't say anything negative, and there was no mistaking that she was glad to see me *and* Tuesday.

My father was waiting outside in the car. As the three of us headed out together, my leg was still pinching me, though I didn't say anything yet.

"Load," I told Tuesday, and we all piled in for the twenty-minute ride to the bookstore. My dad dropped me, Tuesday, and Mamá at the front of Books & Books while he went to park the car.

"Get busy," I told Tuesday, and he did exactly that outside the doorway.

When Tuesday had finished his business in the grass, we went inside to meet Ketsia, the children's program coordinator, who couldn't have been more welcoming. This whole trip, frantic as it was, was turning out to be fun, meeting new people and reconnecting with others. Fun, once we'd gotten that escalator bounce behind us. Ketsia was all smiles and said she had heard a lot about Tuesday and was eager to meet him in person. She was good with children and maybe even better with dogs. With all the attention she was giving him, he was thrilled to meet her too.

As we began setting up for the presentation, the kids had already started to gather in the reading area of the store. Some parents were there, too. Ketsia had set up a pile of *Tuesday Takes Me There* books that I would sign after the presentation and a copy for me to read aloud. I mentioned the Florida heat and she filled Tuesday's portable water bowl while I unpacked my Sharpie pen and his paw-tograph stamp. My dad went to sit with my mom in the back. Two of their closest friends, Josefina and Julieta, also came. I've known them since I was a child. It was very kind of them to make the effort.

The kids were arriving now. Once they focused on Tuesday, they were overcome by his furry charisma, cuteness, and charm. They jockeyed and jostled each other a bit, getting as close to him as possible. A little girl asked if she could pet him. "Sure," I said, "he'd love to meet you. Say, hi, Tuesday." The kids all seemed to delight in him. The parents delighted too. So did Ketsia. So did I. That good feeling Tuesday brings to any room, it's almost always infectious.

I started the children's presentation as I usually did, by sitting on the floor at roughly the same level as the kids who sat in a semi-circle in front of us. I don't like towering over smaller people. It's intimidating. Yes, children are used to parents and teachers all being taller, but I enjoy relating on a different level. Being way up there, I'd found, impedes free-flowing conversation and a natural exchange. We were all there to learn together. That requires some give-and-take. So before I started reading, we just talked.

"How's your summer going?" I asked one of the boys who was sitting up front. "What are you doing?"

"Going to camp," he answered tentatively.

"What kind of camp?" I asked, gently prodding him to tell me more.

Slowly, he overcame what seemed to be a touch of shyness. "Acting camp," he told me and the other kids.

"That's so cool!" I said. "I never did acting camp."

This broke the ice and soon others were sharing their stories too. One boy said his family was going to the beach. Another child, a girl, said she was taking swimming lessons. No one mentioned summer school. *This must be a smart crowd,* I thought.

We chatted a bit longer, and then I explained that we were going to read and share a new book that Tuesday and I had written called *Tuesday Takes Me There*. I told them, "It's about a trip Tuesday and I took together and some of the amazing things we saw. Tuesday keeps taking me places, and we wanted to write a story about it. And I have to tell you"—here I chuckled quietly to myself and threw Tuesday a knowing glance—"that in the past two days, oh boy, from New York to Washington to Denver to Miami, oh boy, did Tuesday take me there!"

I could tell the kids were eager to hear the story. I was eager to tell it. There is something about the wonder and enthusiasm of a room full of inquisitive children. I knew I was still exhausted from our extensive travels, but the energy of all those kids in the room and my parents in the back had fully washed over me. I was energized.

My parents had seen me speak in public several times before, but always to adult audiences. This was different. They hadn't seen a children's program before. I'm not sure what they expected from me, their child who didn't have his own kids, in front of a roomful of wide-eyed children. My parents had seen me at my worst in the early years of my PTSD when even a handful of friendly adults would have been an impossibly difficult situation. I'm pretty sure they were happily surprised by how at ease I was interacting with the kids.

I got a lot of questions about Tuesday.

"How did he get his name?"

"What does he like to eat?"

"Why does it say, 'Do not pet'?"

"Does he have any tricks he can do?"

I answered all the questions as well as I could, often following up with questions of my own. "Do you have a dog?...What's *her* name?...What *should* Tuesday eat?...Can you tell me what it means to be a service dog?"

This was a great group of kids.

"Here's a tough question," I said. "Who knows the answer to this one? How long have humans and dogs been friends?"

I looked out at the adorable, wide-eyed, speechless children.

"Well," I said. "Where did humans live thirty or forty thousand years ago? Before we had houses and apartments and buildings of any kind?"

"In caves," one boy answered.

"That's right," I said. "In caves."

"And what do we call the people who lived in caves?"

"Cave men," several of the children answered at once.

"What about cave girls?" I asked with a laugh. "Weren't there cave girls back then?"

A little girl knew the answer to that one. "Yes," she said quite decisively. "Cave girls. They *had* to have cave girls." She erupted in laughter.

"Yes," I told her. "They did."

And then a boy said, "And cave boys!"

"That's right," I said. "Cave boys. Not just cave men and cave women. Also cave boys and cave girls." The kids were chattering excitedly, imagining themselves living in caves.

"And what else did they have?"

I wasn't sure if they would know what I was getting at. But these kids were smart, and Tuesday was rolled up on the floor right at my feet. The kids who were up front were close enough to reach out and pet him. I glanced down at Tuesday, knowing the children would pick up on my not-so-subtle visual cue.

I caught the eye of a little boy in glasses and a Miami Heat T-shirt who hadn't said anything yet. But he spoke up clearly now.

"Cave dogs," he said.

Yes!

"That's right. Cave dogs. Even all those years ago, even before people lived in houses and apartments, even before we had schools and playgrounds and highways and swimming pools and backyards, when all they had to live in was caves, people were already friends with dogs. People and dogs have been friends for a very, very, very, very long time."

They loved this. Now they were imagining themselves in prehistoric caves with their own pet dogs.

Several of the children—the boys, mostly—asked about my leg. I was wearing shorts, as I'd been doing so often, ever since the procedure. Leg amputees have a difficult time managing socket comfort. The heat accumulates inside the socket. Having to remove the prosthetic periodically to wipe down the leg, air out the liner, and refit the prosthetic to the residual limb is a challenge.

And since we were in Florida's unforgiving climate, everyone else was wearing shorts. So why not? I didn't try to hide the leg. It was plain for everyone to see. The kids were fascinated by it. That's a big difference between children and adults. Kids don't hide their curiosity. They don't believe it's impolite to see something new and ask about it. These kids seemed most focused on the whole "bionic" idea.

"Can you take it in the bathtub?" one boy asked.

"Yes, I can," I told him. "This new leg is waterproof. And I clean it every day, just like I groom Tuesday every day. You have to take care of the things you love."

"Can you run fast?" another child asked.

"Not yet," I told him. "One day, I hope. Tuesday loves to run, and I can't wait to play sports with him."

They all clapped at that.

Then, I started reading. I won't blow the story for you here, but the tale we tell with great illustrations isn't so different from our real lives. A children's book doesn't have to be fantastical to be fun and interesting. Tuesday and I keep traveling together. He takes me to interesting places. We meet cool people and see amazing things. All with friendship and love.

The kids listened intently. The adults did too. Of course, what seemed like a simple story time was much more. That's the thing about advocacy. With the right tools, we are able to make our points while also making people smile. None of this was lost on Tuesday, who had a giant grin on his face. He loves being directly involved.

The kids clapped their small hands together enthusiastically when the story was done. A lot of parents clapped, too. Many of the people in the bookstore got their books autographed and, especially, paw-tographed as well as posed for pictures with Tuesday. It's a good thing he loves people as much as they love him. He got and gave dozens and dozens of hugs that day. No one appeared ready to leave. We talked to people and answered questions for almost an hour. The children kept making hilarious and astute remarks. I'd come there that day to educate and entertain—but here I was, the one on the receiving end.

When the crowd finally thinned and we'd personalized our last book, my parents, their two friends, Tuesday, and I all walked over to have lunch at the Books & Books Café. It was really our first chance to talk.

My father at last said something about my changed appearance. He remarked, with sincere approval in his voice, that I seemed to be getting around pretty well on the new leg, especially considering how little practice I'd had. "It's remarkable," he said, nodding his head.

I loved hearing that.

Given how far I'd come to be here—and not just geographically—I could tell my parents were proud. Witnessing me in this situation, handling a room of inquisitive children and adults, delivering a serious message, and making it fun all the while. That parental pride was something I wasn't sure I would ever see again—not after I'd returned from war such a changed man. And here it was on full display. My mother, who isn't a very expressive person, said unequivocally, "Gosh, Luis, that story was wonderful. It has real educational value, I think. Tuesday taking you to all those American landmarks and learning what they mean."

I'm an adult now. I've been to war. I've been to college and to graduate school. I've faced challenges I was completely unprepared for. I have been to places I never imagined I would go. My relationship with my parents had been strained for a long time as they'd confronted those experiences, my failures, and successes. But sitting in that bookstore café, I couldn't help but notice that things had come full circle and I was so glad they had.

I mentioned that I might need their help with something. The new leg fit quite well, I told them, except for a small spot just below my groin where it was pinching. I winced a bit as I spoke. "That's not a place I really like to be pinched," I said with a laugh. My father smiled knowingly.

Suddenly, I was their little boy again, seeking parental magic. "Mamá, maybe you can help me fix that," I said. "We could make a little cushioning lip or something to stop it from pinching. Do you have duct tape at home?"

"We have duct tape," Papá piped in.

"Great! I'll bring some cloth when I come over to dinner tonight," I said. "We'll figure it out."

They dropped us back at the hotel around 1:30 P.M. Tuesday and I still had a lot more sleep to catch up on. I got four more hours—Tuesday had quite a snooze, too—before my dad walked over from the condo to collect us for dinner. As we headed over together, the pinching I had been feeling definitely hadn't gone away. When we got up to the apartment, my mom was already waiting with the duct tape, ready to get busy. She insisted we take care of my leg before she and my dad showed us around the new place.

"Let's do it now," she said. "No reason for you to be hobbling around in pain. Let me have a look."

Clearly, Mamá hadn't lost her can-do focus.

I took off my leg. I can only imagine how strange that must have been for them to see for the first time. But Mamá didn't miss a beat. She took the cloth I brought and, together, we fashioned it into a careful lip, securing it just at the right spot with the duct tape. It wasn't a one-person job. She held the leg and the cloth while I taped it down. It was a highly efficient mother-son operation. It was nice for us to do something together. As a mother, I'm sure she liked the idea of helping her son with something that would make his walking less painful. She didn't say that, but I could tell that it was true.

I tried on the leg with the new lip in place. She didn't have Bill's training or experience, but I knew immediately that it didn't matter at all. The improvement was night and day. I couldn't feel any pinching at all. Finally, I said to myself, we really do have the fit right.

My mom proudly gave Tuesday and me the nickel tour of their new condo, with my dad tossing in occasional comments. We reviewed the modern kitchen, the spacious bedrooms, the two gleaming baths, the comfortable living-dining room, and the broad balcony with a view of Coconut Grove Marina and Biscayne Bay. We lingered outside closets large enough to pass for bedrooms in some of the tiny apartments Tuesday and I had rented in New York City. This place was sweet.

"The condo is beautiful," I said back in the living room at the end of the tour.

My dad smiled and reached into his pocket. He gave me a key. Their home was mine.

As I took a seat on the sofa, Papá went to the kitchen and got me a beer. He poured glasses of wine for himself and Mamá. His hosting gestures weren't quite done. He also refilled Tuesday's water bowl in the kitchen. We chatted about the new apartment, their move to Miami, and the pleasures of a comfortable retirement in a city with no snow and lots of sunshine. Papá was seventy-four. My mom was seventy-one. "This is our last move," my mother said decisively. "We're not doing that anymore."

The visit was hitting all the right notes for a family that had come together better than ever. I wished my brother and sister and their families could be here. Mamá had made a delicious dinner of steak with rice and salad. She remarked about how well behaved Tuesday was, even making a favorable comparison with her human grandchildren, my sister's kids.

"I love *all* my kids, of course, and *all* my grandkids, of course," she said. "But it is a pleasure having Tuesday over." I'm not sure how serious she was being, but she laughed and added: "He is better behaved than the grandkids and—" she glanced at the family photos—"some of the kids."

I have never understood how someone could not be an animal person. For the first time, I thought, maybe she was making progress. Or maybe the credit all went to Tuesday.

"Listen," my mother said. "Let's make this a regular thing."

"Sure," I said, not quite certain what *this* was.

"Let's make you coming down like this a regular thing," my father clarified.

"Of course, of course," I said. We'd made vague promises before. This time I actually meant it.

We agreed that for the next couple of weeks—or however long I could stay—we'd have dinner together each night. We'd gather like a real family. I would do all the other things I needed to do. Tuesday and I would keep up with our work and our advocacy, getting around to our various events. But every night that we could, we'd make the effort to get together for dinner. That might sound like a lot. But we had a lot of catching up to do, my parents and me. I was going to enjoy my homecoming.

I still didn't quite think of Miami as my home. Even with my own front door key, this was my parents' home. But *homecoming*—that was still a good word. People often say, "Home is where the heart is." Well, wherever your parents are certainly holds a piece of your heart. So in a way, I guess you could say we really had come home.

CONCLUSION

Friends Forever

I WALKED 10,000 STEPS YESTERDAY WITH TUESDAY BY MY SIDE. THAT'S not an estimate. It's an exact count. Back and forth down the hotel hallway, ignoring the stares of curious guests.

On the long road to full mobility, I constantly look for fresh ways to motivate myself. My new Fitbit, the wearable fitness technology, is an excellent scorekeeper. It tallies every step I take and measures the distance covered while tracking my heart rate. At 10,000 steps a day, I'm hitting the fitness goal suggested by the American Heart Association—for someone with two God-given legs. And I'm doing it on an above-the-knee prosthetic leg, which takes far more strength and stamina than walking the old-fashioned way. It's a process of constant self-discovery...this new version of me.

I'm not sure how many steps that is for Tuesday, whose stride is considerably shorter than mine. Has anyone invented a Dogbit yet?

Of course, next week or next month, we will need to find a more challenging goal. Pushing myself with Tuesday's encouragement— that's the only way I'll ever get fully proficient on this amazing bionic leg. As Triathlon Tom told me soon after we met at the VA clinic in Denver, "You have to walk the leg. It won't walk you."

I am still determined to engage in athletic pursuits with Tuesday.

I haven't stopped smiling at the thrill he got from our wheelchair mini-Olympics in El Paso. I'm sure he'd love bicycle and kayak racing even more. I'm not there yet. But don't worry, Toopy, I will be. I promise.

I'm a little more sober now about the challenges faced by all amputees, especially those who've lost a leg (or two). But not for a second am I sorry that Dr. Jones laid out the option for me. I made the decision—yes, the shocking decision—and Dr. O'Shaughnessy went to work. Now, even my parents understand what got me there. I am so happy we feel like a family again. While my mobility will be a work in progress for some time, at least the trajectory is ever upward, which is infinitely superior to a slow, glum slide of feeling worse each passing year. I had to make a change. I had to act. I had to take a risk. To thrive, not just survive! For me, being confined to a wheelchair— even a racing model, even temporarily—was like rolling straight to the netherworld. The trip was just as harsh as the destination.

Tuesday's doing just great. He remains the light of my life and omnipresent companion, my dependable service dog and best-est of friends. As I told those veterinarians in Tampa, he isn't like a member of the family. He *is* a member of the family—the most important and certainly most-loved one.

Like all of us, he continues to age. He is still quite fit and energetic. He hasn't lost a speck of his boyish magnetism or an ounce of his irresistible charm. I swear it isn't only because of his thick blond mane. He's a good soul and an optimistic one, always up for whatever comes our way. I know he will make a world-class role model and a master-level teacher to Promise, as Lu does her thing and the new puppy finally comes to live with us. Tuesday and I are still discussing our successor strategies, how we will show the newbie that we love her, how we will teach important lessons to her, how we will make her a full-fledged member of our currently all-male pack. At the same time, we are sketching out the perfect next chapter for

Tuesday. Will he become more of a therapy dog? More of an international goodwill ambassador? You just know that someone will want to make a movie of his life! I know this much for certain: We will be advocating, educating, event-hosting, book-signing, and spreading furry love from city to city and town to town.

So who is Promise?

Lu has a particular puppy in mind, a golden-haired girl who displays the earliest makings of a first-in-class working dog. I'm not sure which of Daisy's offspring she is eyeing. But I know that Lu will find the perfect match for me and bring me fully into the process whenever the time is right.

Until Tuesday opens with a short poem I wrote.

"Split in Half"
I happened upon a tree struck by lightning;
the aftermath of a wild and violent thing.
A tree split in half.

How do we come upon such things?

What happened here?

I have seen men and women split in half.
I've split people in half.
I am split in half.

Are two halves really a whole?

There are holes.
Deep and lonely holes,
split in half.
A tree with holes.

The poem is a soldier's eye view of PTSD, and it sprung from the disconnection in my life I felt after war. My time in uniform truly did split me in half, creating damage I never believed could be repaired. Then, like manna from heaven, Tuesday arrived and my wounds began to heal. Oh, there's still a lot of scar tissue. But scar tissue is easier to live with than festering holes, and scar tissue often grows back even stronger and more resilient than untouched skin.

To this day, I can still relate to the words in that poem. They speak of a widespread condition. But they no longer define me. My outlook is far brighter now and far more outward-looking. My life is more productive too. Tuesday gets much of the credit for this blessed transition, and I get some too. As a human being, I am so much closer to whole.

The quest for wholeness is crucial to the human condition. Indeed, it's central to the mission Tuesday and I are on. Our mission is not just for the benefit of disabled people or sufferers of PTSD. It is for everyone in hope and in need. Over the past decade, I have experienced two versions of this healing journey, one for my mind and one for my body. I would hate to say which was more daunting or which will be more difficult for others who struggle. But here is a lesson I have learned: When the mind is healthy, you are at last prepared to confront the challenges of the body. But the real triumph occurs in healing them both. In so doing, the spirit is restored.

With the help of Tuesday and many wonderful people and organizations, I see healing everywhere we travel and in the beautiful correspondence we receive every day. People are healing in much the same way I learned to walk again, step by step by step, until they have achieved greater wholeness.

Tuesday and I will continue to travel. I'll keep telling him, "Say hi, Tuesday," and he'll keep sidling over to thousands of people a year. I have no doubt he'll keep lifting the spirits of every one of them. Our advocacy—for ourselves and for others—will not end. Through these efforts, we will do all we can to help create better families, better communities, a better nation, and a better world. Isn't that what leadership is all about? The U.S. Army defines leadership as "providing purpose, direction, and motivation to accomplish the mission and improve the organization." I have never heard a better one or a more telling touchstone to live up to.

I'd like to think I keep making progress. I have learned to be more thoughtful in how I expend my energy. Every night, I remember to leave my leg by the bed along with accessories needed to don and doff it efficiently. I try to bring more balance into my life. All of us have so much to juggle daily: work, family, friends, health, spirituality, and also the struggle, turmoil, and conflict of the world around us. Is it any wonder that we rarely find the time to focus on ourselves? I take comfort in knowing that while life ahead is certain to include madness and melancholy, it, too, will include beauty, splendor, and peace. With love in our hearts, faith is fortified.

Tuesday continually teaches me. Appropriately, we pass it on and pay it forward.

Tuesday and I will keep traveling as long as the two of us can. Lovingly, we will introduce Promise into the equation and—who knows?—there may be others over time. We are constantly seeking allies, human and canine. But as long as a veteran is suffering, as long as a disabled person is being shunted aside, as long as mental health is an elusive condition, as long as the love of a canine can make a difference to someone, we will have places to go and people to visit and work to do. Together with the many people we've met already who share our determination and the new friends made along the way, we will continue to march ahead.

This is what dogs and people together are capable of. We have been each other's friends since prehistoric times. I am certain we will always remain so. Countless humans and canines have shared this special bond together. Our relationship will evolve. It will continue.

Together, we will never forget what we learned at the start: There is no hole so deep, no challenge so large, no dream so far away that things can't be improved by an outstretched paw, a burst of warm doggie breath, and the gentle smoosh of a soft, wet nose.

Go say "hi," Tuesday. Go say "hi."

AFTERWORD

BY ELLIS HENICAN

And that was where the book was supposed to end—with Luis and Tuesday gazing into the future, still fueled and inspired by each other's commitment, preparing for fresh and important adventures ahead.

What happened next was not supposed to happen. Our hero, Luis, was not supposed to die. Certainly not this way, taking his own life, yet another terrible tragedy of the invisible wounds of war. This big-hearted warrior and his loyal canine companion had so much left to accomplish, so much more to share with you, his supporters, readers, and friends.

Luis had made huge progress since the days of *Until Tuesday,* when his post-traumatic stress disorder had left him a prisoner of his anxious mind. With Tuesday's love and devotion, he'd literally turned his life around, becoming a man dedicated to helping others with PTSD; advocating on behalf of veterans, soldiers, and other people with disabilities; launching the multiyear, cross-country journey of healing that became the prime purpose of his life. For this highly decorated former army captain, that was an even greater achievement than his two tours in Iraq, his two Bronze Stars, and his Purple Heart.

And always at his side—paws forward, tail wagging, ready to go— was his not-so-secret weapon, the golden retriever Tuesday, spreading comfort, happiness, practical assistance, and unconditional love.

"People can't help themselves," Luis said as we sat together, writing the new book, *Tuesday's Promise*. "Once they see the love in his eyes, they are changed forever. He brings out the best in everyone."

As if to prove it, Tuesday looked up right then, flashing his thousand watts of canine charisma straight at me. All I could think was, "The next sentence we write had better sing!"

I have worked on books with many people of great achievement, top players in politics, sports, business, law enforcement, pop culture, and the military. But I'm not sure that any of them touched as many people or changed as many lives as Luis and Tuesday did. They were that irresistible!

Like other people who cared about Luis—friends, family members, readers, and fans—I was caught completely off guard by his death on December 2, 2016. *Tuesday's Promise* was already in the publisher's hands. The title was chosen. The editing was finished. The design was done. All that was left was for the presses to roll and the publicity campaign to begin. We know Luis was very much looking forward to traveling around with Tuesday to local libraries and neighborhood bookstores, inspiring adults and awestruck children, posing for pictures, sharing snout nuzzles and doggie hugs, signing (and paw-tographing) his brand-new book.

His death was news across America. *The New York Times* ran a full obituary: "Luis Carlos Montalván, Advocate for Soldiers With PTSD, Dies at 43." The *CBS Evening News* broadcast a moving tribute: "Sad ending for Iraq War vet who shed light on PTSD." U.S. Senator Al Franken, who had worked with Luis to pass the ground-breaking Service Dogs for Veterans Act, took to the Senate floor in a very moving tribute to honor the passing of his ally and friend.

"Luis," the senator said with tears in his eyes, "I want you to know that while you are not with us anymore, I am proud of you. I am so proud that you were brave enough to serve your country for seventeen years and then brave enough to share the story of the hardship that you faced afterward. I am so proud of you for giving hope to our other veterans who face the struggles you did."

Let me put your mind at ease about one thing. Tuesday is in the best possible hands, those of the woman who trained him, Lu Picard. "He will live out his days with our family, an ambassador for canines and all they are capable of," says Lu. "I would do that for any of our dogs." Tuesday is healthy, active, and engaged, impeccably behaved as always, though some who've seen him have detected a touch of sadness in his once-dancing eyes.

———

I believe I speak for many when I say we have lost a fellow traveler and a treasured friend. For more than a year, Luis and I worked closely together on what I now see was his last letter of love.

You now hold that love letter in your hands.

It is a love letter to Tuesday, the light of his life. It's a love letter to veterans, soldiers, and others who struggle with disabilities, a message of hope and admiration for these noble souls. It's even a love letter to the politicians, military officials, government bureaucrats, and others who sometimes stand in the way. We will fight you with the power of love, he wanted them to know.

This book is, just as importantly, a love letter to you—his friends, his readers, his allies, and all the other special people who have stood by him and Tuesday along the way.

You have his thanks, his admiration, and his plea and promise for the days that lie ahead: Please carry on. We will get there.

———

This was the book Luis wanted to write, the story he was eager for you to read. No one has changed a word.

With Luis's death, some parts of *Tuesday's Promise* take on added poignancy. This hits hardest in Chapter 22, "Older and Wiser," where Luis reflects with his typical openness on Tuesday's aging—and what that means for the two of them. A few lines are actually hard to read.

On page 229, Luis declares, "most likely I will outlive Tuesday." That seemed obvious when the sentence was written, though events overtook it. One has that same feeling again eight pages later with the story of Rainbow Bridge.

"Do you know about Rainbow Bridge?" Luis asks. "According to a story that has brought great comfort to many when they need it most, that's where our animals go after their time on earth ends."

Luis continues: "The way it's told, there is a multi-colored bridge 'this side of Heaven' and a green meadow beside it. 'When a beloved pet dies, the pet goes to this place.'"

Whoever dies first—the human or the animal—waits for the other in this peaceful meadow. Once reunited, they pass together across Rainbow Bridge—healed, whole, and happy—and into eternity, loving companions until the end of time.

Tuesday will continue the mission that he and Luis were so dedicated to. Their many friends will provide whatever assistance and comfort Tuesday may need.

Whatever else may happen as this healing journey goes on, you and I know this much for sure: Luis is waiting in a meadow somewhere for his beloved Tuesday. And he's not crossing any bridges alone.

ACKNOWLEDGMENTS

Thanks to all of the wonderful people of the Hachette Book Group. Tremendous thanks to Krishan Trotman and Mauro DiPreta.

Lots of gratitude for the terrific team at Foundry Literary+Media and Peter McGuigan. Great thanks and respect to Ellis Henican who was a pleasure to work with.

Though Osseointegration didn't make the book because the manuscript was submitted prior to my surgical procedure, my heartfelt thanks go to all of the amazing folks involved with the Osseointegration Group of Australia. Special thanks to Prof. Munjed Al Muderis, MD.

To the following, we are grateful for your love and support:

Carol & Charlie Brown, Judy & Ken Noon, Colleen McLaughlin, Marna & Arthur Ginsburg, Anita Campana, Noël Thayer, Kathleen Sangen, Will Tanner, Amy & Ted Gavin, Loretta Stadler, Mary Beth & Bill Hewitt, Lisa Scudieri, Sandy Sandberg, Deborah Gallagher, Melanie Huff, Bronwen & Scott Pence, Daniela Tomatti, Judith Jaeger, Jeannine Jennette, Kathy & Ed Paulson, Darby Kelly, Penelope Harrison, Joanne Singleton, Constance Hopkins, Elizabeth Meyers, Pamela Champeau, Pam & Steve Goldsmith, Jaime Bruce, Lu & Dale Picard, Kristi Flesher, Andrea Morris, Jose Kirchner, Mary Belmont, Roxanne Roberts, Robert Smith, Diane & Lou Bonita, Mary & Ken Seversen, Lindsay McKenna, Richard Colom, Lynn Burton, Lisa Baca, Chris Cooper, Mark Reed, Jane Eckert, Carol

Whitener, Dana Piercr, Mark Oldstrom, Lainie Deschamps, Andrew Fish, Steven Zacharius, Trish & Lee Keene, Pam Kemp, Goli & Adam Tiffen, Anna Ingenito, Kathleen & Rick Schoen, Elizabeth Rider, Brook Longmaid, Brooke & Ed Maxwell, Curtis Murray, Donna & Charlie Rosenblum, Carol Anne Adamson, Patricia Peterson, Lynn Hunter, Anna & Lars Commes, Charlene McKenney, Susan McGee, Ernie Hsin, Karen Levine, and Aline & Tony Pelkey. To the roster of thanks, Ellis adds key members of his literary posse: James Gregorio, Janis Spidle, Larry Kramer, Jesse Savran, Claire Harris, David Lamb, Bret Witter, Ben Selkow, and Roberta Teer.

Tuesday and I wish to profoundly thank all of the people, animals, and organizations we've met across the world. Inspiration truly goes both ways.